Saving
Zimbabwe

Saving Zimbabwe

LIFE, DEATH & HOPE IN AFRICA
BOB SCOTT

STRUIK CHRISTIAN BOOKS

SAVING ZIMBABWE

Published in 2010 by Struik Christian Books
An imprint of Struik Christian Media
A division of New Holland Publishing (South Africa) (Pty) Ltd
(New Holland Publishing is a member of Avusa Ltd)
Cornelis Struik House
80 McKenzie Street
Cape Town 8001

Reg. No. 1971/009721/07

Text © Bob Scott, Compassionate Justice Books 2009

Unless otherwise indicated all Scripture quotations are taken from
The Holy Bible, New International Version (NIV) © 1984, International Bible Society;
Used with permission.

Project management by Lana Coetzee
Edited by Tony van der Watt
DTP design by Sonja Louw
Cover design by Joleen Coetzee
Cover image by Gallo Images / Getty Images
Interior photography by Bob Scott
Printed and bound by CTP Printers Cape Town
Duminy Street, Parow 7500, Cape Town, South Africa

ISO 12647 compliant

ISBN 978-1-4153-0986-5

www.struikchristianmedia.co.za

DEDICATED TO

Jeremy Russell, Matthew Marais and Laura Russell who lost more in one moment than most of us will ever lose in a lifetime. To Stephen, Neville, Guide, Thabani, Roy, Nkiwane, Esinath and all the Zimbabweans whose hope for a better life was stolen from them in one tragic moment.

ENDORSEMENTS

'This book is a call to all sons and daughters of Zimbabwe, black or white, Ndebele of Shona, Kalanga or Sotho, to put their difference aside and work together towards making Zimbabwe the jewel of Africa again.'
— MUCHENGETWA BGONI, ZIMBABWEAN DIASPORA

'Bob Scott is a genuine ambassador of peace and reconciliation. His book Saving Zimbabwe is a tangible act of faithfulness, making clear the ongoing story of Jesus at work in the world. There's no corner of reality that Jesus does not steward and call his people to. Bob shines the light on Zimbabwe and the transforming work God is doing there through the hearts and hands of his people.'
— CHARLIE PEACOCK – AUTHOR OF NEW WAY TO BE HUMAN

'This book will serve many different groups of people: those who love Africa, those who love Zimbabwe, those who love Jesus, those who want to see reconciliation, those who are looking for hope, those who want to serve and help, those who need a vision and those who want to practically apply the principles in their own life – as demonstrated by the people of the Community. Many, many people will benefit from it.'
— JOHANNES BARATTA, MANAGING DIRECTOR, DEUTSCHE BANK GERMANY

'Saving Zimbabwe is a powerful story. It has all the potential to show all Zimbabweans who feel disenchanted with their leaders that Christianity, when properly lived, can bring blessings and favour to everyone involved. It is profound and moving. I think it's a must read for anyone who wants to reaffirm his or her faith in the promise of Zimbabwe. It inspires hope and presents a blueprint for the future. Thank you for having such compassion for mankind.'

— ARTWELL MOYO, ZIMBABWE

TABLE OF CONTENTS

ACKNOWLEDGMENTS

I n writing my first book I have come to learn that it takes a whole community of people to bring an inspiration to life. I feel indebted to so many for helping me give expression from my heart through written words. First and foremost is my wife Elizabeth who has not only been my greatest source of encouragement throughout this exhausting journey, but has also had the challenge of trying to help me correct my many abuses of the English language. She too felt this story needed to be told and has endured at my side to see this project reach fruition. Thank you for believing in me.

Editing is a complex process and I am grateful for Jackie Macgirven who put her heart and soul into this story. Her editing suggestions and insights definitely enhanced the project, helping me clarify my thoughts to better communicate the burden in my heart. I want to thank Abby Vogels for her many hours of detailed work on the copy and Dale Jimmo for her expertise on the book layout. In the course of writing I was privileged to discover a new friendship with the very talented artist Ken Westphal. His contribution to the graphic design work on this book was extraordinary.

I would like to thank Jeremy Russell for sitting with me for hours sharing not only his own story but the back stories on his amazing family. Your father John was an incredible man whom I deeply respected. I owe a debt of gratitude to Mike Town, Terry Hartley and Noel Alexander who are all intimately knowledgeable about the story and helped confirm that my facts were accurate and my writing reflected the heart and soul of the people of The Community of Reconciliation.

Thank you to my soul mate Muchengetwa Bgoni whose input from the African perspective was vital to ensure that this story was told honestly and from all perspectives. It is my hope that this labour of love will help 'set the captives free' and that you will be able to return home soon to rebuild your nation. I hope to be there at your side, brother.

I want to give special thanks to a number of people who have been a source of great encouragement to me over the decades. Angela Gutshall for your unending prayers and not giving up on me. I did get up! Charles Lynn, for your wonderful insights on geopolitics, water and religion. Thanks for the encouragement to tell my story transparently. Bill and Debbie Corum, without whose support this project would have never seen the light of day. Your strength held me up. Bill and Penny Biedermann, not only for your support on this project, but your compassionate heart for the downtrodden. Johannes Baratta, my long time friend who has always seemed to understand what's in my soul. You are truly one of my closest Band of Brothers.

Please accept my heartfelt gratitude.

FOREWORD

D ecember 7, 1941, November 22, 1963 and September 11, 2001 are dates that live in infamy in American history. What makes them unusual is that we each know exactly where we were and what we were doing when we received 'The News'. December 7, 1941 was the day the Japanese attacked Pearl Harbor. My father and his best friend were comfortably seated at the Sunday matinee at the LaGrange movie theatre when the film stopped and the lights came up. The theatre owner took the stage and told a horrified audience that America had just been attacked.

On Friday November 22, 1963 I walked in after another long, boring day of first grade, to find my mother sitting in shock watching our small black-and-white TV. The look on her face told me that something terrible had happened. She could barely utter the words, 'President Kennedy has been shot in Dallas.'

For a younger generation, the events of September 11, 2001 will be the moment in time when they look back and say, 'Everything changed that day. My life has not been the same.' Thanksgiving 1987 was such a moment for me on a very personal level. It was the day that I received the news that 16 of my dearest friends had been massacred across the ocean on a humanitarian project in Zimbabwe.

For anyone who has experienced the call that a loved one has been killed in an accident, you know exactly what I'm talking about. For those of you that thankfully haven't, I can only describe it as initially unreal and ultimately devastating. You are never the same afterwards. Something dies in you.

I was a young associate pastor of a dynamic, growing church that was going places. God was moving and the future couldn't have been brighter. The sense of invincibility and divine destiny was woven through everything I was doing. I was a man on a mission that included not only my home church in Kansas City, but the African nation of Zimbabwe. I believed that God had a destiny for that country and its people.

I have spent the past 22 years carrying the story of these amazing people in my heart. I have rarely spoken about it because I've had so many unresolved conflicts in my soul over the whole situation. For me it was 'the death of vision' but taken to an unimaginable level, as 16 people really died! You may be familiar with Proverbs 29:18: 'Where there is no vision the people perish.' This certainly was the resulting 'domino effect' of the massacre.

I finally came to terms with the fact that the haunting images of death and destruction from 1987 are forever etched into my psyche. They will never be removed. The ripple effect has touched every aspect of my life and in many cases negatively. I have more than a few haunted shipwrecks lying at the bottom of my ocean that stare up at me from the depths. I lived in fear for years that at any moment I'd be pulled under, never to be heard from again.

Time plays a significant role in our lives in bringing two concepts into balance. When we are young, our focus on the future and our perspective on the past are completely askew. As children, the future seems so far away. We fantasize about what we want to be and where we want to go one day, but it is all wanderlust. None of it is based on reality, as we have little understanding of life. It is virtually impossible to see clearly what life holds for us further down the road. Life seems out of focus and the horizon hidden.

At the same time, because we are young, we have no history either. This means we have no perspective and therefore life has virtually no context. We live in the moment and are only concerned with our most immediate needs. As we journey down life's highway and grow older, our future starts coming into focus and our past starts to bring perspective. This has certainly been the case for me.

In early 2008, something I thought had died many years ago started to resurrect. I started feeling emotions and passions I hadn't felt in years and they were bubbling up with an energy of their own. At first I tried to suppress them as I wasn't sure where they were coming from, nor was I interested in feeling more pain or living through more disappointment. I was caught off-guard as my heart was being pulled back to the people of Zimbabwe.

One day as I was ruminating over all these mysterious thoughts and feelings, out of the depths of my soul came the words, 'Do not let the lives of your friends be shed in vain. The story is not over, in fact, it's just beginning.' These words would not leave me alone for weeks until one day I came to grips with the fact that I had been entrusted with a message. For reasons only God knows, like a pregnant woman, I was carrying in me a profound story that needed to be told.

Once I got past all my fears and insecurities about writing, I set my mind and heart to telling our story. It's a big story that covers a host of people and generations. While it is the story of Zimbabwe, it's also the story of many other people around the world. It's a story that sadly has repeated itself like a broken record as mankind fails to gain understanding and wisdom from history.

I'm old enough now to have perspective, and from my perspective the cure for what ails the world will not be found within our own hearts.

I have seen too much, the evidence is too overwhelming; mankind is plagued by the terminal disease of selfishness. It is at the root of all evil and has consumed humanity like a ravenous beast. If there is any hope that, as the prophet Isaiah dreamed, the lamb will ever lie down with the lion and wolf, the human soul must be re-wired. In the place of out-of-control self-centredness, mankind needs a new heart, one that is motivated by true selfless love, one for another.

The people of The Community of Reconciliation had that kind of love, but it came not from their own innate goodness as they were all too aware of their own human frailties. It came because they had a spiritual encounter with God himself that transformed them. That transformation couldn't help but transform the people around them. Transformation of the soul is the soul of transformation!

I hope our story, while at times gut-wrenching and unbearable, will be both thought-provoking and inspirational. It's a story that is in progress and this book is only the first volume in an ever unfolding divine drama.

To put some form to a number of concurring and intertwined story lines, I have divided the book into two parts:

Part One, 'The Road Behind,' chronicles the martyrdom of my friends and their simple but extraordinary lives. It also recounts the history of the Zimbabwean people and addresses the elements that contributed to this violent collision of cultures.

Part Two, 'The Road Ahead,' explains the current situation in the nation and what I believe is a general road map for significant and lasting change in the country. It is my hope that this story will help inspire others to join with the Zimbabweans to rebuild their nation.

Thank you for taking the time to read this book. Like all those associated with this story, I hope you will never be the same again, nor will the people of Zimbabwe.

– Bob Scott

January 2010

Part One:
The Road Behind

The past is our definition. We may strive, with good reason,
to escape it, or to escape what is bad in it, but we will
escape it only by adding something better to it.
– Wendell Berry

CHAPTER 1

A Journey into
Uncharted Territory

If you can find a path with no obstacles,
it probably doesn't lead anywhere.

— Frank A Clark

I t was a grey, overcast day at New York's JFK Airport, one where it felt like the clouds were just a few feet above one's head. The events of the past twenty-four hours had left me in a dark, introspective mood. Talking was out of the question. It almost seemed irreverent. As we were finding our seats for the long-haul overnight flight, the captain announced that we were temporarily fogged in. He suggested we get comfortable as it was possible the flight would be delayed for some time.

My feelings and emotions were churning like the ocean during a massive storm. On the one hand, I was frustrated and wanted to get on with the trip. I needed to get to Zimbabwe and find out what had happened to my friends and to comfort their families. On the other hand, their deaths were so violent that I was filled with anxiety about having to face not only the unpleasant sights but also a lot of people in anger and excruciating pain. I was not sure if I really wanted to experience what I was about to be exposed to. I felt totally inadequate. It soon dawned on me, however, that it really didn't matter. I was on an airplane headed overseas to a huge funeral and there was no turning back now.

Suddenly, the flight attendant's announcement interrupted my inner world of thoughts. Due to the weather delay, the captain was going to make the evening news available. It looked like it was going to take quite a while for the fog to clear and he thought it might be a nice gesture to keep everyone occupied.

What happened next is a memory so etched into my psyche that I will never be able to forget it. It's like a newsreel stored in my head. It sends a chill up my spine as I recall the sound of the musical intro to ABC's Evening News blaring over the plane's loudspeakers. Then there was the distinct Canadian voice of news anchor Peter Jennings saying, 'Tonight's top story: sixteen missionaries were massacred in Zimbabwe yesterday …' At that moment it seemed like my whole internal gyroscope started spinning out of control. I felt dizzy. There on the TV screen on an airplane in New York City was a picture of my friend Gerry Keightley holding his baby son Barnabas, along with pictures of his two beautiful daughters, Deborah and Glynis, when they were little children. I was stunned to see them on TV. I had no idea that anyone outside of Zimbabwe, aside from a few folks here in the States, even knew about what had happened the night before.

In the US, the Friday after the Thanksgiving holiday is always one of the busiest shopping days of the year. No one has time to sit and watch the news, much less care about or even want to hear about a massacre in Zimbabwe. The story was a morbid one and, after all, it was the first day of the holiday season.

As I sat stalled on the tarmac in that suddenly claustrophobic jet I thought, *There are my friends on TV. They have become a news story because they are now dead. How sad is that? No one seemed to think that leaving behind their comfortable suburban lifestyle for the sake of racial harmony, in a country torn apart by racism, was newsworthy when they were alive. Now they are dead because of it, so we'll tell the story on a day when no one cares! This is warped.* The whole scenario was causing me intense emotional pain and I felt a consuming anger rising up inside me. I was so emotionally conflicted with so much sorrow and anger in the same moment.

As I looked around, I saw children playing in the aisles, people reading the newspaper and others with headphones, listening to music. I was beside myself. Everything inside me wanted to run up and down the aisles ripping newspapers out of people's hands. I wanted to make all of them watch the story. It was important to me that they knew that these people had died for something good, something really good. They had demonstrated that by the grace of God, black Africans and white Africans could live together. They were not just talking about it, they were doing it. They had established a genuine expression of the Kingdom of God that modelled racial harmony, feeding the oppressed poor and forming a self-sustaining, small village economy. They died not because it was a flawed truth but because it was a powerful, working truth. They had demonstrated that age-old hatreds could be put to rest. They called their little expression, 'The Community of Reconciliation'.

> *These people had demonstrated that by the grace of God, black Africans and white Africans could live together.*

Sitting there in stunned silence, it hit me again that these were my dear friends with whom I had worked so closely over the past few years. I wanted to tell everyone, including the press, that they had it wrong. These were not missionaries from far away; these were ordinary local African people, friends and neighbours who just wanted to do the right thing. They wanted to demonstrate the love of God in the simplest way. They wanted peace, not conflict. They wanted to help people out of difficult times, whether white or black. These were good people, really good people. Did anybody care what they had been living for?

It was a terribly excruciating experience to see that few had cared about what they had been doing when they were alive, and that they were only newsworthy now that they were dead.

To over 350 people on that plane, it was just another news event about another tragic story somewhere far away. While they were comfortably numb to it, I was filled with raw and painful emotions that kept escaping from their self-imposed exile to the deep recesses of my soul. These human beings were not just a story or a photo on a screen. They had become family to me. I sat in that aircraft seat like a caged animal using what little bit of self-control I had left to keep myself in my seat. If I had given in to all those raw emotions just for a second, I'm sure the airport police would have carried me off that plane wrapped in a straight-jacket, screaming into the foggy night.

I was really upset at ABC News for the 'missionary' reference as I thought it took away from the true nature of the story. Not that I have an issue with missionaries, but this was not about people coming from somewhere else to help the poor Africans. This was about indigenous black Africans and their white neighbours saying, 'Let's live in peace together, side by side. Let's change our history. God made us one people in Him, let's live like it.'

For hundreds of years, the South African Dutch Reformed Church had either turned a deaf ear to, or in the worst cases, sanctioned the hideous concept of Apartheid. This political ideology sanctioned by the church stood for two of God's diverse ethnic groups living side by side, but in different communities, with different standards. The inequality was substantial, with the white population getting the vast financial benefits of the arrangement. The people of The Community of Reconciliation believed that God had a very different expression in mind that celebrated diversity in harmony. They understood that each group brought something unique to the table and that the only one who sits at the head of God's table is God.

I couldn't keep from thinking of my dear friends John and Elaine Russell, who were in their 70s. They had lost nine family members in this tragedy. That number seemed unimaginable. Losing one loved one is difficult enough, how could anyone survive the loss of nine?

As I would later learn, the Russells were just returning to Zimbabwe from visiting with their youngest son Jeremy here in the States, when the raid and subsequent massacres took place. As they got off the airplane in Johannesburg, they noticed that there was an unusually large contingent of people there to greet them. It was then that they learned about the attack and murders. They had lost two daughters, two sons-in-law, a daughter-in-law and four grandchildren! How I ached for them. Adding to the pain was the immense distance, the sense of separation from them and the inability to even give them a hug or utter a kind word.

Why do bad things happen to good people?

As the magnitude of it all hit me, the tears welled up. *How tragic,* I thought. *They don't deserve this. Why do bad things happen to good people? This just doesn't seem right. I thought if you obeyed God and lived righteously He would protect you.* None of this made sense; this whole scenario felt wrong, very wrong.

After a few more hours of what seemed like reliving a lifetime, the plane finally took off. As we roared down the runway I was thrust back in my seat by the power of that huge aircraft. It all seemed like a bad dream or a metaphor for what lay ahead. I was no longer in control of the situation. I was being unstoppably carried along by the jet as we soared into the darkness.

How did all this happen so suddenly? Yesterday I was enjoying a beautiful Thanksgiving with my family.

My date with this unforeseen destiny started out unusually in that it was actually a beautiful day. Kansas City Thanksgivings traditionally were cold, overcast and often rainy; this one was warm and sunny. The air outside was clean and fresh and there was a sense of anticipation over this family holiday.

Thanksgiving is an American celebration of the friendship between the 'Pilgrims' who left England to settle America and the indigenous Indians who were already living here. The contemporary Thanksgiving celebration involves family and friends at a large meal: usually a roast turkey with many side dishes made from foods native to the United States.

It is a form of harvest festival. The first Thanksgiving is believed to have occurred at the Plymouth Plantation in Massachusetts during the autumn season of 1621.

Traditionally, we gathered our whole family and headed to my mother-in-law's house for an all-day event. It was an experience unlike any other. With seven children of her own, each bringing their brood, Peggy's little white, single-level home on Blue Ridge Boulevard was always packed with people. I was particularly thankful for the pleasant weather as it meant the massive gathering of hyperactive grandchildren could play outside.

The sense of anticipation of seeing all their cousins in one place usually had my kids wired by early morning. This led to frequent, incessant questioning about whether or not we were going to be leaving soon. I was always fascinated by the sense of excitement that the children had about Thanksgiving. I think the fact that it was an 'event' and at Papa and 'Gre-Gre's' house was what made it special.

Once we had our assigned portion of the feast prepared, we loaded the children and food in the car and headed on our merry way to Thanksgiving Madness. My son Kyle was five and my daughter Jessica three. They looked so cute buckled in the back seat of the car, beaming with expectation. Kyle, who always had enough energy for three kids, couldn't wait to get there to play football with his uncles and cousins. Even at five he already had the natural intensity of a competitive athlete and the heart of a soldier. Jessica had a baby doll in her arms that she was mothering to death. She loved the 'American Girl' collection and my mother, Elaine, always made sure that her dolls were finely dressed.

Upon arriving at the Callahans', the kids were practically out of the car before it stopped. Their little legs ran as fast as they could to the back yard to see who else was already there and to make sure they wouldn't miss anything. Once they had scoped out the whole situation, I heard their mother yelling out the back door for them to come inside to give their Papa and 'Gre-Gre' a big hug and kiss. Papa was a big outgoing man and gave big bear hugs, while 'Gre-Gre' had a favourite chair she loved to sit in to watch all the 'goings-on'. With a beer in one hand and a cigarette in the other, she'd sit there quietly for hours and just smile, taking the whole scene in. One by one, more cars arrived and more kids piled out, each making the same mad dash to the back yard to see who was already there.

It was a tradition that late morning and early afternoon were always spent watching football. Around half-time, dinner was ready. First, the kids' plates were filled, then the adults lined up at the serving table. We were a football family. My brothers-in-law were die-hard Kansas City Chiefs fans. It just so happened that this Thanksgiving the Chiefs were playing the Detroit Lions and thankfully with the nice weather the kids were all outside. My in-laws had one of those old wooden console TVs that sat on the floor. If the weather had been bad there would have been virtually no way to see the screen with all the people standing around in the house, so this year we actually got to watch the game uninterrupted. Thankfully the Chiefs beat the Lions 27–20 or my brother-in-law Pat would have been in a grumpy mood the rest of the day. The late game was the Dallas Cowboys vs. the Minnesota Vikings, but before the game started, I decided to mosey outside to see how my father-in-law Bob was doing in the back yard.

Bob was a big man who had had a rather tough life, growing up on the violent streets of East St. Louis, Illinois. He had married my mother-in-law, Peggy, and they had a house painting business together. He was as blue-collar and redneck as they come. You could always expect beer, barbecue and country music. He and Peggy were also very involved at the Elk's Lodge in south Kansas City. The Elk's Lodge is a social and fraternal club founded in 1868. For a number of years Bob was the 'Grand Poobah', or leader at the Lodge. He ran that place like it was his domain. He loved to cook and it was a common sight to see him standing behind the grill cooking for the whole crowd.

For all of his street toughness, underneath he was a big soft teddy bear who really loved his step-kids and grandkids. When he knew 'the family' was coming over, he'd fire up his grill, crank up the country music and start barbecuing. This year he was smoking a turkey in a new smoker he had just purchased. As I stepped outside and looked around, there he was, standing next to his grill with his big barbecue fork in one hand and a beer in the other. He had his chef's apron on, but he was so big it looked more like a bib. At that moment he was watching all the grandkids run around the yard. The boys were playing football, the girls had their dolls and the moms were seated together on the patio furniture, all talking at once. It was quite a sight to see and the volume level was staggering. I remember thinking to myself, *He's in his element now.* Bob loved having lots of activity around him all the time. I think he quite enjoyed the chaos.

> *Nothing could have prepared me for this call or how this crisis was about to take me to my knees and pillage my status quo 'normal life'.*

After walking back into the house to watch the Cowboys game with Pat, I sat down in one of the armchairs, thanking God that all that noise was outside. Around half-time, they announced that the turkey was ready. Peggy kicked into gear and started setting out the food, plates and utensils to feed this crazy mob. The cousins came pouring into the house and jostled into line, jumping up and down while their moms filled their plates and sent them back outside. Once the munchkins had cleared out, the adults started lining up. I was so looking forward to tasting some of Bob's smoked turkey, as it looked and smelt delicious.

After piling my plate high and having just sat down to devour the amazing feast of turkey and trimmings, the phone rang. I was really surprised when I learned that the call was for me. Why would anyone be calling me at my in-laws' house on Thanksgiving? I was hoping it wasn't someone from the church who needed counselling. It's awfully hard to have compassion for someone when you know you have a big plate of delicious food that's getting cold.

My brother-in-law and I had started this church a few years earlier, and sometimes people's needs would cause them to be invasive. It wasn't uncommon for someone who was in the middle of a personal crisis to try and reach us no matter where we were. Nothing could have prepared me for this call or how this crisis was about to take me to my knees and pillage my *status quo* 'normal life'.

Once the phone made its way over to me, I was surprised to hear the distinctly South African voice of my pastoral colleague, Noel Alexander, on the other end of the phone. Noel wasn't one to show a lot of emotion and I could tell by the unsettling sound in his voice that something was wrong. Very wrong! He told me to sit down; he had something dreadful to tell me. It's amazing all the things that ran through my mind in that moment. In an effort to help immunize myself from the impending pain, my mind raced ahead, trying to uncover every possible scenario, so that when I finally heard it, I wasn't going to be totally shocked. Well, even though my mind covered a myriad of scenarios, what I was about to hear wasn't in any one of them. I could feel Noel's voice struggling to come up with enough strength and find the right words.

> *Suddenly it was like I was a spectator of my own life.*

After a brief pause he stammered, 'Bob, all the white brothers and sisters on the farms in Zimbabwe have been killed. They've been massacred Bob, all of them, even the children.' I couldn't believe what I was hearing. In fact, I was so stunned I asked him to repeat what he had just said. My worst fears came true when he told me again the news of the massacres. In that moment the sense of shock generated strange sensations in my body. It started in my head, and soon had completely consumed me into what felt like some sort of dimensional bubble or alternative reality.

Suddenly it was like I was a spectator of my own life. I felt like I was having an out-of-body experience. I was watching people's mouths move, but couldn't hear a word they were saying. I could tell by the expressions on their faces that they were all having fun, laughing and enjoying the meal and each other. I remember my mind going numb, and then my body, as all the feeling just drained out through my feet. I was sitting there in a chair with a whole plate of untouched food on my lap and a phone to my ear, but I had no idea what I was doing there.

As I tried to find my mental and emotional equilibrium, I started asking really dumb questions just to buy time to try and get a hold of myself and clear my head. I finally had one cognitive thought and asked what had actually happened. Noel explained that he had just received a call from Joseph Huidekoper in Montana, and that he had been frantically trying to track me down. Joseph and his new bride Joanna had lived and worked for a couple of years with my friends who had just been massacred in Zimbabwe. Noel told me that from what had been communicated to him, a group of political dissidents had raided the New Adams Farm, killing eight people, and then raided the adjacent Olive Tree Farm, killing eight more. Both properties were a part of The Community of Reconciliation.

This just wasn't supposed to be the way the story ended. Someone had decided to rewrite the script, and violently at that!

I sat there in shock and asked myself, *How could this have happened?* These were really good people who were doing something simple and yet extraordinary. I thought, *Bad things don't happen to good people; how can this be?* I hung up the phone and just sat there, my mind racing to figure out some rational explanation for this tragedy. This just wasn't supposed to be the way the story ended. Someone had decided to rewrite the script, and violently at that. My paradigm of the Christian life and God's ways took a huge hit in that moment. In fact, they got nuked.

Before we hung up, Noel and I decided to meet at the church offices immediately to try to sort through this overwhelmingly tragic news. Neither of us really knew what to do next. It was fortunate that Gary Kroeze, who had introduced me to this group of amazing Zimbabweans, was in Kansas City at the time. He was having Thanksgiving dinner with Jim and Sallie Collins, who were members of our church. The Collinses had recently returned from an extended stay in Zimbabwe where they had been working on developing simple technology solutions that would benefit not only the people in the Community, but also those in the surrounding region.

I put the phone down and just sat in the chair looking around, struck by the incredible irony of it all. Here I was sitting in America, with life teeming everywhere around me. Three generations of family members were laughing, joking and eating together, celebrating the gift of life and family. The warm autumn sun was shining down brightly and the birds were in the trees singing at the top of their lungs. Life surrounded me; I was immersed in it. At the very same moment, a continent away, sixteen lifeless bodies were being loaded up and driven to the local morgue in Bulawayo. Those weren't just any bodies. They were the bodies of my friends and, in a spiritual way, my extended family. Just a year earlier we had sat together and shared meals, friendship and our dreams for this community. We dreamed of a peaceful and prosperous Zimbabwe where the colour of one's skin was irrelevant. We dreamed of a land whose soul was transformed by the very same values and principles that beat within Jesus' heart. Amazingly enough, it was materializing and almost everyone in the region saw the transformation taking place. Centuries of racism and resentment that had tarnished a nation so filled with promise were slowly being washed away by a love not of this earth.

> *We dreamed of a land whose soul was transformed by the very same values and principles that beat within Jesus' heart.*

I felt very alone as I sat there in that chair. No one at the house had any idea as to what I was feeling. I still hadn't touched my food and frankly I had lost my appetite. I didn't want to say anything because I didn't want to ruin everyone else's holiday and yet I needed to leave. What do you say to people in a situation like that? I had no idea. I was still in shock. I finally excused myself, telling them I had to leave to attend to a personal crisis. I told my wife I would meet her at home later that night once I figured out what was going on.

I headed to the church offices to meet with Noel and Gary. I was lost in thought about all the people who had lost family members, how they must be in total shock and how hard this was going to be for them. It suddenly dawned on me how similar John Russell was to my father-in-law, Bob Callahan. Both men had had hard lives and grew up tough. Both were fiercely independent and self-made men. Both were blue collar and not scared of a hard day's work. Both ran trade companies and were leaders. Both men, while seemingly tough on the outside, were big teddy bears on the inside and absolutely loved their children and grandchildren.

I traversed the library of my mind looking for some past experience or material I might draw on, but I came up empty. I was in uncharted territory.

This Thanksgiving, November 26th 1987, while Bob Callahan was celebrating the joy of life and family, John Russell was in mourning, having been left to deal with the calamity and destruction the Angel of Death had left him.

In the same moment, I found myself overcome with a very sobering sense of my own immaturity. I thought, *I am way too young and inexperienced to deal with something of this magnitude.* Other than Elizabeth Elliot's story of the martyrdom of her husband and his four friends in 1957, I didn't know a single person who had gone through a similar experience. I found myself overwhelmed by the sheer magnitude of the situation. I kept repeating to myself, *Sixteen people have just died! Sixteen!* Frankly, I was lost. I traversed the library of my mind looking for some past experience or material I might draw on, but I came up empty. I was in uncharted territory. It's embarrassing to admit, but I found myself momentarily feeling sorry for myself. I was bemoaning the fact that I wasn't sure I was up to this and I had no idea what I was even supposed to do. *I can't fix this,* I thought, *it's just too devastating. I am not even sure what to think. There is so much I don't understand about what happened and why.*

Waiting next in line on this emotional and mentally volatile ride were thoughts of guilt over my feeling so pathetic in the midst of a crisis. I didn't like how I was dealing with the whole situation. I felt like a boy, but needed to be a man. With hindsight, I am sure that I was still suffering from shock as my brain just could not seem to think clearly about anything. It felt like I was in a fog and struggling to focus on what was ahead of me. I still had that strange sensation as though I was somehow in another dimension. Everything inside me wanted to get away and try to process all that had just happened alone. What I really needed was time and solitude which, over the course of my life, have served me well. They have helped me calm my emotions and by isolating myself from all the other voices, I can hear my own thoughts and get in touch with my feelings. Unfortunately, that opportunity never materialized and I was left to compartmentalise my emotions until some unknown point in the future.

When God entrusts you with a compassionate heart such as I have, one of the very real struggles is to separate your own pain from that of others. At times, all those emotions can get tangled into one large knot that seems impossible to separate. I had dealt with the death of my father a few years earlier, but this situation was altogether different. How does one process the tragic deaths of sixteen friends at once? I could barely get past mourning for the first few friends who came to mind when I realized that I still had fourteen more to go. It seemed that there just wasn't enough of me or that my heart simply wasn't large enough. This was perplexing and gave my inner demons more fuel for their bonfire of guilt. In the end I had to lump everyone into one big group called 'The Community' and mourn them together, which took away some of the personal nature of it but made it possible to process some of my grief.

I wondered about the remaining family members scattered around the world. My thoughts turned again to the Russells. *What about John and Elaine? What about Dave and Sharon's families in the US who are now so far away from their dead children?* At that point it was all coming too fast and furious and I was unable to process it.

Despite the state of chaos that my mind and emotions were in, I had no choice but to force myself to rise to the occasion right then and there as people were going to be looking to me for direction and answers. After all, it was through my encouragement and leadership that so many people in Kansas City had been involved with this project. They were going to be looking to me not only for direction, but how to respond to a crisis of this magnitude.

Just then another wave of emotion swept over me. What about the families from the church that had spent time on the farms? What if the Collins, Corums or Hartleys had been killed? It would have been unbearable, and yet what I was already feeling seemed unbearable. Could something be more unbearable than what I was already feeling? That seemed like such an oxymoron. Sometimes emotions can wreak havoc with the mind. When you need sanity, they betray you and seem to want to drive you toward insanity.

> *Sometimes emotions can wreak havoc with the mind. When you need sanity, they betray you and seem to want to drive you toward insanity.*

I kept telling myself, *If there was ever a time to stand up and be a man, it's now.* It was like I was giving myself an internal slap on the face to wake up out of this mental stupor and emotional chaos. If I was going to be remotely helpful at this meeting I needed to do something with these unbridled emotions as they were tearing me apart inside. I wanted to let out an enormously loud scream. I decided at that point to do what I had done so often in the past, which was find a nice cabinet in my soul and stuff every emotion I had in there. Once firmly packed, I chained the doors, and locked them securely. To make sure that there would be no chance of escape, I took that cabinet and rolled it into a cave even deeper into the recesses of my soul so that it would never see the light of day. There it has remained for many years until recently.

As I walked into the meeting room, Noel Alexander and Gary Kroeze both met me with an extended tender hug. Noel was his typical stoic South African self with little to say, and yet there was that strength of soul that was always evident with him. Gary was trying hard to hold it together but his eyes were filled with tears. While he was a tough Montana cattle rancher on the outside, on the inside he was as tender as they come. Later when he just could not hold it in anymore he blurted out in a moment of pain, 'I should have been there, I should have died too.' He was really struggling with the guilt of being alive while his dear friends had crossed over to heaven. My friend Mike, the senior pastor, decided to come by the offices to see if he could lend any support. I remember being so thankful for his willingness to do anything to help. Although he had not visited the Community and so didn't have the personal connections that we did, he knew we were in pain and just wanted to be there for us.

I do not remember much of what the four of us discussed in that room other than recapping the phone call from Joseph and praying, asking God for strength of soul and direction. I know that there were some extended moments of silence as no one knew quite what to say. Since Gary and I had the most to do with the people at the community, it was decided we should go there and take whatever time was necessary to help comfort family members and the Africans and help with funeral arrangements.

The events of Thanksgiving 1987 swung open a door I couldn't kick closed and, believe me, I kicked hard. In fact it would indelibly reshape me, my destiny, my view of life and my view of God for the rest of my life.

It's now been over 20 years since fate stood like a bully in my path, forcing me down a road I did not want to travel. Years later, I'm still dealing with its awful and yet uncharted repercussions. On the other hand, as the prophet Isaiah proclaimed, 'Woe to him who quarrels with his Maker ... does the clay say to the potter, "What are you making?"' (Isa 45:9).

I had no idea when I woke up that Thanksgiving morning what God was 'making' out of me and certainly no idea of the ghastly circumstances that had taken place while I had slept. I was a young pastor trying to be obedient to the perceived call of God on my life. I simply wanted to help Jesus build his church. I had no idea the wilderness journey He was about to take me on.

CHAPTER 2

ON THE JOB TRAINING

In a time of drastic change it is the learners who inherit the future. The learned usually find themselves equipped to live in a world that no longer exists.

– ERIC HOFFER

A s our flight headed east over the dark tumultuous seas of the Atlantic, I had ample time to reflect on the journey that had brought me to this implausible moment. In spite of how far I had travelled and how much I had learned, in light of the moment I was but a child in my own mind in terms of understanding.

As a child of the '60s, being self-absorbed was the mindset of the day and I had jumped in with both feet.

While Zimbabwe, then called Rhodesia, was in the midst of political, economic and religious turmoil, back in the US I was on my own spiritual journey that would ultimately change the course of my life. In the summer of 1975, I had a rather deep spiritual encounter that radically altered my self-centred, self-indulgent pursuit of self-happiness. As a child of the '60s, being self-absorbed was the mindset of the day and I had jumped in with both feet.

Without understanding it until years later, by the time I was eleven I had already developed my own pseudo form of existentialism. Simply defined, existentialism is a philosophy whereby each person is free to determine right and wrong personally. You determine the moral and ethical compass you will use to direct and govern your individual world. There are no absolutes. Hence, you are god of your own world.

In the end, they all seemed to be determined to get to the same goal ... to be happy.

I decided to do some research by observation and see what goals people had for their lives. It soon became clear that there were a variety of ways people chose to achieve their goals, but in the end, they all seemed to be determined to get to the same one ... happiness. I decided that my new goal in life was to be happy as well and to do whatever it took to achieve that end. It was just a few years before my 'nirvanic', existential bubble burst. I saw it happen not only in my own decadent heart but also in those around me. Selfishness leads us to do inhuman things. I saw the depths of depravity that people would descend to in order to get what they wanted. I observed the blatant disregard and devaluing of human life and the indignity that selfishness breeds. I didn't like what it was doing to me and who I was becoming. I needed to change. This philosophy was turning me into a self-absorbed monster that just consumed material resources and people. I was a serial narcissist.

Once God got my attention by showing me the ugliness of my own heart, I became profoundly affected by the lifestyle and teachings of Jesus. After reading the historical record of Jesus' life, I was fascinated by the way that one man with some rather simple truths built on principles like Mercy and Justice could change the world forever in just three years. His impact was even more far-reaching and extraordinary than that of other men I greatly respected like Abraham Lincoln, Mahatma Gandhi and Martin Luther King. It wasn't long before it dawned on me that those great men had all died standing for the very same principles that Jesus had first laid out in his teachings thousands of years before. It seemed to me that truth, no matter the person it came from, was still the truth. What was a mystery to me at the time was why they all died at the hands of their fellow human beings. Didn't everyone want to know the truth? Why would anyone want to kill those who stood up for equity and justice? What were their killers so afraid of?

There is a story that the historian Luke recounts about when, very early in his public life, Jesus enters a Jewish synagogue in his home town of Nazareth. Standing before his family and friends, He reads from the writings of the prophet Isaiah, whose words were recorded on a scroll. In this moment, for all to hear, He defines, or frames, his life's purpose with these words:

> *The Spirit of the Lord is upon me, because he has anointed me to bring good news to the poor. He has sent me to proclaim release to the captives and recovery of sight to the blind, to let the oppressed go free, to proclaim the year of the Lord's favour.*
>
> – LUKE 4:18–19

As I read what Jesus said about Himself and his life's purpose and put aside all that others had told me about Him, it seemed that He was quite simply deeply concerned about the plight of the poor and the oppressed. He wanted to free the broken and heal the blind. That, after all, was his personally stated mission. As I read more about Him, I was equally touched by the many times the historians commented that 'He was moved to compassion and therefore … ' The 'therefore' was always followed by some form of action.

What was a mystery to me at the time was why they all died at the hands of their fellow human beings.

It soon became clear that this remarkable man genuinely cared about the plight of the people He saw as oppressed. In fact, He cared to such an extent that He did something about it. He was proactive. He challenged people's conventional thinking. He was a catalyst for change. People were different after being with Him. I found it interesting that his biggest conflicts seemed to be with those who liked to talk about truth from a place

19

of self-righteous arrogance. I drew the conclusion that Jesus was a 'Spiritual' man who really disliked institutionally sanctimonious or 'Religious' men. He seemed to have a disdain for people who externally ascribed to a system of regulations that looked good on paper, but internally had hearts that were hard and without compassion. It really bothered Him that they evaluated themselves as good or bad based on how well they religiously followed a set of rules or 'Laws', as they called them.

Jesus seemed to be a 'man of the heart'.

Jesus seemed to be a 'man of the heart'. He was drawn to genuineness, sincerity and the simple faith that people had. He certainly seemed genuinely interested in the plight of the 'little guy' and was committed to changing their lives. However, He didn't often do it in the way that they expected, but in the way that they needed. I identified with Him as I think He saw the religious community of his day much the same way as I did. He seemed revolted by the condescending self-righteousness of those supposedly 'in the know'.

At that point in my life, the church in general seemed like the 'Tin Man' from the Wizard of Oz – lacking a heart. Most of what I had been exposed to were churches whose primary goal was to get bigger. A building programme was the sign of a successful and healthy church. There was something unsettling about it inside my soul. For me, that just wasn't enough. There had to be more to all this. After all, a man had lost his life teaching the truth about what love really looked like. He had asked thought-provoking questions to expose what truly motivated people. He had demonstrated this otherworldly love by feeding and healing the poor. In the end it cost Him his life. Just like Lincoln, Gandhi and King, He was fully committed. Just like them He believed that the world could change; that people could make a difference. And therefore He offered them hope of a better world based on better principles and values.

Just like them He believed that the world could change; that people could make a difference.

I was a now young man on a mission. I was going to leave no stone unturned until I found satisfaction to my many questions. One in particular was really bothering me. *Why, if the Church was Jesus' chosen vehicle to teach and demonstrate the truths that He had held so dear, did it seem like it was so irrelevant and ineffective in the current culture?*

From where I stood, the world was a mess. It seemed that racism, oppression, hatred and greed, as well as many other insidious attitudes, were at the heart of conflict after conflict. The world was tearing itself apart and the victims, typically, were the innocent. Why weren't the governments and leaders of the world breaking down the doors of 'The Church' to get the answers from us? After all, didn't we have the teachings and wisdom of God?

Why did no one seem to care what we had to say? What had we done or not done to relegate ourselves to this sad place of insignificance? Was there not any current expression of Christianity on the earth that impressed people and got their attention? Was anyone making a significant impact?

> *What had we done or not done to relegate ourselves to this sad place of insignificance?*

Something seemed to be wrong … or was I missing something? I thought to myself that maybe it was just like this in America, and that in other places in the world the church was changing the world in significant ways.

As I continued on this journey of discovery, I was constantly amazed at the things I read about the unusual movement that Jesus had started. For example, I noticed in Luke's historical account in The Acts of the Apostles that the early Christian community had an unusual lifestyle. There was a very interesting social dynamic that developed with his followers. It seemed that even though the traumatic events of the crucifixion had scattered them due to the fear of possible repercussions, Jesus had gathered them back together after his resurrection.

Even though most of Jesus' inner circle of followers lived 190 kilometres away in northern Israel, they remained in Jerusalem for an additional fifty days. Luke records that the eleven remaining disciples, Mary, Jesus' mother, and his natural brothers, all stayed in Jerusalem and joined together in prayer. The record doesn't state how they provided for themselves, so one is left to speculate that there must have been other local followers who looked after them. Soon the city was packed as pilgrims from all over the region were streaming into the city to celebrate the Jewish Festival of Pentecost which pronounced the beginning of the autumn harvest season. This was typically a time of great joy and festivities with lots of parties.

Luke records that at nine o'clock one morning, a violent wind came rushing into the building where they were all praying. It appeared to observers something like 'tongues of fire' had settled on those present. Soon they were speaking in multiple foreign languages and the Pentecost sojourners who had come from all over the known world could understand them in their native languages. As you can imagine, it created a huge uproar. People were in utter shock.

As the record states, these men were not learned scholars or professional government translators. Something supernatural had happened to them whereby they could now speak in a previously unlearned foreign language. I'm sure that it must have been a mind-bending experience for those who were speaking as well as those listening.

Then Peter stood up and spoke to the crowd that had gathered after hearing all the commotion. He tried to explain what had just happened and then dropped a bomb by saying, 'the guy you just crucified and killed a few months back, well ... He is the one that just did this! He's the one that created this mess but He did it for a reason ... to get your attention.'

The record says that people were 'cut to the heart' and that 3 000 people joined this little group of followers that day. Things suddenly got really complicated as the 3 000 people who had just joined the group were in the same situation as Jesus' followers. They didn't live in Jerusalem and were far from home. This was a potential logistical nightmare. What were Jesus' disciples going to do with this throng of new converts who wanted to stay in the city and learn more about their newfound faith?

As I'm reading this account, I'm imagining this happening to 3 000 self-centred, spoiled Americans on vacation in Hawaii. Can you imagine the chaos that would ensue and how demanding all these people would be? I feel sorry for the poor people working behind the front desk at the hotels that day. It's a frightening picture to imagine. I'm sure the TV networks would have been there in short order, blaming the government for not being better prepared and FEMA for not handling the crisis better.

I was gripped by reading Luke's account of the developing situation and how different the response was to this logistical crisis. He states:

> *All the believers were together and had everything in common. Selling their possessions and goods, they gave to anyone as he had need. Everyday they continued to meet together in the temple courts. They broke bread in their homes (must have been some locals' homes or newly bought homes) and ate together with glad and sincere hearts, praising God and enjoying the favour of all the people. And the Lord added to their number daily those that were being saved.*
>
> – ACTS 2:44–47

The English have the saying 'bowled me over', and that's what I was. There is no possible way that this situation could have resolved itself so peacefully unless something profound had taken place in people's hearts. What would cause a man to want to give up all that he had for the sake of others? I came to the conclusion that this was exactly what Jesus had stood for. This unplanned collection of people had taken on one of the distinct character qualities of its leader. These ordinary people were doing something extraordinary because their hearts had been transformed and out of it came a new expression of relating to one another. Years later, historians would define this situation as the first expression of 'Christian Community'.

What would cause a man to want to give up all that he had for the sake of others?

While I was in awe that one man's message could have such a profound impact on people and utterly transform their self-centred nature, I was equally impressed by the way that this new form of Christian expression affected the surrounding society. Luke records that *they enjoyed the favour of all the people.* Now that was significant impact. Something was happening there that was so genuine that those they came in contact with in the larger society noticed it and respected it. This really intrigued me and I set course to better understand this new expression and unique concept of Christian Community.

> The Christian community's biggest challenge has never been one of words but of deeds.

After many months of studying and visiting with a number of groups with a community lifestyle, I came to some conclusions. There was no denying that the form of community where everyone had everything in common could be a powerful expression of people's faith as long as it was rooted in humility. I also concluded that it wasn't for everyone. In fact it probably wasn't for most people.

It also seemed to me that this unusual but powerful expression of community was actually better suited for crisis-driven environments or circumstances. For example, situations where people were reacting to sudden positive influences like what happened during the Pentecost Feast. This was a spiritual dynamic that created a practical problem. The solution was that people's hearts had been transformed and they wanted to be generous. No authority was forcing them to do what they were doing. It was a reaction of the heart responding to a wonderful problem.

The other side of the spectrum would be negative situations like the intense persecution that the Anabaptist groups (i.e. Amish, Mennonites and Hutterites) experienced in Europe. They were trying to find ways to survive. Economic crisis would be another example. During the depression, many families moved in together and shared whatever resources they had. When floods, hurricanes and tornados devastate whole communities, you often see people banding to together in various types of new communities to help each other through. These powerful external forces can become a great motivation for people to band together in some type of community for survival. One way or another, when it's done right, it can make a significant impact and, as Luke wrote, people will look on the community with favour.

The Christian community's biggest challenge has never been one of words but of deeds. We have lots of verbal expressions. We have volumes of written material from the past two thousand years explaining what we believe. There is no shortage of voices telling the masses what it means to be a Christian. The volume of written and spoken words is staggering. But what about putting these words into action?

The question that was eating at me was: whose deeds are speaking in such a way that it significantly matters in someone else's life? Was there anywhere in the world where the non-Christian community was so impressed by the authentic and practical expression of faith that they actually admired Christians? Were we looked up to anywhere in the world? Did anyone care what we had to say?

The question that was eating at me was: whose deeds are speaking in such a way that it significantly matters in someone else's life?

If Jesus defined his purpose as setting captives free and fighting on behalf of the poor and oppressed, shouldn't that be what we, his followers, are doing? His first followers took on the characteristics of his kind and generous heart during Pentecost; shouldn't we also be taking on his compassion and energy for the downtrodden orphan and widow?

Jesus used ordinary men and women to do extraordinary things thousands of years ago and that has never changed. That is God's way – to use broken people with 'clay feet' who have a genuine heart to demonstrate his love for the world in practical and meaningful ways. It is really quite simple.

The 1980s was, for me, a decade of exploring and great adventure with seasons of vast learning. In early 1982, I was asked by a close friend if I would help him plant a new church in the Kansas City metro area. In the first few years, I spent a great deal of time getting the infrastructure in place. We had tried to avoid people's continual pressure to satisfy their needs by calling our gathering a 'prayer meeting'. We believed that if it was a prayer meeting, we had less responsibility to provide the typical church amenities. After all, it was 'just a prayer meeting'. That didn't exactly go over well as the church kept growing and people kept complaining. The responsibility fell on me to make it all happen and I worked as diligently as I could to keep the masses content. Eventually I established all the important facilities that people expected when coming to church.

In time, I started to articulate more and more to my colleagues on our ministry team the burden I had for the oppressed poor. While I wanted to be a team player, taking on responsibilities for the day-to-day administration of the church wasn't what was burning in my soul. The church oversight team decided in late 1983 that, since the oppressed poor were such a huge part of my heart, I would go on a six-week exploratory trip overseas. My task was to look at various 'missions' projects to assess the possibilities of partnering with them for our yet to be developed Missions Department. I was extremely excited! Other than visiting Tijuana, Mexico, this was my first real adventure into the Third World and I was so very ready. People kept asking me if I was scared, which mystified me as that emotion wasn't even on my radar screen. I was so intent on having my limited American worldview blown wide open that fear wasn't even a thought. I was more in the 'bring it on' mode. I wanted a reality check. I wanted to see the truth and smell the stink that you can't get from sitting at home.

My first stop on this great adventure was a week in Madras (now Chennai), in India, to view an organization that had a number of orphanages and a small school.

After landing at the Madras airport at night and meeting my hosts, we boarded a yellow-and-black three-wheeled taxi with go-kart sized wheels. This was known to the locals as an 'auto-rickshaw'. I wondered if we were going to survive the ride, and anyone who has had the same experience knows exactly what I am talking about! We darted in and out of traffic, between buses and trucks that could have crushed us like a bug, and I am sure I saw my life pass before my eyes on a number of occasions. By the time we stopped I was coughing from the huge amount of diesel exhaust I had inhaled. It seemed that every time we stopped at a traffic light, the buses' exhaust pipes were at the same height as my face. I have no idea how the Indian public transportation drivers do it. They drive on both sides of the road, zooming in and out of traffic, avoiding wrecks often at the last second. Somehow I lived to tell this story.

That night at the hotel I found it hard to sleep. I'm not sure if it was jet lag or the constant sounds of the city. It could have been that I was just excited and full of anticipation. I was used to the serene quietness of suburban life behind closed doors and windows. Here everything was open to listen to and smell. The sounds of the city are a constant hum in the background of daily life. The smells vary from the stench of raw sewage to the sweet fragrance of the abundance of flowers.

After lying there restlessly for some time, I got up to look out the window just to observe what was happening on the street. The road in front of the hotel wasn't well lit, so it was hard to see. I did notice that the sidewalks seemed to be moving, which was a strange sight at 2 a.m. I thought at first that I was dizzy from jet lag but soon realized that something else was going on. I decided to be adventurous and take a walk.

Everywhere I gazed, there were thousands of people walking in lines like ants.

As I came out the hotel entrance I saw that the sidewalks on both sides of the street were packed with sleeping people. Whole families were curled up together, lying on thin mats on the dirty concrete. As far as my eyes could focus there was a sea of people camped outside for the night. I was amazed, and wondered if these were pilgrims on their way to some sacred shrine. Later I learned that this was a nightly occurrence all over India and most of these people didn't have a home or couldn't afford to pay for lodging. I was overwhelmed that so many people in one place could be homeless.

The warm Indian sun came up the next day and I met my hosts for breakfast. After a meal of eggs and rice served on a fresh banana leaf, we headed off to see the city of Madras. I soon realized that India was filled with people; lots and lots of people. Everywhere I gazed, there were thousands of people walking in lines like ants. Both sides of the street were packed with people going in opposite directions.

Focused on one life at a time, it was very possible to make a significant impact on some person's life.

The whole city of Madras was alive with commerce. Man and beast were pushing and pulling carts filled with produce and goods, moving from one neighbourhood to another. The continual sound of vehicle horns blaring back and forth created a sense of anxiety in my soul. The abject poverty that I had read about was evident everywhere. After witnessing children rummaging through a garbage dump for food, I knew that this certainly was a place where one could make a significant difference in another's life. The need was so huge.

It occurred to me that if I looked at the poverty of the entire nation of India, the puny little light I had to contribute would get swallowed by the immense darkness. But if I realized the value of each life and focused on one life at a time, it was very possible to make a significant impact on some person's life.

I felt a particular compassion for the little children who were innocent victims of this poverty. They didn't ask to be brought into the world nor suffer the loss of their parents. It was clear that, if done right, an orphanage could change the course of these children's lives in a significant way.

Over the next few days we continued to visit various facilities in southern India. Riding the Indian trains was a highlight. The British had their share of flaws in the attitudes in which they had once managed the country, but one thing that they did exceptionally well was build the railway infrastructure. It is the circulatory system and lifeblood of Indian culture. For a moment, while sitting on the steam train and listening to the chugging sound, it felt like I was in the middle of a Rudyard Kipling novel.

As the Indians sat on the roof of the train carriages, I was watching out the window, taking in the beautiful Indian countryside. It really was a magical moment.

At one point in our journey we visited the home of the mission's founder, who was born and raised in India, and was now getting on in years. He was a gracious and distinguished man who exuded a gentle kindness. He and his wife lived simply, but were gracious hosts. For several hours he shared with me the history of the organization and what had motivated him to start it. It was clearly evident that he was a man with a caring heart who had given his life to raise these orphaned children whom no one else wanted. He had fed, clothed, housed and educated them at great cost and sacrifice to himself and his family.

As I listened to him share and felt his heart, it was soon evident to me that something was off that I couldn't put my finger on. Later that day the thing that was making me feel so uncomfortable dawned on me. It was the contrast between the 'feeling' that I had talking with him and the 'feeling' I had the first few days in the country while talking with his son. His son was being groomed to take over the mission's leadership and he had a very different 'vibe' about him. I didn't sense any of the heartfelt compassion or humility that radiated off of his father, and that puzzled me.

That night the son invited me to his home for dinner and to meet his new bride. Both his new house and his new wife were beautiful. It was all very impressive and yet I slept restlessly that night. I got up early the next morning to walk and see if I could get this restless feeling out of my soul. As I was walking down the street I noticed something missing ... people. Where were all the people? I soon realized that we were in some sort of isolated community. As I looked at the houses I noticed they had the names of the people living there, along with their occupation, engraved in brass next to the front door. There were doctors, lawyers, business owners, etc, all living in this walled subdivision. This was the elite of Madras.

It suddenly dawned on me what was causing my unease. The founder of the ministry and his son were on different planets. Their lifestyle, values and ministry philosophy were like night and day. They had completely different hearts. This perplexed and disappointed me. Why was he so different to his father? What had happened to his heart? The next day we met the father again, this time at one of the orphanages. I took advantage of a few minutes we had alone and asked him some probing questions.

As I listened to him share, the pieces of the puzzle started falling into place. The father understood that he was getting on in years, and realizing that some day his son would take over the ministry, decided to send him to America to get a ministry education. While there, he learned that in American churches, perception is much more important than substance. He learned that in order to get funding from the American churches, he had to look like a success. In order to get American ministers to come over he had to give them the best in hospitality. He had to live like royalty and treat them like royalty or he wasn't going to get the support he needed to sustain the mission.

What have we done to him, I wondered. *Have we ruined him?* He had been taught the perception game and it had completely desensitized him. I left India with a profound sense of sadness about what kind of impact the American church was having on the world. While I had gone there in search of participating in something that was special and could make a significant impact on people's lives, I wondered if we, the American church, were making things worse. What were we doing to these young hearts and minds? Had we destroyed a young man's life by removing the heart of compassion that his father had given him? Had we replaced it with a self-indulgent, self-centred form of Christianity that was justified by a perverted belief that God wanted him to have all this? The whole experience had left me in turmoil, as the direction they were going was the very opposite to that in which I was headed. I also felt somehow guilty by association for producing this sad state of affairs.

I travelled next to Nigeria to hook up with my friend Gary Kroeze. During the flight I was left to the ponderings of my soul. Was I too hard in my assessment? Maybe I needed to look at the end result; children were being fed, clothed and going to sleep at night with a roof over their heads. I came to the conclusion that, at my age, I didn't understand enough to evaluate others, as I simply wasn't experienced.

I realized that while what I had seen in India was good, my heart was looking for something more. I wasn't sure what it looked like but I thought I knew what it felt like. Something that had been ruminating in my mind for several years was the question of whether the world of missions and humanitarian aid would always be the same dance of well-meaning people from overseas coming to the US to request funds for their various projects. It was comforting to know that my home country was the most generous nation in the world. As I understood it, the vast majority of funding to try and make a dent in the war on poverty came from the US. In fact, I believe the US gives more than the rest of the world combined. My question, though, was whether we created a welfare mentality and if we were possibly robbing people of their dignity by not helping them become self-sufficient? Was it even possible to do that?

Over the course of the trip I started to formulate a two-pronged philosophy. On the one hand there were situations that called for what I termed 'crisis mode missions'. On the other hand there were situations that needed a long-term solution which I called 'economic development missions'. Crisis Mode Missions were situations where, due to sudden or catastrophic circumstances, people needed immediate aid. Whether it was the result of Mother Nature's violent tantrums in the form of tornadoes, hurricanes, flooding, etc, or long-term crises like drought which brought on starvation, action needed to be taken quickly or people were going to die. Long-term solutions were just not a possibility as too many lives were at stake.

But what happened after that? Did the people of that area just wait for the next crisis to gain more assistance? This seemed so short-sighted to me. Why couldn't we help them rebuild stronger and better designed dwellings that would withstand high winds and harsh climate? What about flood control? Often after the floods there is no water at all for months on end. Why couldn't we build dams to catch the water in the rainy season so that people could irrigate in the dry season?

What about drilling wells for clean water? So many people on the African continent drink water contaminated with dangerous bacteria and diseases. Most of the African population is sick and listless due to water-borne diseases. Children are most often the victims. One well can support thousands of people and sustain a basic village economy. Why can't we drill wells for these people? How hard could that be? My head was filled with so many ideas and questions. What about teaching agriculture and small business? The Israelis had turned their desert into a garden. Why couldn't Africa do the same? For these projects I used the term 'economic development missions' as they were long-term and self-sustaining.

At my next stop, Nigeria, I would further develop my thinking as I saw exactly what not to do. When I finally arrived it was so incredibly hot that I instantly started perspiring. I wanted to ask someone for an iced tea but was afraid as to what I would get. I had done that at a restaurant in India and they had brought me a hot cup of tea with ice cream floating in it!

For a 'Cheesehead' from Wisconsin, the intense heat of Africa was a huge challenge. As I left the airport in Lagos my first observation was that there were so many Africans wearing wool in the blazing heat. I had a whole suitcase full of light coloured cotton clothes that I had packed, and it seemed more logical that a person would want to be dressed in lighter fabric in this inferno. It wasn't long before I was inquiring of my host about the logic behind wearing wool in the heat. He let out a huge laugh and said, 'Bob, you Americans and Europeans are so concerned about how you smell and therefore do everything you can to not sweat. We Nigerians on the other hand don't mind body odour and we work at making ourselves sweat as it helps to cool you off.' It's similar to the concept of a car radiator. The perspiration actually cools you off. I must say, I was intrigued, and by the end of my time there found myself caring a lot less about how I smelt and much more about how cool I was. Vanity can only get you as far as the point where you decide to chuck it all for the sake of a little cool comfort.

Our first few days were spent in Port Harcourt, which is west of Lagos on the Niger River Delta. I was busy learning about the country and the work that was going on there with this particular organization. The opportunity to experience an African church on Sunday was a real treat for this white boy from Milwaukee. Who said 'white men can't dance?' One morning in a Nigerian church could cure any white man of his lack of rhythm. The spirit of the music just seems to get inside you and soon your legs and feet have a mind of their own. I really enjoyed myself and soon found that the sounds and rhythms of Africa agreed with me. To this day, whenever I need cheering up, I dial up one of the African albums I have stored on my iPod. If I'm in the car I'm sure those who drive by me must think I've lost control of my muscles. Their first inclination may be to call 911 to let them know there is a white man driving a car who is completely out of control!

On our second night we were on our way home from a meeting at about 1 a.m. when we came to a roadblock just outside the city guarded by a group of Nigerian soldiers. It was pitch dark as there was no power anywhere in the area. Electricity in most of Africa is a hit-and-miss proposition. In most cases you have no idea when they plan on turning it back on. Our host tried to remain calm but you could tell he was worried at the soldiers pointing their AK-47 rifles straight at us. He gingerly got out of the car and began to speak to the soldiers.

While he was doing that the other soldiers began to walk around the car and told us to get out. We stood there for quite a while with guns pointed straight at us as they searched the car. It then dawned on me that this could very well be the end of my life. If these soldiers, who were clearly angry at us for some reason, decided that they wanted to do away with us, nothing was going to prevent it. We were out there in the pitch dark and no one would have seen or heard what happened or where our bodies were buried.

I was relieved a few minutes later when our host signalled to us to slowly get back in the car. He carefully drove away, continually looking in the rear view mirror for any sign of the soldiers changing their minds and opening fire on us. Once we were out of sight, I learned that a military coup had taken place in the government that night and a curfew had been put in place. This news had not reached us or we would never have been driving around at that time of night.

It was a really scary moment, but after pondering on it for a while, I realized that this was Africa. It was similar to the time of the Apostle Paul when he travelled across Asia Minor preaching his message of hope, fearing bandits and wild beasts lurking in the darkness all around him that could have killed him at any moment. In order to get his message out he was prepared for whatever eventuated, and lived by faith in God's plan for his life. I had a whole new appreciation for him that night and what he meant when he said, 'I have a sentence of death hanging over me' (2 Cor 1:9–10).

Over the next week we travelled extensively through the Niger River Delta, visiting remote villages by boat. At each stop, the whole village came down to the river's edge to greet us with lots of pageantry. Some of the children who had never seen a white man were wide-eyed with surprise as they observed these ghostly-coloured creatures being led into their village. Soon the chief of the village would come and extend to us an invitation to speak to his people. Honestly, I was at a loss for words. What do you say to people whose worldview is so different from your own? I always wanted to say something deep and meaningful, but had no idea what that was for them. I think in the end it mattered little what I had to say; it was the fact that I had come to visit them that meant so much. Even though I have no idea what our host pastor shared with the people, I'm sure they had some good laughs at our expense as there was always laughter.

As we continued to travel around the region I began to notice a lot of rusted tractors and other farming equipment standing in the fields. One day we drove past a huge vacated facility that looked like an abandoned town. When I inquired about it I was told it had been an automated pig farm. Over the course of several days I saw hundreds of pieces of rusted equipment and empty farm buildings. At this point my curiosity had reached its peak and I asked one of the Nigerians what all this was about. He then gave me a quick lesson on the 'Green Revolution' and the Foreign Aid policies of the US Government in the 1960s.

Apparently it was called the Green Revolution in 1968 by former director William Gaud, who noted the spread of the new agricultural technologies and said, 'These and other developments in the field of agriculture contain the makings of a new revolution. It is not a violent Red Revolution like that of the Soviets, nor is it a White Revolution like that of the Shah of Iran. I call it the Green Revolution.'

In an effort to increase agricultural production to help with the rising demand for food, the US Government had sent the best of its high tech equipment to underdeveloped countries all across the world. They shipped over hundreds of millions of dollars in the latest of tractors and farm implements. They built huge self-sustaining pig and poultry facilities to increase the production of meat. The Ford and Rockefeller Foundations were also instrumental with funding and education. The experts of the world had descended upon Nigeria and set them up with everything they needed to feed the masses.

Things didn't exactly go as planned as there were a few unexpected fundamental problems. The fact that all this was simply handed over to local people who had never asked for it or even understood all that was happening, was a problem. There was no sense of ownership or responsibility, as after

We imposed on them our god of technology that they didn't want to worship.

all, they didn't have to earn it or work for it. The Nigerians had been ploughing for hundreds of years behind an ox. That was what they knew and felt comfortable with. From our western worldview this was archaic, but for them it was a way of life.

It wasn't long before the tractors were in need of repair or maintenance. This was a bit of a mystery to the Nigerians as they knew more about how to deal with an ox than a tractor. You feed it and if it remains healthy it works. If it breaks down you simply get a new one. As the tractors and other farm equipment began to break down, they simply left them in the fields, walked home and rounded up their oxen to finish the job.

This scenario happened over and over again until, sitting in fields all over the country, there were rusted monuments to our failure to design solutions around what the Africans actually needed. We imposed on them our god of technology that they didn't want to worship. It wasn't long before the pig and poultry facilities began to break down and people just divided up the remaining livestock and returned home to the family farm.

The gospel may have put their soul in heaven but they were still living in hell.

As you can imagine, this had a profound effect on my thinking. I was on a journey to gain understanding of the Third World and how I could make a significant impact. I was embarrassed that our government could have been so arrogant to assume that high-end technology was the solution to everything.

I did understand that technology could be a life saver and had been behind some of the best solutions to combat hunger and disease. The problem here was that there seemed to be no preliminary research done to understand the culture and to design solutions around their unique cultural needs. We just descended on the country with the mentality that 'if it works in America it will work here.' It is an undeniable truth that Africa needs technology but it needs technologies that are simple, inexpensive and don't require a lot of maintenance.

As I finished up my time in Nigeria I again was made aware of the huge need. One fourth of all of Africa lived in this single country. My hosts were doing all they could to reach the remote island people with the message of the salvation. They too had been educated in the US and were doing exactly what they had seen other American ministries do when they came to Africa: set up a tent and preach. Success was based on crowd size and converts. Again I was internally conflicted. All this was good as people were being saved, but I wondered about tomorrow.

What would happen when they woke up and their living situation remained the same? The gospel may have put their soul in heaven but they were still living in hell.

Did any of the Africans feel today that they had been set free from a life of oppression and poverty? I told myself that this liberating message somehow had to translate into a genuine and tangible expression, or it was just empty words. I needed to see substance, the Africans needed to see substance and I wanted to find out what that looked like. How could we make a significant impact?

CHAPTER 3

LOVE IS AN ACTION

Silence in the face of evil is itself evil: God will not hold us
guiltless. Not to speak is to speak. Not to act is to act.
– DIETRICH BONHOEFFER

M y time in India and Nigeria had been eye-opening to say the least.
I had left the very ordered and somewhat predictable lifestyle of the
West and been introduced to the chaotic and unpredictable lifestyle of the
developing world. There, nothing is sure,
and planning for the future is a shaky proposition. It was clear to me that when I returned home there would be much research
to do. I had a whole lot more questions than
answers, but my heart was gripped by the
plight of so many people who seemed absolutely powerless to change the awful
course of their life. The look of hopelessness
in people's eyes was haunting. It reminded
me of the black and white photos I had seen of Nazi death camp survivors.

*My heart was gripped
by the plight of so many
people who seemed
absolutely powerless to
change the awful course
of their life*

After a brief stop in Kenya, Gary and I caught a flight from Nairobi
to Harare, Zimbabwe. Our final destination was a farm community located 40 km from the city of Bulawayo. This is the second largest city in the
country and is located in an area called Matabeleland in the southern

part of the country. This region is populated by the Ndebele people who have lived there for nearly two hundred years. My travelling partner had been telling me for the better part of a year that I really needed to see and experience this community as it would have a profound effect on me.

Gary was an ex-cattle rancher from Montana and had gone on his own unique journey with God. He was at least twenty years older than I was and our backgrounds couldn't have been more different. This, I'm sure, was part of my curiosity with him. While he wasn't much of a public speaker, he had a very different disposition when one-on-one. From the pulpit he tended to come down pretty hard on people. Sometimes I wondered if he thought he was still driving cattle. When you got him away from the public forum and alone, you would find that he was really a very tender and compassionate man underneath it all.

He was a paradox to me and while he was confusing at times, he stimulated my thinking and forced me to figure out where I stood on various issues. He held his opinions firmly, and our relationship was a classic case of 'iron sharpens iron'. Gary knew that I was wrestling with much of what I had just observed in India and Nigeria. I was already on overload and wasn't sure how interested I was in seeing another project. He assured me that our time with the people at the New Adams Farm would be a very different experience. Gary had been introduced to the people there a year earlier by another friend. He had been very impressed by what he had seen and was sure that I would be too.

As we flew south over the countryside to Bulawayo, the landscape changed from lush green vegetation to barren red ground interspersed with pockets of trees. The region had been stricken with drought since 1980, which ironically was the year of the country's formation as the new nation of Zimbabwe. You could see the devastating effect that the lack of water was having on the plant life. Zimbabwe's rainfall in the southern part of the country was sporadic at best. When it did rain, the ground was so hard from baking daily in the hot sun that the water simply bounced off the hard surface and ran rapidly down toward lower ground. This could be devastating as streams of water joined each other, creating even larger walls of water that could wash away anything that got in their way. Soon after a torrential downpour, all the water would be gone, having taken with it everything in its path. The local people were left struggling to find enough water to even drink, let alone irrigate their crops.

I had a lot of nervous energy surging through my system as I was sitting on the plane. I was both excited and scared at the same time. The environment that I was entering was one filled with a lot of tension and some danger. President Robert Mugabe's 5th Brigade was currently active in the region, committing genocide against the very Ndebele people that I was about to visit. After years of white-on-black and black-on-white violence, now things had deteriorated to the point that the Africans were killing each other. At this point, it was all a bit confusing for me and yet I wanted to understand why.

As we continued to fly, I wondered what kind of people we were going to find once we arrived. It wasn't but a few years earlier that this country was in the midst of a horrible war. Everyone living on the farm had been involved in that conflict one way or another. Some had even been a part of the Rhodesian security forces. I was curious to hear their stories and discover what the motivation was behind such a radical project like The Community of Reconciliation. Something had obviously happened, as they were living and working with the very people who only a few years earlier had been their mortal enemies. What had changed them? What had possessed them to leave the comfort and safety of the city and move out into the bush with all its dangers? For me, understanding people's motivation has always been extremely important. It is perhaps the single most significant issue as, in my mind, it determines whether or not something is genuine or simply a facade. It is the difference between true spirituality and false religion. One is life and the other is death.

After landing at Bulawayo Airport and being greeted by our hosts, we

What had possessed them to leave the comfort and safety of the city and move out into the bush with all its dangers?

headed out to the bush country near the Matopo Hills, where the New Adams Farm project was located. The farm was not far away from where mining magnate Cecil John Rhodes was buried. There wasn't much to see along the way as everything was dusty and barren and not particularly appealing to the eye. As we drove through the gate entrance to the farm community, I was surprised to see a beautiful large stone rectangular building with thatched roofing. It was actually quite impressive in its size and appearance. Other than photos in magazines, I had never seen thatching done so well. The base and walls of the building were built with rock quarried out of the hills on the farm property. We got out of our vehicles and made our way to what I later learned was called the 'community centre'. There, people were milling around as it was almost time for lunch. Meals were often a group event and so people were coming in from all directions. We were greeted with warm smiles and affectionate hugs. Gary re-acquainted himself with everyone and introduced me one by one to most of the group.

One of the first people whom I met was Simon Rhodes, a tall, lanky, brown-haired fellow who was born in Harare, formerly known as Salisbury. As we got to know each other better, we discovered we were the same age and our birthdays were just a few days apart.

I found Simon to be a wonderful source of information on a vast array of topics. It wasn't long before I was asking hundreds of questions and Simon was kind enough to answer them all. I thoroughly enjoyed talking with him as he was easy to communicate with and transparently honest. He was a bit of thinker and philosopher like I was, so we spent quite a few hours discussing Zimbabwe's history and the current geopolitical situation. He was convinced that there was potential to make a significant impact in that region of the country, though it wasn't without its risks.

Simon was married to a sweet woman named Rina and they had been married almost four years. He had worked seven years as a policeman and in 1982 left the force to pursue a ministry calling. After attending Bible School and working at a local church, he heard about the vision for the community. He was so deeply touched that he relocated his family there to be a part of the team.

Simon was troubled by Zimbabwe's less than stellar past when it came to cross-cultural issues, so he wanted to do something about it and to change the direction in which the country was headed. He felt that a modest expression of genuine Christianity might just heal the wounds of a nation torn apart by resentment and war. In time he would help co-pastor the African church located in the village of Mbezingwe, which was not too far from the farm.

I was soon escorted into one end of the community centre where there was a huge kitchen area. Spread across one of the countertops were stacks of fresh vegetables that looked absolutely delicious. As they were preparing the food, I was introduced to Jean Campbell, an engaging Scottish woman in her mid-fifties. Jean was one of the few people I met during my stay who wasn't actually from Zimbabwe. She had come to Africa several years earlier as a linguist and had spent some time in Uganda before relocating to Zimbabwe.

Working side by side with Jean was Esinath, an African woman with a wonderfully warm smile and charming personality. Esinath lived in one of the villages near the farm. She was a single mother with five children. Her husband had fought with Joshua Nkomo's Ndebele soldiers in the Bush War and never returned, so it was presumed that he was dead. Being a war widow, the people at the community had taken her in and made her a part of the family.

After washing up and getting a proper UK hug from Jean, I went back outside where I noticed a young woman sitting on the grass in the sun playing her guitar surrounded by lots of children. She had a beautiful voice and the children obviously adored her. She would get them singing and dancing so that it seemed at one point that I was looking at a scene out of 'The Sound of Music'. I was told that her name was Gaynor Stewart and that she was a young woman from nearby Bulawayo. She had decided to move from the city as she too wanted to make a contribution and help fulfil the vision for the farm community. As I observed later,

Gaynor had the same effect on the African children in the village. There was always a competition, especially among the girls, as to who was going to sit on Gaynor's lap during church services.

Lunch was wonderful and almost everything we ate was produced right there on the farm, which I found amazing. I had my first introduction that day to the delightful taste of fresh passion fruit juice. It is a taste that has remained one of my favourites to this day, especially on a hot, dry summer day.

I enjoyed meeting everyone and in time got acquainted with the whole group. The two men who bore the primary leadership responsibilities were Gerry Keightley and Tony Davenport, both of whom had been part of a home Bible study group in Bulawayo. They had gathered in early 1982 to discuss how they could be used by God to make a difference in their country, which was so violently torn apart along racial lines. Over the course of time, a vision for The Community of Reconciliation emerged. Tony, who was an economist/accountant, handled the legal matters and wrote the original vision for the community. He was in his mid-forties, quite sharp and married to a woman named Pauline. They had three children; John, Sarah and Nicola.

I was particularly intrigued by Gerry Keightley who, as a new Christian, had a certain childlike passion. It was clear that Gerry had a unique stature about him. While he tried to be meek and self-effacing, it was clear that he was a natural born leader and a man on a spiritual quest.

Gerry was born in 1947 in Bulawayo. His journey with God had brought about quite a personal transformation. As a young man he was very outgoing, had many friends and was always the life and soul of the party. He was your stereotypical man's man, drinking all night with the guys and working hard the next day. He had started out his business career working at Barclay's Bank. Three years later he accepted a position to work for Dunlop Tyres as a sales rep. After a three-year stint there, he made a move over to Caltex Oil were he spent the next eleven years.

During his busy career, Gerry found time to marry Marian Elaine Russell, who was the daughter of John and Elaine Russell. Marian was born in Durban, South Africa and had moved to Rhodesia with her family as a little girl in 1951. She was both a beautiful and gracious woman, and was longsuffering in putting up with a lot of Gerry's late night parties with the guys. Marian and Gerry had two beautiful daughters, Deborah and Glynis. While they had carved out a life for themselves, Marian's heart was deeply spiritual which at times created tension in their relationship as Gerry just wasn't interested.

Things got really complicated in the 1970s when civil war broke out and Gerry was called to serve in the Rhodesian military. The war experience affected him in a very sobering way. The unethical and morally reprehensible things he saw were a wake-up call as to how depraved men can be in their lust for power. The result was that he took stock in his own life and came to the conclusion that his values were completely askew and that he had better re-evaluate some things. It was just a matter of time before he became completely captivated by the life and teachings of Jesus and asked himself if there was a better way. After further reading and meditation, he came to the conclusion that it wasn't just a matter of changing his mindset; he needed to change his lifestyle.

Gerry grew tired of listening to people talk about wanting to make a difference; he wanted to make one himself. While he wasn't sure what it all looked like, he knew he wasn't going to find it while living a comfortable suburban lifestyle. He was intrigued, like I was, about Luke's account of the early church and how their expression of lifestyle as a community gave them favour with the larger community of people they lived among. Gerry wanted to bridge the huge chasm of race that had driven Zimbabwe to war. He believed that God's ways could make a difference and he set out on a journey to see what type of expression of faith might do just that.

After further reading and meditation, he came to the conclusion that it wasn't just a matter of changing his mindset; he needed to change his lifestyle.

When we first met in 1984, Tony, Gerry and the whole group were still wrestling with exactly how this was going to take place. They had taken the first step in 1982 by selling their suburban homes and pooling their proceeds. They had purchased an underdeveloped 2 600-hectare farm near the Tribal Trust Lands. This was where many of the indigenous Africans lived and they were the exact group Tony and Gerry wanted to reach out to. The previous owner of the farm had drilled several times for water, but only got dust. Because these were the very people they wanted to build the bridge of reconciliation with, this location was very important, and they proceeded.

Once they had the deed in hand, they added the word 'new' and 'Adams Farm' became 'New Adams Farm'. They were well aware when they purchased the land that the region was in real trouble. Both drought and war had ravaged not only the people but the land itself. Initially, they lived in tents, cooked on open fires and took showers under a 200-litre drum hanging from a tree. While working round the clock, they managed to maintain a 24-hour prayer cycle with each person taking a two-hour shift. Transporting the children into town for school wasn't an option. Two of the women were former school teachers, so the children were well educated at home.

It was really an amazing site to behold as there, sitting on the edge of a valley that was barren from lack of water, was this virtual 'Garden of Eden'.

By the time I met them, they had erected a few more buildings on the property (including a prayer chapel), and were reclaiming the land by irrigating from the wells they had drilled. I was very surprised to see a huge 4,5-hectare garden. It was really an amazing site to behold as there, sitting on the edge of a valley that was barren from lack of water, was this virtual 'Garden of Eden'. It was very impressive.

I remember one night a few of us gathering at the community centre, sitting around the fireplace and having a long discussion about land as there seemed to be more to it than just being ground or an asset. At times over the past few years I had wondered if there was something spiritual about land. It seemed like such an oxymoron for something material like land to be considered spiritual.

In reading the history of God's interaction with mankind, I had noticed that in God's way of thinking, stewardship of the land was extremely important. In fact there were only three things that were given the privilege of a 'Sabbath' rest: God, Man and the Land. Letting the land rest every seven years was so important to God that, years after his people refused to do so, He sent them into slavery for every Sabbath year they had missed. I thought that was a pretty strong statement from God's perspective on how important land management was. It seemed to me that God was indicating there was some symbiotic relationship between man and the land. Man was allowed to sow, reap and prosper from the land for six years, but on the seventh year the land was to be given time off to rest and rejuvenate. From Day One when He put Adam in the garden to manage it, there has been a responsibility on the shoulders of mankind to take care of the earth.

It seemed to me that God was indicating there was some symbiotic relationship between man and the land.

As I stood looking out over this huge lush garden made possible by water, and watched black and white Africans working side by side, something in my soul gushed up to the point that I had to turn to the person next to me and say, 'This is good. No, this is really, really good. Actually, this is incredible!' It truly was a beautiful sight to behold and the feeling of seeing something reclaimed from abuse was extraordinary. I was amazed at how I was reacting to the whole moment as it felt so profoundly spiritual and yet it was so incredibly simple. I could see right in front of me that not only had they reclaimed the land and made it beautiful, but

It truly was a beautiful sight to behold and the feeling of seeing something reclaimed from abuse was extraordinary.

they were feeding themselves, the Africans working with them and those in the surrounding villages who had no means of sustaining life. I wondered to myself if this simple and yet profound expression of Christianity could be what my heart was longing to see and be a part of?

After hundreds of years of distrust, this was not a problem that was going to be solved overnight.

One of the questions I was finally able to ask Gerry when we were alone was, 'Do the Africans really want you here?' I was concerned that, given the history of Zimbabwe, New Adams Farm would be seen as white farmers taking the land from the Africans and using them as cheap labour to build their personal wealth. It was clearly evident to me that the Africans working on the farm were very happy and yet, since I was new to the culture, I didn't want to make any assumptions. Gerry assured me that while it would take time, walls of suspicion were being broken down and bridges of trust built. After hundreds of years of distrust, this was not a problem that was going to be solved overnight.

As we talked further, it was clear as that Gerry had a long-term plan of seeing the Africans actually living on the farmlands together with them in some form of community expression. This really excited me as I could not think of anything more profound than former enemies living side by side, loving one another and taking care of each other. What an amazing demonstration of the grace of God that men's hearts could be so deeply changed that, instead of shooting at each other, they could live together genuinely caring for one another. I thought to myself, *This is exactly what the world needs. This is what the United Nations has been trying to do for years but has failed miserably at achieving. Why is that?*

As I thought about it I came to the conclusion that the UN tries to solve its problems through political solutions. The problem with that is that institutions cannot address the real root issue, which is the self-centred, greedy and often wicked heart of mankind that, left unfettered, leads to corruption. As we have all come to see, even the best of intentions will get derailed when the heart has not been transformed. There are vast opportunities for Christianity to make an impact. There is so much conflict across the globe that has left the world torn and broken. Just maybe, I hoped, the Christian community could rise to the challenge and do something so simple and yet so profound that the people in the area might take notice. Could we actually speak without words? My head and heart were overcome with the wondrous possibilities!

Even though I was a guest, I wanted to roll up my sleeves and jump in to help with the daily workload so I could get a firsthand experience of their daily lifestyle. I wanted to immerse myself in the New Adams environment so that when I left I would be 'wearing it'.

One day Gerry, Gary and I were hiking on the property as they were discussing the possibility of developing a cattle herd. It was time for lunch and instead of heading back to the community centre, Gerry asked us to walk with him toward one of the villages. After we had walked about ten minutes in the hot sun, we came out of the bush

> *Institutions cannot address the real root issue, which is the self-centred, greedy and often wicked heart of mankind.*

to a clearing where I saw Simon and a few of the Africans standing around an open fire. As we got closer I noticed that they had two pots resting on logs and they were busy cooking something.

Once we joined the group I was introduced to Stephen, Roy, Thabani and Nkiwane, Africans living in the villages around the farm. Thabani was fluent in English, which made conversation much easier. He explained to me that they were making a typical Zimbabwe bush meal. In one pot was a white substance that looked like a thickened version of American grits and was called 'sadza' – known in South Africa as mielie-pap or mealie-meal porridge.

In the other pot, which was actually shaped like a wok, they were browning chunks of a lamb they had just butchered and had added a variety of cut up vegetables from the garden. When it was done, the pots were removed from the fire and placed on the ground, and we all gathered around, sitting on logs and staring at the food.

I was actually really looking forward to the meal as I was starving, and the fact that it was a traditional Zimbabwean meal only added to my excitement. I was puzzled, however as I did not see any plates or utensils and wasn't sure how we were going to eat this feast. At that point Gerry offered up a meal prayer and then let out a laugh as he told us to 'dig in'. He knew I had no idea how to 'dig in'. He reached into the maize pot and grabbed a fist-sized portion. The consistency of the 'mealie-meal', as they called it, was so thick that it stuck together like a snowball. He fashioned a bowl shape by pressing with his thumb. He then reached into the lamb stew, scooped out a portion and devoured it. This looked like a lot of fun and reminded me of India a few weeks earlier where I had eaten breakfast on a banana leaf with my hands.

I reached into the pot and grabbed some mealie-meal. I was shocked at how hot it was in the palm of my hand. Of course the Africans had a good laugh at my expense as they could see the painful look on my face as I tried to figure out how to form a ball while it was burning a hole in my hand! After a few tosses in the air it cooled off and I was finally ready to attempt to scoop out some stew for myself. This too was a skill as the stew was just as hot as the mealie-meal and it burned my fingers. My pride, however, was not about to let anyone know that my fingers were burning. As the food made its way to my mouth it cooled off enough not to burn my tender tongue. I was pleasantly surprised at how good it tasted and soon everyone was helping themselves and laughing and enjoying the moment.

The Africans were curious as to where we came from and what brought us to their part of the world. For the next few minutes as we sat there eating, I shared with them some personal history and the journey I was on to understand the world outside of America.

As I sat there surveying the whole scene it suddenly hit me: here were white men and black men, sitting around a meal, dipping hands into the same pot and enjoying one another's company. I was caught up in the moment and the implications started to overwhelm me to the point that I got teary-eyed. In that little segment of time, over something as simple as a shared meal, we were reversing hundreds of years of appalling history in that region. The bad blood that had developed between the two races that resulted in armed conflict could be changed. Men of different races could eat out of the same pot.

The moment was not lost on Thabani either. As we discussed afterwards, this simple act of 'fellowship' had profoundly affected the Africans as well. None of them could ever remember a white man eating out of the same bowl as them. Being treated as equals in the way that Gerry, Tony and the New Adams people had, was a whole new experience for them. To be eating out of the same pot as a white man said more to them than any sermon ever possibly could. It was another huge girder laid in place for the relational bridge that Gerry was slowly building to them.

> *To be eating out of the same pot as a white man said more to them than any sermon ever possibly could.*

Halfway through lunch we were joined by Robert Hill, whom everyone called 'Rob'. He was a tall thirty-five-year-old with sandy hair and a beard. He had been one of the first people to move out of the city of Bulawayo with Gerry and Tony after purchasing the property. He had helped get things up and running.

Rob was one of those people who didn't say a lot but you knew his mind was always going. He had spent four years at university studying zoology (animals) and entomology (insects) before graduating in 1971. After graduation he was immediately called, as most white males were, for two years' mandatory service in the Rhodesian army. Being a pacifist, those two years were extremely hard for him. Following his service, he went to work at a Government research station doing experiments on how insects were affecting crop yields and what could be done to control them. Rob was part of the original Bible study group that had developed the vision for the farm and The Community of Reconciliation. He told me that, in time, he wanted to start a bee colony to create a honey business.

He also loved making cheese and he had plans to start producing it as the dairy herd increased.

After lunch we all walked back to New Adams to work in the garden. There I met Joseph Huidekoper, who had recently come over from the United States and was working diligently on the irrigation system. Joseph was a big, strapping twenty-year-old with bleach blond hair and thick black glasses. He was a sort of gentle giant with the kindest heart. He and his family had known Gary for a number of years as they were from the same church in Montana. Joseph was so excited to be there, though I did wonder how his pale complexion was going to stand up against the unforgiving African sun.

A few nights later Gerry, who was always full of surprises, had another one for me. After dinner, while it was still light, Gary, Simon, Gerry and I headed out on a journey through the bush. I had no idea where he was taking us. We seemed to be heading along a path toward the village of Mbezingwe. Then he told me that Simon had arranged for us to spend a few hours with the village chief. This sounded really interesting. I had met a lot of chiefs while in Nigeria but had never had the opportunity to sit with them and talk for any extended period of time.

As the sun was setting we entered the chief's small round hut and were directed to sit on one of the circular mats on the clay floor. Three or four African brothers working on the farm joined us, and one of them translated. As we all found a place to sit, the sun finally set and it was almost pitch dark in the hut. Someone lit a paraffin lantern and at that point I started to make out a few faces in the shadows.

For the next few minutes no one said a single word, so I just sat there waiting for something to happen. I figured that there must be some type of protocol as we were, after all, in a chief's hut. I certainly didn't want to blow it so I sat there quietly like everyone else, wondering what was supposed to happen next. Finally the chief leant over and began talking to one of the villagers, who in turn translated for us. 'The Chief would like to welcome the people from New Adams Farm and the visitors from far away across the ocean in America.' I thought to myself, *Does the Chief have any idea where America even is?* He seemed so far removed from the outside world that I could not imagine how he would even know where we came from. It is possible that just knowing we were from a land over a great ocean of water was all he needed to know.

Gerry thanked the chief for his greeting and expressed his gratitude for the honour of being invited to meet with him. The next few minutes were spent exchanging pleasantries back and forth until, suddenly, we were back to an extended period of silence. Gerry then asked the chief to give us a brief history of the region, which he did in only a few words, followed by another long period of silence. This pattern of minimal conversation followed by extended silence went on over several more exchanges until I was about ready to lose my sanity. I had never been in a social setting with so much silence. What made matters worse was the fact that as I looked around the room into the shadows, no one else seemed to be bothered by this type of interaction, or should I say lack of interaction. For someone like me who has a bit of attention deficit disorder, this was almost like torture. My instincts kept telling me to say something just to keep the conversation going, as we do in America. I reeled in my emotions and reminded myself that I was in another world and that the same rules might not apply. As it was still way too quiet, I started a conversation with myself inside my head.

> *I was struggling with these long periods of silence because I was, sadly, a product of my burgeoning information technology culture.*

My mind is strange in that I can be the prosecutor, the defendant and the judge all at the same time so that I can get all the perspectives:

Shame on you for being bored! Your thoughts are so disrespectful. Why are you having such a difficult time sitting there? Nobody cares that your butt is falling asleep!

Why are you feeling guilty? This is so outside of your natural environment and what you are used to. You have no training for situations like this and nobody explained to you what you were getting into.

> *If I was going to understand their world I needed to 'dial down' on the inside and just learn to go with it.*

Now Bob, this is an opportunity to learn and experience cultures outside your current paradigm, just relax and try and take it all in and learn something.

After a few minutes of non-stop dialogue in my head, I started to calm down enough to reflect on the situation. It suddenly dawned on me that I was struggling with these long periods of silence because I was, sadly, a product of my burgeoning information technology culture. Everyday back home I was exposed to endless amounts of information that were continually bombarding my mind, like reading materials, radio, TV, advertising and telephones. Each of these mediums demanded a response from me. I was an information junkie. This was in 1984, even before cell phone usage was the standard protocol. The Internet, too, was still a tool of science and it would be another six years before the World Wide Web came into existence!

As I pondered the whole situation I was struck by the cultural contrast. The people in the village have no electricity and so no telephone or radio. From time to time a newspaper would make its way around town but the information was controlled by the government. The beginning and end of their world was their village and the life that went on there. They weren't worrying about the Russians attacking the US or Europe. They didn't care that the Middle East was in continual conflict or that the socialists were trying to take over Central America. They were simply worried about where their next meal was going to come from. How were they going to keep their ox alive so that he could plough the field? Would there be rain soon? They lived a simple subsistence level existence that was in rhythm with the rising and setting of the sun. They were never in a hurry. Where did they have to go? They had no alarm clocks, no Microsoft Outlook reminders flashing to tell them that they were late for a meeting. Their life moved at a very different pace from mine and if I was going to understand their world I needed to 'dial down' on the inside and just learn to go with it. I closed my eyes, took a few deep breaths and just sat there enjoying the silence.

After a few more brief moments of conversation followed by more silence, it dawned on me that the chief spoke only when he had something important to say. What a contrast this was to my world of continual mindless babble where you are forced to sift out the important stuff as though it were a rare mineral. I started to wonder if maybe these Africans in their simple ways had something to teach me. Besides the cultural experience, the one thing that was clear was that the chief was very glad Gerry and his group had come to the region, and he was grateful for all they were doing with and for his people. It was very assuring to know that the chief was pleased with everything that was going on and that they had his blessing.

As we walked back to the New Adams Farm that night, I was struck by the number of stars I saw in the night sky. It was truly an awesome sight to behold and it was the first time I had seen the Southern Hemisphere's view of the heavens. There were so many stars from one end of the horizon to the other. As we walked through the bush, I could not help thinking about Abraham. It is recorded in the 15th chapter of Genesis that God promised him that his descendents would be as many as the stars above. From where I stood that night, that was a lot of family!

By trying to implement another man's vision or strategy, we often cut ourselves off from the grace God has for our own lives.

As our time on the farm was coming to a close, I asked Gerry if we could have some time alone. I wanted to have a heart to heart conversation with him about what he saw for the future. We decided to get a good night's sleep and in the morning he wanted to show me something.

After breakfast we went on another hike and as we walked we talked very openly about a number of issues. He was still trying to work out in his heart what their expression of 'community' was going to look like. There were some internal philosophical issues within the group that still needed to be ironed out as they weren't all of one mind yet. He wanted so badly to do it 'right', but wasn't always sure what right looked like. I encouraged him not to succumb to the outside pressure that religious-minded people can often bring, but to do the thing that God had put in his own heart. By trying to implement another man's vision or strategy, we often cut ourselves off from the grace God has for our own lives.

From where I stood, Gerry and the people on the farm had the right heart. Their compassion and humility were not just pious words but actions demonstrated daily in everything they did. I could not imagine God with a bigger smile.

Soon we came to the edge of the New Adams Farm property and Gerry showed me a 1 400-hectare property that was adjacent to their land called 'Florencedale'. He had had his eyes on this land from the day they had relocated there because it had much more potential for water than New Adams did. The property was now available but they did not have the resources on their own to purchase it.

I knew from my time in Africa over the previous few weeks that water was in many ways the most significant component to survival. Simply put, 'Water is Life'. With his desire to expand the community population not only with more people but also livestock and small businesses, the need for water was essential. Africa has the most underdeveloped water storage infrastructure in the world. In the United States there are 6 150 cubic metres of water stored for each person. In Ethiopia it is 43 cubic metres. In South Africa, the continent's most developed country, they are still able to store only 746 cubic metres per person. Only 36% of Africa's people have access to basic sanitation and 288 million people do not have access to safe drinking water. Water is a huge problem and the difference between life and death.

Gerry understood that water and finances were the biggest limitations they faced, and that these would, in the end, determine how much they could do and how many people they could realistically help. I assured him that my heart was with him 100% and that while I was not in a position to make financial commitments, I would share everything I had seen with men of like mind in the States to see what we could do to help.

After saying our good-byes the next day I headed off to the airport to begin the return trip to Kansas City. During the journey, I took the time to reflect long and hard about all that I had seen over the past six weeks. I had so many thoughts running through my head and yet one thing really grabbed hold of my heart: The Community of Reconciliation.

They decided to rename it 'Olive Tree' as a symbolic gesture of peace between the peoples of Zimbabwe.

After taking a few days to catch my breath and get re-introduced to my family, I met with my colleagues on the Senior Council at the church and shared with them all that I had experienced. It was decided after lengthy discussion that in some form or fashion we would support all three projects I had visited. At the same time I was also free to focus my heart on the New Adams Farm/Community of Reconciliation project, as it was obvious that that was the one that had touched me the most deeply.

Within a few weeks I met with various men in the church and shared what I had observed. A number of them expressed their interest in helping me raise the funds necessary to help Gerry purchase the additional 1 400 hectares. It took some time, but between the church and a number of key private donations, we were able to raise the needed funds. I was so excited to see the monies wired over as it really was the first significant investment we had made in their project. After purchasing the property they decided to rename it 'Olive Tree' as a symbolic gesture of peace between the peoples of Zimbabwe. In honour of the moment they planted an olive tree on the land.

Over the next couple of years I continued to correspond frequently with the folks at New Adams, keeping updated on developments and the always shifting political environment. While I felt so far removed due to distance, what they were attempting to accomplish was so close to my heart. Gary Kroeze became more directly involved in the community, spending extended periods of time there helping them establish new agricultural projects. He would frequently return to Kansas City to update us on how things were progressing. I was particularly interested in how Olive Tree Farm was developing, not only because we had a personal investment there, but also because it was the next phase in fully integrating the community.

MAP OF THE COMMUNITY OF RECONCILIATION

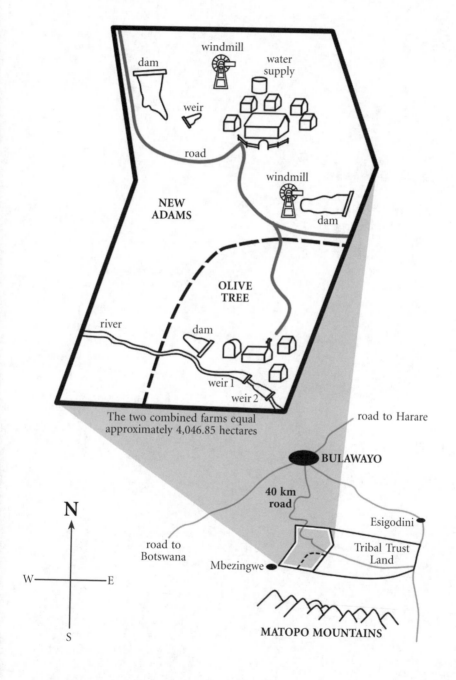

windmill

dam

water supply

weir

road

windmill

NEW ADAMS

dam

OLIVE TREE

river

dam

weir 1

weir 2

The two combined farms equal
approximately 4,046.85 hectares

road to Harare

BULAWAYO

40 km road

N

Esigodini

road to Botswana

Tribal Trust Land

Mbezingwe

W———E

S

MATOPO MOUNTAINS

CHAPTER 4

An Emerging New World

Following the light of the sun, we left the Old World.

– Christopher Columbus

S o many wonderful memories; so many incredible people, I thought to myself as the loud humming sound of the airplane's huge Rolls Royce engines broke in on my nostalgic journey. What an honour it was to have met such amazing people. After a brief meal and a feeble attempt at sleep, I found myself lost in thought about all that had transpired over the past few years of the community.

In June of 1986, I returned to Zimbabwe to see firsthand how things were progressing. So much had happened in the past two and a half years and so much more was about to take place, it seemed like the right time. I asked Noel Alexander, one of my closest colleagues on the church staff, to go with me. He was born in South Africa and I felt he would bring a fresh set of eyes to the situation. I was so passionate about the project and wanted to make sure my zeal did not blind me to things that I might overlook in my enthusiasm.

Noel had joined our ministry team a few years earlier. Although he was relationally quiet and reserved, when you put him behind a pulpit, the fire in his soul exuded a commanding presence. He was nicknamed the 'Major-General' due to his demeanour, and could be intimidating if you did not know the tenderness of his heart. Middle-aged and balding, his hair was long, wiry and wavy on the sides. Often when I looked over at him during meetings, it seemed like the wind was blowing through his hair. He seemed to be in perpetual motion even when still. I knew that Noel saw Africa as having unlimited potential for saving lost souls and he was an evangelist at heart. I hoped that our time there would join our hearts together for an even more comprehensive vision, which was to use the gospel not only as a means of saving souls but of saving lives.

I hoped that our time there would join our hearts together for an even more comprehensive vision, which was to use the gospel not only as a means of saving souls but of saving lives.

Much to my surprise, another young friend of mine expressed an interest in going with us on this venture. Robert McGeorge, who was twenty-five at the time, originally hailed from the Phoenix, Arizona area. Robert was the youngest of three boys. His cousin, Jerry Reardon, was one of my closest friends and very active in helping raise funds for the project. He had a wonderfully engaging personality and seemed to be friends with almost everyone. There was something about Robert. I just sensed one day God was going to use him in a significant way. At this juncture in his life he was ready for something serious to impact it. A trip to a war-torn region in Africa where people were laying down their lives to help others live was just what he was looking for. Soon the three of us were in the air on another great adventure to see how the funding we had raised was being implemented. We were in for a wonderful surprise.

Since we had to travel via Johannesburg, Noel requested we spend a day there so he could visit his father and mother who still lived there. We shared a lovely dinner with them discussing life and culture in South Africa. I remember so vividly his father giving me a lengthy lecture in his distinctly South African accent on the many merits of eating garlic.

The next morning we flew up to Harare, then down to Bulawayo and finally drove the last 40km out to the community. The minute we crossed the cattle barrier onto the property, it was evident that things had changed significantly. It was no longer a quiet oasis in the bush, but a virtual beehive of activity. Soon, people were gathering from all directions, including Gary Kroeze, who had been there for the past few months helping them with all the new development. There was a tremendous amount of excitement in the air and many new people to meet as the community population had grown substantially.

Gary had extended invitations to more families from the Montana area, where he was from, to join him. One of the first couples to accept was Mike and Francie Town. Mike had grown up in Great Falls, Montana and later moved to Choteau where he became acquainted with Gary. Mike and I soon discovered that we had both attended a Torchbearers Bible School. I had gone through the training in Estes Park, Colorado in 1975–76, and he had been to the school in Sweden in 1978. While his school experience sounded more exciting, having been overseas, I teased him that my school had more well-known people attending. Billy Graham's son, Franklin, had attended the Estes Park School the year before I had.

Mike and Francie had three children at the time, two boys, Seth and Judah, and a daughter, Lilah, who was precociously cute with a mischievous smile. She had a certain glitter in her eyes that made me wonder what she was thinking. Mike had worked on a Montana cattle ranch for a few years, so of course – with his 'cowboy' background in mind – he was deemed *exactly* the right man to manage the vegetable gardens! He had a great attitude about it and was in process of developing a deep life-long bond with the black Africans who worked with him.

Another Montana transplant, David Emerson, had come over in July of 1984, a few months after my first visit. Dave was responsible for tool and general farm maintenance. He loved to move around the now expanded community lands of 4 000 hectares on an off-road bike. One day he offered Noel an opportunity to take the bike for a ride. After he had been gone for what seemed like over an hour, I started to worry that he might not come back. Suddenly, with a dust plume in his wake and the front tyre almost off the ground, Noel came flying back home, grinning from ear to ear. The bike and the wide open spaces had reduced the Major-General to Peter Pan!

Dave and Kathy Marais were also a new addition to the community and had moved into one of the homes on the New Adams property. Kathy and Gerry's wife Marian seemed very similar, and soon I learned that they were in fact sisters. Kathy, the younger of the two, was outgoing and friendly and full of stories, as she and Dave had done quite a bit of sailing around the world.

Dave was born in Pretoria, and was thirty-three years old when we met in 1986. His family had moved to Zimbabwe like Kathy's, and they had met during their teenage years in Bulawayo and became high school sweethearts. After dating for five years they finally got married in 1975. Dave volunteered to join the Rhodesian military forces. He completed an officer's course and graduated as a second lieutenant. He had fought in the bush war and was stationed in Salisbury (Harare) at the time.

Like Gerry, he was deeply disturbed by what he had seen and struggled with it internally. He left the army in 1977, having made the rank of captain. For the next two years Dave and Kathy got away from all the violence and travelled the world on a 38-foot yacht they had built with Kathy's older brother, Malcolm. Jeremy, Kathy's younger brother, joined them for part of the trip, where he learned to sail. He enjoyed the experience so much that he eventually rose to the rank of captain, sailing people to various ports around the world.

During a voyage to the Caribbean, Dave and Kathy both had an encounter with God that would alter their lives forever. While they loved the travelling lifestyle, they knew it wasn't conducive to the family life they wanted. So in 1980 they returned to South Africa to start a very successful metalworking business called 'Genesis Enterprises', manufacturing refrigerators. Three years later Dave accepted a position with Woolworths of South Africa as a buyer. While business was good and they were doing well financially, the tug at his heart to do something meaningful and significant was just too much. They decided to make a radical lifestyle change and moved with their boys, Matthew and Ethan, back to Zimbabwe so they could be a part of the community's work there.

They were very encouraged by the reports they heard from Gerry and Marian and couldn't think of a more noble cause for which to lay down their lives. Dave was now managing the beef cattle herd, which had grown substantially since I was last there. With the addition of the Olive Tree property, they had more grazing land which allowed for expansion. They had also started goat and sheep flocks and were already breeding them.

I had my first taste of goats' milk on this trip. They had also started producing goat cheese and one day I even ate goat meat! The area was still suffering from drought, but fortunately goats seem to do well in dry, arid climates.

The Africans were keen to treat us to another sadza meal as they remembered how special the first one was. They thought Noel and Robert might enjoy the experience as well. We hiked to the Olive Tree property where they were preparing the feast, and on our way we came out of a thicket and were met by the most putrid odour. There, in front of us, were all the entrails of some animal covered with flies. It turned my stomach as I smelt it rotting in the sun. As we walked approximately another ten metres, we came across a severed goat's head that we surmised belonged to the rotting guts. We had a good laugh about it when Noel stated, 'Well gentleman, I do believe we have just witnessed the fate of what has become our dinner!' Soon we found our party and our prospective meal. As we were standing alongside everyone else in a big circle, I think the three of us from Kansas City were the only ones wondering what we had got ourselves into. Surprisingly, we really enjoyed the goat meat stew and thanked our African hosts for a hearty bush meal.

Of all the wonderful new members of the community whom we met, none had a greater impact on me than John Russell. John and his wife Elaine were out of the country when I had first visited the community in 1984. They were so excited to meet us this time, and rightfully so, as John was very proud of his family and all they had accomplished so far. Marian and Kathy were both his daughters, and his sons-in-law Gerry and Dave were giving oversight to the project. John's daughter-in-law Hazel had recently moved from South Africa with her daughter Laura, so John and Elaine were surrounded by family. Although they had a place in town, they had built a home on the New Adams Farm where they spent most of their time.

John was a hardworking, self-made man who had endured a lot in life. Both his parents had passed away by the time he was eight years old, so he was brought up by an older sister. After finishing school and getting an engineering degree, John spent the next twenty-one years working for the Road Motor Services of the South African Transport Service. During his employment there, the Second World War broke out and he enlisted with the South African military. He was a natural born leader and eventually reached the rank of sergeant-major. After being captured during the North African Battle of Tobruk in 1942, he was shipped to a POW camp in Italy. Later they were moved to Poland where their prison camp was located right next to the infamous Jewish death camp in Auschwitz. He was forced to witness unspeakable horrors that, like most men of his generation, he buried in his soul and rarely talked about. It would haunt him for the rest of his life. Years later he recalled one night in particular when he was woken by the sound of hundreds of wooden shoes as they walked over the cobblestones. The next day when he was able to look outside, he witnessed carts of dead Jews being transported to the furnaces.

During one winter his group was marched over a thousand miles from Poland to Germany. Again, he was forced to watch as many men fell due to frostbite and exhaustion. Those who fell were simply shot dead on the spot. Along the march he contracted frostbite but endured the pain and made it all the way to Germany where he was encamped at Stalag 17. After the war he was in such bad shape that he was sent to London, where he spent time recovering before returning to South Africa.

In 1951, with the racist policies of the South African government taking a turn for the worse with the implementation of their Apartheid policies, he decided it was time to leave and moved his family to Rhodesia. Once there he went to work for Fox & Booklers, a large transport contractor.

In time he was promoted to manager of one of their subsidiaries that was engaged in quarrying and civil engineering. In 1962, he left to form his own company, Russell Construction Company Private Limited. He grew the fledgling company from nothing to become a million dollar company by the time he retired in 1982.

Within the black African community, working for Russell Construction was considered a real privilege as John paid his black employees the same wages as his white employees.

John was a man of principle with strong ethics. He was well known in the country for being one to work hard, expecting his employees to work hard and rewarding those who did. Within the black African community, working for Russell Construction was considered a real privilege as John paid his black employees the same wages as his white employees. His integrity produced such a loyalty within his company that whenever riots broke out from racial tension, his black African employees made sure none of his assets were harmed. He was affectionately called 'Boss Papama' which meant 'Boss Hurry Up' as he was a man who knew how to get the job done.

John really loved his son-in-law Gerry, as he saw a lot of himself in him. In 1979, when Gerry decided to commit his life to God, it came as quite a shock to John and yet he knew there was something very right about it. Over time, as God reshaped Gerry's heart and gave him a vision for racial reconciliation and establishing a

The transformation was amazing as this hard and driven man became so meek and tender-hearted.

community that could practically serve the poor, John became increasingly intrigued. John's only exposure to Christianity had come from more traditional institutions and, as we have already discussed, they didn't exactly have a stellar record of representing the true heart and nature of God.

In 1983 and at the age of 70, after seeing the genuineness of Gerry's and Marian's faith and that of Dave and Kathy, John finally got down on his knees and humbled himself before God. The transformation was amazing as this hard and driven man became so meek and tender-hearted. When I first met him he reminded me of John Newton, the now famous slave trader who wrote the classic hymn *Amazing Grace*. John couldn't talk about his life and the strong sense of God's grace he felt without tears running down his face. He was amazed that at his age, God had given him a chance to make a difference in people's lives. It was a privilege in his mind. As he had done with his business, he threw himself into it with all his heart.

I was struck by the sense of purpose everyone seemed to have.

He and Elaine loved to garden and were always experimenting with various plants to see how they would hold up under the hot African sun. He loved concocting organic pesticides and was always at war with some creature trying to eat his plants. Elaine was a trained nurse with a compassionate heart. She was also an expert in teaching the blind to read Braille.

John's skin looked like leather from hours baking in the hot Zimbabwean sun on construction jobs. By his own admission he had been quite a character and not a very good father. He was typical of many Europeans who had grown up in Africa, in that they were hardened by its primitive environment. If you've ever seen the movie *Out of Africa* you would understand how difficult it is to carve out a slice of life on this rugged continent.

When I visited the farms in 1986, John took me under his wing and showed me around. He was so proud of what was happening there. He told me on more than one occasion how grateful he was that in the later years of his life God had granted him the opportunity to be a part of something so significant. He was a wonderful father figure for me as my own dad had passed away a few years earlier.

John had decided that when our group arrived he was going to take care of us. He planned a trip to Victoria Falls and the Hwange Game Park, which was very exciting for us. Before having fun, however, we had a lot of work to do. So much had transpired since I was there in 1984 and John, Gerry and Dave were excited to show us around. I was particularly interested in how the Olive Tree Farm was developing as so many people back in Kansas City had helped make the purchase of the property happen.

On the New Adams Farm they had erected a few more dwellings as well as facilities for maintaining cattle. They had built a 'cattle dipping' run where they would move the cattle through fencing that would only allow a single animal to pass at a time. The cattle would go down an incline into a basin of water mixed with chemicals that would kill ticks and other parasites. It was a fun procedure to watch and even the little children got into the action, chasing the cattle through the fences.

As we jumped onto the back of the trucks to head to Olive Tree, I was struck by the sense of purpose everyone seemed to have. When I had visited a few years earlier they had the heart of compassion but were still working out what that looked like practically. On this visit you could tell that things had grown substantially as more people had come to join the community's vision and they all were on a mission to do something significant for the people in this region.

It was clear that without adequate water resources, no matter how well intentioned they were, they would not be able to reclaim the land, nor feed, clothe or house people.

As we drove to the new property it was evident that drought conditions had not let up. I noticed there was less underbrush and a lot more barren ground that was as hard as concrete. As we baked in the hot June sun, John and Gerry stopped to show us some new water management plans they had for the property. I was surprised to see a large yellow earthmover sitting on an area that had been completely cleared, with an earthen dam at one end. John, who was an engineer, proudly climbed to the top of the dam and explained to us what his strategy was.

He explained that if it should rain, it would happen only between October and March. When it rained it was rarely a soft shower but more often a torrential downpour that bounced off the hardened soil and ran to the lowest point. His plan was to catch it in large enough amounts that it would create a lake so big that even with evaporation they would still have plenty of water. It was clear that without adequate water resources, no matter how well intentioned they were, they would not be able to reclaim the land, nor feed, clothe or house people. Water was the single biggest factor determining the practical impact they could make on the region.

John loaded us back into the trucks and took us to another section of the property. He pointed out how the land sloped down into what looked like a shallow ravine. Then he showed us how he had dug a trench at one end of the ravine in preparation for laying the foundation on which to build a concrete weir. Weirs are also known as 'low-head dams' and are typically concrete walls that are used to raise the depth of a stream. Once he got us in the right position, we could see how the ravine had run with water in the past, but with the current drought conditions it was bone dry. I asked him how high he had planned to build the wall and he said, 'Twenty to thirty feet.'

It was then I realized how big the scope of this project was and the fact that they needed more help, not only with manpower but finances. I learned a few days later that John had actually arranged and paid for the earth-moving equipment and earthen dam out of his retirement funds. It was clear that he was not only invested spiritually, and this said a lot to me.

Gerry thought it might be a great idea if we visited a friend of his who had done the same type of water management on his farm, so the next day we headed off in a couple of vehicles to visit Noel 'Boetie' York who had a huge cattle ranch a few hours' drive away. Boetie was built like a rugby forward: thick and powerful. He wasn't a religious man but was fascinated by Gerry's transformation and what he was doing in Matabeleland.

Driving into Boetie's property was the antithesis of entering the community. Instead of finding a peaceful environment with an 'arms wide open' policy, we drove up to a compound with 10-foot high fencing and two guards armed with automatic weapons standing at the gate. The stark contrast really took me aback, but since we were guests I didn't want to say anything at first.

Boetie was thrilled to have guests from the United States, and was all too accommodating. Before lunch we took a drive on his property to see the weirs he had built. He had three vehicles waiting to take us on a tour and we were asked to sit in the middle one which was an open-top Land Rover. As we took our seats, about 6–8 black Africans emerged from behind a fence that was covered in vines. They too were fully armed with automatic weapons and sat in the vehicles both in front of and behind us. For me it was a surrealistic moment as I felt like we were entering a battle zone much like the streets of Beirut or Bosnia.

Even though the Bush War was long over, there was still some dissident activity in the country. Former Ndebele soldiers, who had been disenfranchised by the war and the current Shona leadership, had fled to the bush where they had buried weapons left over from the war. They had banded together in small groups, some out of fear that Mugabe's Shona security forces would try to kill them. The political dissidents who were active in the region were still trying to overthrow the Shona-led government, and many of these disillusioned soldiers had joined their cause. Boetie later explained to us that his brother-in-law had been shot and killed just a few months earlier while ploughing his fields. This really got my attention and I made a note to myself that I needed to have a talk with Gerry and Dave about their security measures as I had not seen anything put in place.

Soon Boetie had us standing on top of one of the concrete weirs he had built on a small stream. The wall was 9.14 metres high and the water behind it stretched back as far as the eye could see into a huge lake and marshy area. It was quite a sight given this was in the sixth year of a seven-year drought. It was amazing to see how much water could be stored in the right topography by simply constructing a concrete wall. I didn't really need to see any more after that, as the visual I was getting made it obvious that if Olive Tree was going to reach its full potential, it needed water, and lots of it. Weirs were definitely the way to get that accomplished, so all I needed to know was how much money they needed to get the project completed.

On the way back to the York homestead we took a detour so Boetie could show us his herd. It was amusing to see, in the middle of a sea of thousands of brown cattle, a zebra! With his black and white stripes he certainly stuck out from the rest. They decided to drive some of the cattle back to the kraals for feeding, and the zebra stayed right in the middle of the herd. As they headed for the feeding troughs, he did too. Boetie's wife told us that the zebra had shown up a few weeks before and seemed to have forgotten that it was a zebra and was now acting more like an ox. She said they had tried to chase him away but he kept coming back, so they finally just gave up and decided they would let him think he was an ox.

They were fighting a long established pattern of European behaviour that had inflicted untold humiliation and pain on the black Africans.

After further discussion we came up with a second theory that maybe he had discovered he liked the straw and grain that Boetie was feeding the cattle, so decided to try and fool everyone into thinking he was an ox. Unfortunately, he could not change his stripes, but had hoped that no one would notice his unfortunate black and white birth-mark. Matthew, David Marais' six-year-old son, had made the trip with us. At one point I looked over and little Matthew was sitting in the middle of a cattle trough with all the huge beasts around him, eating from it as he talked to them. It was very cute. I think he was hoping the zebra would come over to eat. Once back at the house, Boetie treated us to a barbecue, which they called a 'braai'. He cooked huge steaks and after a few glasses of cold passion fruit juice I was ready to take a nap in the shade. It had been quite an adventurous day.

Once we returned to the community and had a good night's sleep, we spent the next day seeing all the recent economic developments on Olive Tree. One of the issues that Gerry and I had discussed a few years earlier was the need to fully integrate the black Africans into the community. Without this taking place, the community would be seen as carrying on the same historical attitudes and policies that had caused so much hurt and anger already. They were fighting a long established pattern of European behaviour that had inflicted untold humiliation and pain on the black Africans. It had become so ingrained in their consciousness that they just assumed this was how it was always going to be. The community leadership was up against two hundred years of history and abuse. In order to change attitudes they needed some radical departures from the norm. Building an integrated community where the black Africans were a vital part of the daily management and decision making processes could do just that.

Africa is filled with many well-intentioned groups doing projects where their desire is to be compassionate and alleviate suffering. The problem that so often arises is how to avoid creating a welfare society or mentality among the Africans. When simply handed supplies, the Africans, at times (like any other people), take no further personal responsibility for their own welfare and become dependent on Western aid.

I had seen that first-hand in Nigeria when millions of dollars in foreign aid was simply handed over to people. It ended up rusting in the field. Truth be told, there is no quick and easy solution to developmental projects. As a wise man once told me, 'Son, you can't drive a ten-ton tank over a one-ton bridge.' This invaluable truth reminds me that we are only as strong as the relationships we build. While projects are great, it is really about the people we want to serve. When working in a cross-cultural environment, building the bridge of relationship is vital to the long term success of any project.

When working in a cross-cultural environment, building the bridge of relationship is vital to long term success.

The community leadership had been wrestling with how to do this for the past few years. In no way did they want to send the message that their European way of doing things was superior, as that was demeaning. They laboured over how to improve the conditions and economically develop the area but involve the Africans in the process so that they felt ownership and personal responsibility. Due to the nature of their subsistance level and nomadic lifestyles, the concept of maintenance is new to many Africans. It is second nature to Westerners, however, and can be a source of frustration when trying to establish long-term change.

They had overcome centuries of distrust and built a bridge that crossed cultural differences and laid out a road to a new future.

As we toured the developments on Olive Tree, I was very pleased to see that a number of black Africans from the village were not only working there but also living there in newly constructed homes. Even better, some of the white families had relocated there, and were living side by side with their black neighbours. It truly was a beautiful sight to behold and my heart was just ecstatic! They had overcome centuries of distrust and built a bridge to each other that crossed cultural differences and laid out a road to a new future together.

As we walked around Olive Tree, I met Sebastian, a young African from the village who was being apprenticed in the art of furniture making. He was constructing rough chairs and tables much like rustic patio furniture produced in the States. These furniture pieces were not only being used in the living quarters on the farms, but also were taken to various markets and sold for profit.

When you are starving, access to food can be worth more than money.

Stephen, whom I had first met in 1984, had grown in leadership stature since I was last there. He was older than almost everyone else, and was considered a respected elder. He was in charge of all the agricultural projects in development. They had planted banana and pawpaw trees as well as more gardens and my favourite, passion fruit vines. With the earthen dam in place and waiting for the autumn rains, and the future concrete weirs in progress, agricultural development for Olive Tree was being planned on a large scale. They continued to produce more than they needed so they could sell their fruits and vegetables at the markets. At times they would use the produce to barter for labour. When you are starving, access to food can be worth more than money.

Nkiwane, another African, was now in charge of both the sheep and goat herds. Gary Kroeze had worked with Gerry to get some new breeds imported to see how they would react to the environment. Initial tests were promising, and the herds were multiplying. I was recruited one day into helping castrate sheep which, for a city boy, was a painful operation to behold. It is amazing how you can get sympathy pains even when working with sheep!

Finally Neville, who had recently moved from the village, escorted us to the store he managed. As the store was within walking distance of the village of Mbezingwe, it was very convenient for the villagers, saving them the bus fare they needed for the 40 km trip to Bulawayo. Access to the simplest of supplies was a continual problem for the local Africans.

One day we drove to a nearby town to get some supplies. One of the items on the shopping list was cereal. Being naïve and curious, I wanted to find out what the cereal choices were. After all, back home we

The poor in underdeveloped countries have very few choices.

have one whole side of a grocery aisle filled with what seems like hundreds of choices. As we walked into the store I headed over to the 'cereal aisle' only to find one small section at the end of an aisle amongst other food. To my utter amazement I had a choice of Corn Flakes, Corn Flakes or Corn Flakes! Even more amazing, instead of being packaged in the typical multicoloured, finely designed boxes that are all screaming 'purchase me,' they were in white boxes with large black letters saying 'Corn Flakes'. The simplicity of it all was not lost on me. It was then I realized another simple but profound truth about the poor in underdeveloped countries, and that is that they have very few choices. We in the West often wonder why, with all of our government programmes, people don't choose to get out of poverty. Overseas, in many cases, they do not have a choice at all. One of the definitions of poverty could be 'the lack of choices'.

John and Elaine had wanted to show us 'Yanks' the northern region of the country. After all that we had seen during the week and with the endless discussions, it was actually a wonderful respite to get away for a few days and let it all settle in our souls. Noel, Robert and I piled into his station wagon and we headed north to Victoria Falls. We were all filled with a wondrous sense of excitement as we headed off on another great African adventure.

He knew we were on his turf and did not care what we thought about him.

On the way to the Falls we stopped for a day at the Hwange National Park which is the largest game reserve in the country, covering 23 000 square kilometres. The park is as big as the Netherlands. The park is close to the edge of the Kalahari Desert and thus has a diverse ecological system and is home to over 105 species of wildlife. I was ready and armed with my 35mm camera and a long telephoto zoom lens. The experience certainly wasn't disappointing as we saw many different species and my camera was clicking non-stop. I burned through some serious rolls of film. (A note to the younger folk reading this: yes, there was a day when people took photos with film.) The park was home to a large elephant population and every once in a while we would find ourselves stuck driving slowly behind a huge bull elephant sauntering down the middle of the road without a care in the world. It was as if he knew we were on his turf and did not care what we thought about him.

My most memorable experience of our time there happened the next day. After settling in at base camp that night, John asked me if I had enjoyed the experience. I was of course over the moon as never in my life had I been so close to so many unique creatures. I did confess though that my only disappointment was that we hadn't seen a lion. I really wanted to take a photo of a lion. John suggested that if we wanted to, the three of us could get up early the next morning and take his car out for an hour before breakfast. He thought that at that time of the day we just might see one. We talked about it and decided that since we had come all this way we should give it another shot.

As the sun rose the next morning, Noel, Robert and I headed out in search of a wild beast. We decided that Noel would drive and that, since I had the camera, I would take the pictures, leaving Robert to be the bait. It sucks being the youngest! We had been out cruising around for about thirty minutes when suddenly we saw this distinctly male lion cross the road a few hundred feet ahead of us. We were so excited and Noel stepped on the accelerator to try to reach it before it went too far into the bush. We stopped at the spot where we had seen the lion cross but, at first, couldn't see anything through the high grass. Suddenly I noticed that the lion was crouched on the ground less than two metres away! His fur was the same colour as the tall grass so he was well camouflaged. I quickly took a photo through the window just in case that was the only one we got.

He seemed perfectly happy just sitting there staring at these stupid people huddled in a car.

For a few minutes we sat there staring at him, hoping he would come out of the bush, but we soon realized that he was perfectly happy just sitting there staring back at the stupid people huddled in a car. Being an avid photographer, I wasn't satisfied with a blurry photo taken through the windshield of a car; I needed a real photo. Since Noel was born in South Africa and had claimed to have been around lions before, I asked him for his expert advice. He told us that while lions look big and ferocious they actually only attack when they are hungry and in his opinion, this lion did not look hungry.

Noel was so confident in the lion's passiveness that I decided I was going to hop in the back seat of the car and take another photo. All I would need to do was roll the window down just enough to get my long telephoto zoom lens out the window. I got into the back seat and perched on one knee, bracing myself on the floorboard with the other leg, and then slowly rolled down the glass and slid my lens carefully through the window. It took me a while to find the lion in the viewfinder as he was so well hidden, but I did manage to get another photo of him.

Of course this still wasn't good enough as I wanted him out in the open. Noel spoke up and said that since he had been around lions before he was not scared and would roll down his window and yell at the lion to come out. I thought that was a brilliant idea and repositioned myself on the back seat and focused in on the lion. Noel rolled down his window and started yelling at the lion, saying things that made no sense to me but I figured he was the lion expert and knew what he was doing.

I could see the lion twitching like a house cat, when suddenly his tail shot up in the air and with a huge roar he charged out of the bush straight at us. The next thing I remember was my head snapping back and my whole body flying backwards, bouncing off the back seat and eventually landing on the floor. My camera came flying through the air a split second later and landed on top of me. It took me a few seconds to get my bearings. I realized that Noel had popped the clutch and hit the gas so hard that the car shot forward with the speed and torque of a dragster.

Once I pulled myself up and sat on the back seat, we all looked at each other and broke out in uncontrollable laughter. Our hearts were beating so incredibly fast that we could barely talk. I finally caught my breath enough to ask Noel what the heck had just happened. He said, 'My head said "I'm not scared," but when the lion charged my feet said something else.' After taking a few minutes to get ourselves calmed down, we headed back to base camp and I began to wonder if I had even taken the photo. It was a few weeks before I was able to get the film developed and see what I had shot, but sure enough, there was a photo of Mr Lion charging, hoping to make mincemeat out of us.

We raced back to camp to tell John and Elaine about our lion adventure and they had a great laugh at our expense. After a good English breakfast of eggs and sausages we headed to 'Vic Falls' as they called it. The locals call it 'Mosi-oa-Tunya' which means 'the smoke that thunders'. The falls are located on the Zambezi River in the north-western corner of the country. When you stand and look across the river you can see Botswana to the west and Zambia to the north. The first European to set eyes on the falls was Dr. David Livingstone in 1855. He was so captivated by the sight he wrote of the falls, 'No one can imagine the beauty of the view from anything witnessed in England. It had never been seen before by European eyes; but scenes so lovely must have been gazed upon by angels in their flight.'

Having read that, I was filled with great anticipation as to what I would behold. While the Victoria Falls are not the highest in the world, they are the widest and have the greatest volume of water continually falling over the edge. As we approached, I was mesmerized by the number of rainbows. The falls flow over and down a number of deep gorges which create a natural updraft. The air carries the mist up into the sunlight where it is illuminated, producing a variety of rainbows all at once. It is quite magical to behold.

As you can imagine, with that volume of water crashing into the gorges, the sound was like a roaring freight train that you can hear from miles away. Once we parked the car and headed over toward the falls, I noticed that it seemed like it was raining lightly though it was still sunny. I soon realized that it was in fact the mist from the falls being carried away by the wind currents. As you near the Falls you enter a literal rainforest that is the product of all the mist generated by the powerful down force of large volumes of falling water. We spent the next few hours hiking through the rainforest taking various photos of the falls. For a moment we all stopped and thought about what must have been going through Dr. Livingstone's mind when he came face to face with this wonder of God's creation.

After an amazing few days away, we headed back to the community to spend the last days with our friends and to tie up any loose ends. As we approached the farm property I noticed there was a group of about 5–6 black Africans who seemed to be camped out under a tree on the side of one of the hills. I did not recognize any of the people in the group and asked Gerry about them later. He explained that they were called 'squatters' and were a real problem.

Some of the squatters (about eleven in all) had worked for the previous owner of Adams Farm. When the property changed hands they were given permission by Gerry to remain on the farm. The problems developed when they expanded their numbers by inviting extended family and friends to join them. Gerry had made repeated efforts to befriend and employ them, but they refused. It seemed that the squatters were of the opinion, based on their socialist beliefs, that whatever was happening on the community's land belonged to them. They started stealing and killing cattle and taking supplies from the farm stores. Gerry and Dave had tried to invite them to a meal to discuss their situation, but the squatters didn't seem to have any interest in talking. I had no idea at the time that this situation was going to be at the root of the massacres seventeen months later.

After a few more days with our friends, we packed our bags and headed back to the States to share all that we had seen. The first thing I did was get my photos developed as there was no way I could possibly explain all that was going on without a photo album. Noel and I shared our journey with the leadership team and a few key people in the church to gauge their interest level. Their responses was affirming, and my friends Jerry Reardon and Don Steadman kicked into gear and helped raise additional funds so we could get the concrete weirs built.

We set a goal to have the funds raised and the dams in place by the next rainy season in October of 1987. Jerry and Don were amazing as they were able to get some key companies in the Kansas City area to donate funds. The church also agreed to give additional support, and it was clear by the beginning of 1987 that we were going to reach our goals.

Two families from the church decided to add their skill sets to the mix. In January of 1987, Bob and Terry Hartley headed over on a six-month commitment. Bob was an associate of mine at the church and had more energy than ten men combined. Having been a star wrestler, he was in great shape and his muscle and enthusiasm were a huge relief and greatly appreciated by everyone at the community. The work on the dams was backbreaking, but Bob threw himself into it wholeheartedly. Terry, who had a gentle and tender spirit, helped in a variety of areas, especially teaching.

Jim and Sallie Collins, along with their four-year-old son Michael, also committed to working on the farms. Jim had the single greatest gift of fixing things of anyone I have ever known. You could drive your car into his garage and he would just listen to it and tell you what was wrong with it. He was the 'Dog Whisperer' of cars. Jim helped with maintenance on vehicles as well as engineering new buildings and developing various pieces of equipment that could be solar powered. Sally, like Terry, was a teacher and was a great asset in helping teach the African women how to make various products they could sell at the markets to generate income.

In February of 1987, Noel Alexander returned to the community, taking a team of about ten people with him. He was eager to show them what all the excitement was about. One of the team, an ex-con named Bill Corum, formed an immediate bond with the Africans and those in the community. Like them, his life had been profoundly turned around by the message of the Gospel and the teachings of Jesus. He wasn't at all intimidated by how dangerous their situation was as he knew all too well about violence. After returning to Kansas City, Bill talked things over with his wife Debbie, and they decided to go back to Zimbabwe for another three months to help finish up the weir projects. Gerry would later write and tell me that Bill's presence was a source of great strength and helped them with the final push to get the dams completed. Bill and Debbie were the last people from Kansas City to see our friends alive.

While staying there on the New Adams Farm, Noel had the most frightening dream. He was fast asleep when awakened by the sound of men knocking on the windows of the home where he was staying with the rest of the team. He could hear yelling and a commotion outside, when suddenly the windows were smashed in and men started firing automatic weapons into the room at everyone sleeping there. He found himself under the bed hiding from the onslaught of bullets. He was absolutely terrified, and when he finally woke up he was still lying on the floor with his arms up in the air feeling the bed on top of him. He later recalled that the sensation of the bed over him was like a 'spirit of fear' lying on top of him, crushing him. He had to forcibly throw it off or he felt he would be crushed by it.

Little did anyone realize that nine months later that same terror would revisit the communities, only this time it would be real!

CHAPTER 5

WHEN PAIN COMES TO TOWN

There are things that we don't want to happen but have to
accept, things we don't want to know but have to learn, and
people we can't live without but have to let go.

– AUTHOR UNKNOWN

A fter a long and emotionally draining flight we finally landed in
Bulawayo, Zimbabwe. The whole city was in an uproar over the
massacres. Tensions were riding high and fear was in the air. Even though
there had been other white farmers killed over the years, there had never been anything this brutal, and people wondered whether it was going
to continue. Many of the white farmers increased security measures
around their farms and beefed up their firepower. I wondered if things
were going to escalate into another race war.

Gary and I were taken straight from the airport to a gathering at the
home of a relative of David Marais', one of those who had perished. We
were introduced to various relatives of those who had died, including
Dave's parents and his sister, Linda. Understandably, they were all quite
shaken and filled with many questions. Most of them did not really understand what The Community of Reconciliation was all about. Even
though they were family, they had never taken a close look at what was
happening there, and now they were trying to make sense of it all. None
of the three families from the United States or Scotland who had lost
family members were able to make the trip. I felt terribly for them and

wondered how one grieves for a lost child or sister or brother from thousands of miles away. How hard that must have been for them.

Due to the way that the victims' bodies had been mutilated and burned, it was decided that it would be best to cremate their remains. The crematorium in the city was a small one that rarely, if ever, was used. When it was finally decided that all sixteen people would be cremated and once all the calculations were complete, they realized it would take at least a week to complete the task. In the interim, public and private ceremonies were held in and around Bulawayo to honour their memories.

I distinctly remember visiting Gaynor Hill's mom at her home. Gaynor was a special young woman with a beautiful voice and a talent for writing songs. Six weeks earlier, she and her husband Rob had experienced the wonderful birth of their first child. Gaynor's mom had lost so much in one tragic moment. She would never be able to play with her grandson. As you can imagine, she was completely distraught and angry. She was having a hard time dealing with her daughter's death. Having lost a son-in-law and a grandson as well only compounded her pain. During our time together we talked a lot about Gaynor and what made her special. Her mother eventually came to understand that Gaynor had died doing the thing she loved. While no one was happy with the outcome, everything that the community stood for was what beat within Gaynor's heart. If there was no Community of Reconciliation, Gaynor would have found another place to express her heart and it would have been as radical in its commitment to the values of God's Kingdom as what she had died for. While her mother did not have the same deep passion for this type of thing, it quickly became evident to her that she had had a very special daughter and one that she was very proud of.

On our second day in the country we were escorted out to the 'farm properties'. I use those two words soberly. Until a few days earlier, it had been a place where life was celebrated. Now that the people who gave it life were gone, it seemed to be simply a piece of property. The sense of Community was missing. It was an empty feeling, to say the least.

As we approached the New Adams Farm there was a strong police presence. Without them there, we would not have been allowed to even enter. Thabani met us on site. It was the first time I had seen him since arriving and it was evident by the look in his eyes that he was in a great deal of pain. We embraced, holding each other for a minute or two, and as we pulled away we both had tears in our eyes. We did not need to say anything; each knew how the other felt.

As we came around the front of the community centre, the magnitude of what had happened hit me again. However, this time it was not the loss of friends but the hatred and anger I sensed. As I looked around me, it was like being in the midst of a battle zone. Everything was destroyed! All that was left standing at the community centre were the rock walls that were now scarred with black scorch marks from the intense fires that had raged there.

Leaning against a wall at the entry way was the burnt-out metal frame of the motorcycle that Noel had once ridden. Now it was just a hunk of rusted scrap metal. As we walked from one end to the other I saw broken dishes littering the floor. All that was left of the piano that we had once stood around singing was the metal soundboard lying on the floor exactly in its place. There was a burnt-out baby push cart sitting in the middle of the floor of the main room. I imagined that it wasn't but a few days ago that Gaynor or Laura Russell had been pushing little Benjamin Hill around the building. It was a strange feeling, almost like time stood still except that it was burnt.

> *It was a strange feeling, almost like time stood still except that it was burnt.*

Not too far from the push cart was a strange image burned into the wall. A wooden cabinet had once stood there holding dishes, but today there, staring at me was the image of a bald-headed man with long hair and a beard. There was something dark, brooding and ominous about the image. It made me feel uncomfortable.

As we made our way to the various living quarters, the images that struck me the hardest were the things that had belonged to the children.

There was a child's bike already starting to rust that was sitting amongst the rubble of Dave and Kathy's Marais' home. I am sure it was their son Ethan's. As I walked into Gaynor and Rob's home I saw a piece of melted window glass with the words 'In Your Presence Is Fullness of Joy' still visible. I bowed my head for a moment and said, 'I hope you two have found that joy now.' Rusted, burnt-out vehicles were scattered everywhere. They looked as if they had been hit by a flame thrower. The whole scene was very overwhelming and I had to take some time to sit down and regain my composure.

> *The images that struck me the hardest were the things that had belonged to the children.*

As I headed down to the Olive Tree property with Thabani, we came across a black police officer with two black Africans who were handcuffed. One was sitting on the ground and the other was standing. Both had their wrists handcuffed behind their back. As we passed them I heard a loud slapping sound, followed by a scream. As my head spun around I saw the police officer with a two metre long whip unlike any I had ever seen. It was thick and stiff and as it came through the air it let out a whirring noise. When it hit flesh it let out a distinct noise and I knew was extremely painful. Thabani explained that it was actually made of rhino hide and was called a 'sjambok'. Used in the wrong way, it could kill a man. I'd had enough of killing and asked why the officer was whipping the African. He explained that they were a part of a squatter encampment that had settled on the community's property. The police suspected that they were somehow involved in the massacre and were trying to get information out of them as to the whereabouts of the dissidents who had killed our friends.

> *I needed something that was not naturally within me to give ... forgiveness.*

Honestly, I had some very conflicting emotions at that point. On the one hand my pain and anger wanted the officer to beat him without mercy until he revealed the location of the murderers. I wanted them captured and punished for killing and destroying so many people's lives. On the other hand, what about Jesus' mandate for loving your enemies and forgiveness? While I knew that these were attitudes that I was 'supposed' to have, they were far from me. At that moment I asked God for help. I needed something that was not naturally within me to give … forgiveness.

Once we reached the Olive Tree complex I was saddened to see that it was as devastated as New Adams. The roof of the church had been burned off, leaving just the brick pillars. The raiders had tried to destroy all the living quarters but there were still a few buildings standing. There was one with a unique design that I had not seen before. Thabani explained that it was a new home design that Gerry and Jim Collins had been experimenting with. It was an inexpensive way to build a dwelling that would remain cool in the hot African summers as well as hold up against the sometimes harsh elements.

'This is not the last time you will see the blood of your friends shed for My Name.'

As I headed toward it, Thabani ran up and grabbed my arm. He asked me if I was sure I wanted to proceed, as this was the building in which everyone at Olive Tree had been killed. As I continued to approach it, a great sense of sadness and yet reverence came over me. When I opened the front door the smell of death swept past me. There was blood, hair and pieces of scalp strewn from one end to the other. My eyes started watering from both the smell and the extreme sense of loss. I noticed that blood was still slowly draining out through the front door. As I stood there in the doorway, I felt a Holy sensation pass over me and inside me I heard the words, 'This is not the last time you will see the blood of your friends shed for My Name.' It was one of the most sobering moments in my entire life and one I think I shall never forget.

By this time I simply could not take any more and asked Thabani to guide me to the weirs so I could have some time alone. The weirs had just recently been completed and they stood barren and alone, jutting up out of the parched earth like grey giants, waiting for the rains to come.

After asking Thabani for a few minutes alone, I walked out onto the middle of one of them and sat there on top of the wall for the longest time. I ran my hands back and forth over the concrete thinking about how so many people had worked so hard to get these erected. Touching the concrete was like touching them. I thought a lot about the people from Kansas City who had flown here to help complete this project. They had sacrificed so much so that the people here could have water. I took my time and one by one I thought about and honoured the memory of each of my sixteen friends. When I was finally done I looked up, and as far as I could see was clear barren ground waiting for the rains that had not come in many years. I said a prayer and thought, *'How sad that one day these weirs will be full and my friends will not be here to see it.'*

After a few more minutes alone with my thoughts and prayers, we headed back into Bulawayo. The drive seemed to take twice as long as usual. I was quiet and did not say a word the whole trip. I had no words to communicate how I was feeling. The moment seemed bigger than words.

CHAPTER 6

THE DAY THE MUSIC DIED

*Greater love has no one than this: to lay down
one's life for one's friends.*

– JOHN 15:13

The headline in the 29 November 1987 edition of the Johannesburg *Sunday Times* read 'The Massacre'. The first line was, 'The sixteen Christians butchered in Matabeleland went to their deaths in silence, no screams, no crying, nothing but prayers.'
While my friends may have lost their lives
in silence, around the world their tragic
story was being screamed everywhere. As I
later learned, the massacre was the lead story on virtually every nightly newscast
across the globe. As so often happens, the
news media, in the rush to get the story out,
can get it wrong, or at least miss the key
points. In the US media my friends were
called 'missionaries', which wasn't totally accurate, at least in the way we traditionally understand missionaries. In my opinion, it actually took away from the profoundness of their story and what they all lived and died for.

While my friends may have lost their lives in silence, around the world their tragic story was being screamed everywhere.

The people in the group, who relocated from the security of city life in Bulawayo to a rugged bush lifestyle, were all compassionate, kind and generous. They were people who, for the most part, were either born or raised in Zimbabwe. Dave Emerson and Sharon Ivesdahl were both Americans and Jean Campbell was from Scotland, but the other thirteen white members of The Community of Reconciliation who died were from Zimbabwe. These were not well-intentioned missionaries coming in from overseas to help out in a difficult situation. They were local people who had grown up there. At one time they had been on the opposite side of an armed conflict (Zimbabwe's Liberation Struggle) with the very people they were now living with in harmony. Once they were enemies. It was through an encounter with God that their hearts were profoundly changed. It was because they all believed so strongly in the principles of racial reconciliation and equality that they were willing to change their lifestyles. It was for the truths of The Kingdom of God that they gave their lives. They believed in and were committed to justice. They had chosen love over hate, and integration over segregation. They believed in harmony over discord and that loving your enemies was a higher way of life. They gave their lives to demonstrate that it could be done; it was not just a myth or wishful thinking. In a country tearing itself apart with racism, they proved that God's love can, and will, triumph over hatred and discrimination.

It was through an encounter with God that their hearts were profoundly changed.

After the drive back to Bulawayo, I was exhausted. It had been an emotional day and my body clock was still out of sync with the local time. I was tired and decided to rest. After sleeping for an hour or so I woke up with a few lines from Don McLean's song, *American Pie,* going through my head.

Oh, and while the king was looking down
The jester stole his thorny crown.
The courtroom was adjourned

No verdict was returned.
And while Lennon read a book of Marx
The quartet practised in the park
And we sang dirges in the dark
The day the music died.

While Don was singing about the deaths of Buddy Holly and Ritchie Valens, he could have just as well been singing about my friends.

After some dinner, I was ready to delve further into exactly what had happened the day my friends had died. Thabani sat down with me and for the next few hours I painstakingly interviewed him. It was as difficult a process as I have ever been through. The rest of this chapter is hard reading and not for the faint of heart. In martyrdom two worlds clash in a head-on collision. In the natural world it is brutal and gory. In the spiritual world it is beautiful and glorious. They awkwardly co-exist in the same moment. They are diametric and yet one.

That fateful day started out as any other. There was no sense of the impending dark cloud that was about to descend on the inhabitants of the Community. Thabani spent the day ploughing in the fields and doing his daily maintenance chores around the Olive Tree Farm. Thabani was an exceptional young man with a great smile. You could tell within minutes of being in his presence that he had leadership written all over him. His parents had lived in the village of Mbezingwe near Olive Tree. They had sacrificed much in order for him to be able to attend school and get a good education. Good schooling is not always free in Africa. Due to his command of the English language and our ability to communicate so openly, I learned much from him. He helped me understand his people's struggle for survival against not only the military-led genocide, but also the violent Marxist dissidents that threatened them

They believed in harmony over discord and that loving your enemies was a higher way of life.

unless they joined their cause. Years of drought had also devastated the region, leaving many of its people starving. Thabani's mother had died the year before and his father was now working with him on the Olive Tree Farm. Thabani, at the time, was rooming with Dave Emerson as they had become very good friends. Dave, who was from North Dakota, had never in his life expected to find himself not only being friends with a black man, but also rooming with him! It was a wonderful, eye-opening, cross-cultural experience for both of them.

They proved that God's love can, and will, triumph over hatred and discrimination.

With so much work yet to be done, it was decided that it might be best to extend the work day a few more hours. Since the community dinner at New Adams had already been prepared, everyone gathered there and ate together. After the meal, they returned to their various responsibilities to work for a few more hours while it was still light. Thabani continued ploughing on the tractor until around 8 p.m. that Wednesday night. After cleaning up, the whole group gathered again at the New Adams community centre and learned some new songs that Gaynor Hill had written and wanted to teach them.

Music was always so central to the daily life there. I have a beautiful memory of my first morning on the New Adams Farm in 1984. I was so energized from all I had seen the day before that I could barely sleep. The next morning as the sun was coming up I heard the most beautiful sound outside my room. I quickly dressed and made my way outside, until I found myself looking out at the 4,5 hectare garden that fed the farm and so many people in the region. There, with the mist hanging low over the field, were about a dozen African women, some with their babies strapped to their backs, working in the fields and singing. I was absolutely captivated by the sound as there were no instruments and yet the melody was so full and rich that it echoed through the hills. As the women watered and tended the garden, the smile on their faces and the joy in their souls was so infectious. I soon found myself involuntarily moving to the sound of their rhythms.

Thabani continued with his account. After a few hours of singing and sharing their thoughts of the day, everyone headed to their living quarters to get a good night's sleep. In the early hours of the next morning, Thabani was wakened by the sound of Gerry Keightley's voice just outside his window. It was unusual for anyone to be up at that time of the night, much less Jerry. *'Who was he talking to?'* Thabani wondered. He could not make out the unfamiliar voice.

Thabani woke Dave Emerson and they decided to see who was outside making such a commotion. Once they had positioned themselves next to the window, they heard a voice ask Gerry, 'What are you doing here?' Gerry responded, 'The Lord has called me to help feed and clothe the people in this area.' Thabani and Dave dressed quickly to go outside and see if

In martyrdom two worlds clash in a head-on collision.

they could be of assistance. Thabani was bilingual and an excellent translator, and it sounded to him like the voices were Ndebele. As they were in the process of getting dressed, Thabani heard someone ask, 'Is there anyone else in there?' to which Gerry replied, 'Yes, Thabani and the others are all asleep.' No sooner had Gerry finished his words when the door to their room was kicked down and whoever was outside came rushing in with clubs and pushed Thabani and Dave to the floor. They kicked and beat them violently. Thabani and Dave were stunned and confused. They had absolutely no idea what was going on.

After a few minutes of thrashing them, the men stopped and dragged Thabani and Dave out of their room. Once they got outside the house and looked up, standing there in a group were Stephen, Nkiwane and Roy – the African brothers who all lived and worked on Olive Tree Farm with their families. Standing in another circle just off to the side of the Africans, were all the white people who lived at Olive Tree. Once Thabani and Dave were dragged outside, three men ran into their room and ransacked everything, taking whatever they thought valuable. In the middle of all the chaos was one African screaming out orders to the men in his raiding party. His name was Morgan Sango and it was clear that he was their leader.

Sango was also known by the name 'Gayigusi' which, in Ndebele means 'grind the bush'. Sango was a former Ndebele soldier who had fought with Joshua Nkomo's ZAPU troops in the 'Zimbabwe Liberation Struggle/Bush War' years earlier.

In 1980, after Robert Mugabe's Shona tribe had voted him into office as Prime Minister, he used his newfound power to put his cousin Perence Shiri in place as head of the dreaded North Korean-trained Zimbabwean 5th Brigade. He put other friends and family members in key positions of power, and started a campaign to subdue the heavily populated Ndebele area known as Matabeleland located in Zimbabwe's southern region. His motivation was to remove any potential threat from his political rival Joshua Nkomo and the Ndebele people. Mugabe's 5th Brigade committed genocide on the Ndebele citizens. Estimates of the number of people slaughtered range from 20 000 to 60 000. Mass graves were later discovered not far from where the community was located.

These acts of genocide forced many of the Ndebele ex-soldiers to retreat into the bush where they had hidden caches of weapons left over from the war. They became known as political dissidents against Mugabe's government. They raided, pillaged and destroyed wherever they moved, running from Mugabe's security forces. At the time of the raid, things had calmed down somewhat and Nkomo was in negotiations with Mugabe to find a peace settlement between the two tribes. He wanted to stop the hostilities and end the genocide. For some of the Ndebele people, Nkomo's willingness to negotiate a settlement with Mugabe was considered a complete 'sell-out'. When asked later why he had agreed to this peace settlement, Nkomo said that he was tired of all the bloodshed, and did not want to see any more friends and colleagues murdered by Mugabe's security forces. He wanted peace among the people of Zimbabwe.

After the end of apartheid in 1995, the South African Truth and Re-conciliation Commission was established to attempt to bring healing to the nation. Those who came forward to confess their violent acts of racism were absolved of their sins. It was discovered during the meetings that the South African security forces were ordered to stir up trouble in southern Zimbabwe. They were told to keep the two tribes in conflict with each other to prevent any form of reconciliation. The South African government was nervous about the country being run by a single party Marxist government like the one Mugabe was moving toward. The security forces, under the guise of being fellow Marxist-Leninist rebels, supported the Ndebele dissidents with funding and arms. They encouraged them to disrupt anything they could to keep the tensions high so that hopefully the Ndebele people would put enough pressure on Nkomo to make him reconsider his position.

As the three members of Morgan Sango's raiding party pillaged Thabani and Dave's living quarters, the larger portion of the group remained outside. Armed with AK-47s and sporting Rastafarian dreadlocks, they had a terrifying appearance. It was evident by the smell that they had been smoking dagga. Their eyes had that look of craziness associated with Charles Manson photos. It has been estimated that in the main group there were about 20 men. The Africans living on the farm thought that there were more people who seemed to be with the raiding party. It was difficult to see their faces as they were standing back in the shadows. Most agree that they could very well have been the 'squatters', though no one was absolutely sure.

The squatter problem that I had first learned about in 1986 had not been resolved. In fact it had grown worse as their group grew larger. Besides being unco-operative, they would kill cattle whenever they wanted and not reimburse the farm. They would cut the fencing that surrounded the garden areas to keep the wildlife out. The kudu loved to wander into the garden area and help themselves to a delicious meal. Once the squatters cut through the fence, they would steal food for themselves, and in their haste to get away, trample over and destroy other garden vegetation.

Gerry and the black leaders on the farms had tried on numerous occasions to sit and talk with Charles Masuku, their leader. They had hoped to come to some arrangement, but the squatters would have none of it. At one point, some Ndebele officials from the government in Bulawayo made a trip out to the community to talk with the squatters to see if they could convince them to move. They kindly explained to them that they needed to move on, and let them know that the government had land it would provide them free of charge. This still wasn't good enough for them, as they wanted the farm land that the community had worked so hard to reclaim from misuse and the elements. Charles Masuku at that point got very angry with the officials and vowed, 'No one on the farm will see their next meal.'

> *There were no white masters, only a racially integrated family whose love for one another was being poured out on behalf of others.*

There is still some mystery surrounding the motivation behind the raid. Given Charles Masuku's declaration, there is little doubt that the squatters had a significant hand in the fateful events that transpired. They may have been the faces hiding in the shadows. They could have easily recruited Morgan Sango and his raiding party who were not far away, hiding in the Matopo hill country. Whether Morgan was acting on his own, as an agent of the South African security forces or the ZANU-PF (Zimbabwean) government is still unknown. Whether he was a true political dissident or a pseudo-dissident using a political agenda as a cover story is also a mystery. Until a truth commission is established in Zimbabwe, we will never really know. Either way, with Morgan's violent agenda, and Charles's lust for the land, they both had very personal motives that made their one-night partnership deadly. Charles, in asking Morgan to come and eliminate all the white people on the farm, thought that they could take over the land for themselves and that the black African Christians living there would rejoice with them after being liberated from their white masters. Sadly, they either didn't get it or simply didn't want to.

There were no white masters, only a racially integrated family whose love for one another was being poured out on behalf of others.

The local Ndebele government had been very supportive of everything going on at the farms, which in hindsight may have been a fatal problem as the dissidents were still fighting a war against the Mugabe government. Even though the community had no political agenda, the government was keeping an eye on them as they transformed the region. From time to time various government officials, most of them Ndebele, would visit the farms to see how things were developing. When they saw how the land had been reclaimed from the devastation of drought and mismanagement, they were amazed. They witnessed formerly starving people who were not just surviving, but producing enough food to help others in need. They saw how these same people were also able to sell some of their produce at the local markets to earn additional income. When they saw small village economics at work, it excited them, as not only were people learning skills in agriculture, but also in fish farming, carpentry, furniture making, blacksmithing, weaving and a host of other trades. These skills, and therefore the ability to make a simple living, were restoring the dignity and honour to a people who had been so downtrodden and abused that death would have been a relief for many of them. To see a whole region come alive with hope is a powerful thing to behold, and yet, as I learned, one man's hope is another man's threat.

One man's hope is another man's threat.

Once everyone was outside, Morgan Sango demanded the keys to the farm store. Gerry responded, 'If you'd like them I will go get them for you.' Morgan was suspicious of Gerry's motives and asked him if he was trying to be clever. Gerry realized that Morgan was on edge and high and didn't say much more after that. He just waited as the dissidents spoke among themselves.

There were a number of men in the house still rummaging through things they wanted to take, making a dreadful noise. Barnabas, Gerry's 18-month-old son, woke up crying. Gerry said to Morgan, 'Excuse me for a minute; I want to get my son.' Morgan got very angry with him and yelled 'No!' Thabani whispered to Gerry to encourage him to remain calm as these guys were really agitated. Gerry decided at that point not to say another word and see if things would calm down.

It soon became evident that this was more than just a supply raid.

Morgan grabbed Thabani by the arm and demanded to know his name. 'Tell the mother of the crying child to stand out from the group and go and get the child!' At that point Thabani asked Marian if she would go get Barnabas. After Marian returned with her little boy in her arms, Morgan grabbed Gerry and took him to get the keys to the other buildings. While this was going on, they tied the hands of the eight whites behind their backs with wire. When they came to Marian, who was still holding her child, they took Barnabas from her, gave him to Nkiwane and proceeded to tie Marian's hands behind her back.

No one at this point was sure what was going to happen next. It soon became evident that this was more than just a supply raid. '*There must be a racial agenda here,*' Thabani thought. None of the black members of the farm were being tied up with wire. They were simply being forced to stand as a group and watch everything that was taking place. It was unclear what Morgan was thinking. If he thought of himself as a liberator, and that the black Africans would be glad to be 'set free from the oppression of the white man', he was sadly mistaken. The white man had already set them free and treated them as equals. If he thought of himself as a dissident and that by a show of force he would strike terror into the hearts of the local Africans to support his political agenda, he again was mistaken. In the end they hated him for destroying their lives. The events of that night played out like a Shakespearian tragedy where everyone loses something because of the foolishness and evil in the hearts of humanity.

Finally everyone, both black and white, was herded into Nkiwane's house which was located just across the compound area from Gerry and Marian's. The whites, all with their hands tied with wire and the blacks following, were led into the house. They were then forced to sit on the hard, cold, concrete kitchen floor huddled together in a group. Gerry, in the meantime, was *en route* with a few members of the raiding party to the farm store in order to get the money, food and supplies they wanted. Thabani was pulled out away from the rest of the group at Nkiwane's house. He was taken outside and asked where an axe could be found. He assumed they wanted it to break into other buildings. He told them that he had no idea where they were stored as he worked on the tractor and all the farm tools were someone else's responsibility. Then they demanded a garden hoe and he explained to them again that he did not have keys or know how to get access to the garden tools. They ordered him to go back inside and sit on the kitchen floor with everyone else. After some time had passed, Gerry returned with the smaller raiding party. At that point Thabani was asked where all the other food was stored. Gerry, overhearing the question, stood up to answer. The dissidents grabbed Thabani and demanded that he show them where everything was.

As they went along they pulled and dragged him and every so often would stop to beat and kick him. They were extremely angry and hostile; just looking for ways to inflict pain. Once they reached the store he showed them where everything was inside including the milk and butter. In an effort to try and calm everyone down Thabani offered to cook the whole group a meal. He thought that kindness might work; after all, as he had learned from the teachings of Jesus, 'If some one strikes you on the right cheek, give them your left' (Matt 5:9). He also thought about the Proverb that says 'A gentle answer turns away wrath' (Prov 13:1). No one even acknowledged him as they were hell-bent on

> *The events of that night played out like a Shakespearian tragedy where everyone loses something because of the foolishness and evil in the hearts of humanity.*

pulling everything out of the store and stacking it in a huge pile on the ground. When they asked him where more food was stored, he told them some of it was kept at the homes of Nkiwane and Stephen. The dissidents talked amongst themselves and decided that they would not go into either home to take anything. They told Thabani that they wanted-ed to send a message that their anger was directed only against the white westerners and not the local black population. Thabani was now certain that this was more than just a simple raid for supplies and that Morgan Sango wanted to make a strong political statement.

> *In the end the dissidents had savagely massacred eight innocent people who had wanted to do nothing more than love and feed the black Africans and treat them as equals.*

Besides taking food and supplies, they also wanted any electronics they could get to sell for cash. Once all the food, supplies and electronic equipment was pillaged and stacked in a huge pile, Morgan Sango called Stephen outside from the group left sitting in Nkiwane's house. He was gone for a long time and no one knew where he had been taken. Stephen later told us that Morgan had ordered him to perform the executions and because he refused they got into a heated argument. Stephen was sure at this point that the dissidents were going to kill him for refusing to murder his white brothers and sisters. Next, the dissidents started calling out the white community members by name one at a time starting with Glynis, Gerry and Marian's beautiful 14-year-old daughter. As Glynis was being taken away, she turned to her father and asked him 'How should I pray?' He responded, 'Pray for these men as they are now the ones that need our prayers.' No one understood what was going on as there was no noise other than the sound of their hearts beating in their chests.

Next to be called out was American Sharon Ivesdahl, followed 20 minutes later by fellow American, David Emerson. Approximately every 20 minutes another person's name was called; Sarah Lovatt, Marian Keightley, Deborah, the Keightley's 16-year-old daughter and then finally Gerry. One by one they were being led into Sharon and Sarah's home and axed in the back of the head before their bodies were violently mutilated. Finally, Nkiwane was told to bring little Barnabas who was thrown on the ground and axed in the head as well. In the end the dissidents had savagely massacred eight innocent people who had wanted to do nothing more than love and feed the black Africans and treat them as equals.

As they hacked each person to death, Stephen was made to stand and watch his friends die in the most brutal way. Since those who died had never screamed out, the rest of the Africans who were in Nkiwane's kitchen wondered what was going on. Never did they imagine what they were about to be forced to witness. When they were finally called out, they thought it was to be told to return to their homes and go back to sleep. As a group they went outside where one of the dissidents was standing, holding a tape recorder that had belonged to Sharon. He demanded batteries. Thabani, in an effort to be a peacemaker, told him that he would show him and led him to straight to Sharon's house. When he opened the wooden door there were the eight mutilated bodies of his friends. Blood was running down the walls and pieces of skin and scalp were everywhere. At that moment it took all his strength just to remain standing. His mind was racing, '*Oh My God, Oh My God, what has happened?*' Later he confided in me that he was so surprised that he had not heard a single scream from anyone, as each person who walked into that room had to know they were going to die. The bloody and mutilated bodies of their friends and family members were lying on the floor right in front of them.

At that moment it took all his strength just to remain standing. His mind was racing, 'Oh My God, Oh My God, what has happened?'

Thabani shared with me that from what Stephen had witnessed, they had the 'grace of God on them as they were singing and praying as they died'. Morgan Sango made sure everyone knew that he was in charge and personally did the killings. At this point, one of the dissidents forced everyone who was left to view the bodies.

Thabani recounted that a mysterious occurrence happened that none of them could naturally explain. After the first eight people had been martyred, a mysterious shining light shot across the night sky straight for them. It suddenly stopped and hovered over the building where the eight bodies lay. It was so brilliant that it illuminated the whole area, a few hundred metres in each direction. The Africans said that the light was so vivid it seemed like it was midday. At that point the dissidents became confused as they could not figure out where the light had come from or how to turn it off. They started screaming at the Africans on Olive Tree to shut it off, but of course they had no idea as to what it was either. After a few minutes it lifted and returned to the heavens and the dissidents continued with their deadly plan.

Then at gunpoint they forced everyone left to load their stolen goods onto one of the farm trucks. The problem was that the truck's starter had been taken out for repair, so it would not start unless pushed. This of course further angered the dissidents, and they forced the blacks to push the truck to try to start it by popping the clutch. This failed as well. Next they grabbed Esinath, who worked at the New Adams Farm, and forced her to try and get the truck started.

Everyone was surprised to see Esinath there that night as she lived miles away in another village and would walk daily to work on the farm. It was later discovered that the dissidents arrived first at her house in her village and threatened to kill her and her children if she did not take them to the farms. Some have speculated that because she daily walked to and from the farms, the squatters may have targeted her and followed her home. Later they must have given that information to the raiding party. Soon Esinath would be made to watch the murders of her friends on New Adams Farm as well.

When the dissidents realized that the truck full of supplies was not going to start, they argued among themselves. They tried to start one of the farm tractors but this too failed. They made the Africans unload the truck and marched them at gunpoint to the New Adams Farm. Once there, they were forced to sit in a group huddled next to the fence just outside the large community centre not far from the Marais' home. Two dissidents were ordered to stand guard over the group while the rest of the raiding party approached the living quarters. Dave Marais, who had fought in the Bush War, sensed something was wrong. One of his two sons, Matthew aged six, after being wakened by the raiding party, sensed danger and went out the back of the house through a window. With Dave having been a military man, it was quite an internal battle for him not to have weapons at his disposal. I know that everyone at the community had wrestled with this issue. In the end it was decided by all that for them to truly be a Community of Reconciliation, weapons were not an option.

Because there were government security forces in the area looking for Morgan Sango, the dissidents never fired their AK-47s, so as to avoid detection. They went from house to house and forced everyone at gunpoint to the community centre and made them sit on the floor. Like they had done at Olive Tree, they bound each person's hands with wire. While they sat on the concrete floor, the dissidents raided each house, pillaging whatever they could find. When they had finished and everything was piled up, each person was led one by one to a room to be hacked to death silently. They slaughtered the members of the New Adams Farm with the same axe they had used at Olive Tree.

As Hazel Russell walked through the doorway, she turned to Esinath and said, 'We are going home tonight.'

Esinath was called out from the group and told to stand at the doorway of the Marais' home. They gave her a lamp and forced her to hold it while her friends were being killed. One by one, each of the eight white members of the community were called out to Dave and Kathy Marais' house. As Hazel Russell walked through the doorway, she turned to Esinath and said, 'We are going home tonight.' Unlike at Olive Tree, this time the sound of chopping and hacking could be heard by all the Africans sitting outside the house. Esinath started vomiting and quickly passed out. Thabani was beside himself with grief as this was beyond his worst nightmare. He kept asking himself, 'Why is this happening to me? What am I going to do now? This is my family. This is everything that means anything to me. God, why are you letting me survive? Why am I still alive?'

How traumatic!

Perhaps the most horrific moment, if it is even possible to say such a thing, was after Gaynor Hill was killed. Laura Russell was standing holding Gaynor's six-week-old baby Benjamin, when he was grabbed from her arms by one of the dissidents and thrown cruelly to the floor. Once they realized the baby was not yet dead, they picked him up by the feet and swung him around and smashed his head open on the floor. Poor Laura, who had helped take care of little Benjamin, was left so traumatized by the whole ordeal she could barely recount much of anything that went on for months afterward.

Besides watching Benjamin viciously killed, she was physically abused by these sadistic men yet left alive to 'tell the world' what she had seen. They mocked her and told her that she was 'serving the wrong God'. They gave her a message to tell the Mugabe government, the media and Margaret Thatcher (then the Prime Minister of England) that they were 'Marxist-Leninist fighters prepared to fight to the last man to drive Western Capitalist-oriented people from the country'.

Sadly, little Ethan Marais, sleepy and dazed, looking for his mother, wandered into the middle of this tragic moment and was killed alongside his parents. The next day, still scared, hiding in the bush and exhausted, brave Matthew took a short cut to Olive Tree and found the police there. He did not know for sure, but had a pretty good idea that something terrible had happened. Little did he know, the rest of his life would never be the same having lost his whole family.

Once the raiding party had finished killing everyone on New Adams and was ready to return to the bush, they set fire to everything. With the thick thatched roofs, the buildings burned like infernos, melting glass and metal. In the end, all that was left standing were the remains of the rock walls, blackened by the flames. In the Marais' house, where all the bodies were stacked, the dissidents threw in a phosphorus grenade that incinerated most of the bodies and caused parts of the building's roof to collapse on the remains. The trucks and other vehicles were stuffed with grass and set on fire as the dissidents became more and more violent and vocal. They started singing revolutionary songs. Some of them were yelling, others were whistling, and still others were shouting, 'We've done it; we've done it!' Then they brought Laura over and stood her in front of Thabani and said, 'This is the child we have left. Would you like her to be left alive?' He quickly responded, 'Yes.' They told him, 'Then you are to take care of this child. She has a letter. Nobody is to touch or read the letter. No matter where she goes, she must hold the letter. This letter is to be given to the police.'

Then, as had happened at Olive Tree earlier, the mysterious, brilliant, white light came shooting across the night sky. It seemed to come out of nowhere, as it appeared from behind the community water tank which was situated on a hill. This time the dissidents became frightened and started screaming frantically for the Africans to turn it off. Again they tried to explain that they had not seen this light before and had no idea as to where it came from. The black members of the community were terrified as they had no idea what to do. Some of them thought that since some of the dissidents had been threatening to kill them during the whole ordeal, certainly now that they couldn't turn the light off they were going to die. The dissidents were frightened themselves and nobody knew what was going to happen next. Soon the dissidents realized that the light was not going to dissipate and that they were out in the open, exposed. Some quickly gathered what they could in their arms and fled into the bush having never harmed any of the Africans. A few others fled back to Olive Tree and set the church on fire. The Africans

It was at this point that they realized something extraordinary and supernatural was taking place.

from the community remained standing there for a while, staring at the white light as it hovered over the Marais' home. It was at this point that they realized something extraordinary and supernatural was taking place. This was more than just a matter of their friends being martyred. The heavens were proclaiming something and they felt a sense of awe come over them. They wondered if God had sent an angel to guide their friends home. They knew that despite the terror and brutality that they had just witnessed, they were now standing on Holy Ground.

It was evident to all that genuine Christianity, when properly lived out, can bring blessing and favour to everyone involved.

Once the light lifted and headed for the heavens, the Africans were left there to figure out what to do next. They were so overwhelmed by everything they had witnessed that they decided to hide out in the bush for the next few hours to make sure the dissidents had left for good. It was 4 a.m. and the sun was going to coming up in a few hours. Thabani, Stephen and Nkiwane decided that Thabani would see if he could get the tractor started and then head down the road to the next farm to call the police in town. When he finally got to the neighbouring farm, woke the people up and tried to use their phone, he found it was dead. When the dissidents had burned the community centre at New Adams, it had destroyed the telephone lines and all the phones in the area were out.

At that point he returned to New Adams to get another vehicle so he could drive into town. He quickly realized that all the trucks were burned and unusable. He could not find any suitable vehicle. He decided the tractor was his only option. Once he got it started, he headed into Bulawayo, even though it would take him many hours to get there. To add to his mounting frustration, the tractor ran out of gas along the way, so he had to hop off and wait for a bus to come by. When the bus finally arrived, he climbed on and noticed that there were some policemen escorting the bus. He told them everything as the whole bus listened in on his horrible story. While he was telling the police about what had happened, he noticed Alex Dube from

Mbezingwe sitting on the bus looking a bit nervous. He knew that Alex very well could have also been behind the massacre.

Alex had really disliked Gerry and everything that was happening at the community. He was the socialist political activist in the area, as well as one of the village representatives in the government. Over the course of time Alex had paraded himself around the area, flaunting his stature as their representative yet doing nothing but take advantage of his position.

As the people at New Adams and Olive Tree demonstrated their genuine love for the local Africans, Alex only caused trouble. He lost his hold over the villagers and became increasing hostile and threatening. He had tried to tell the blacks that they were being underpaid and oppressed by the whites, which simply wasn't true. The truth was that they were more prosperous than they had ever been, and were being treated as peers. He also tried to convince them that the whites had stolen their property, and that Africa belonged to the blacks. They, however, did not buy into his socialist agenda, and he finally went to Harare, the capital, to complain to the government there.

What he did not realize was that the government already knew what was going on and were very impressed with what was happening at the two farms, not only racially but also in terms of the land management. It was one of the few expressions in the country where racial equality was being practised. It was evident to all that genuine Christianity, when properly lived out, can bring blessing and favour to everyone involved. This was not what Alex Dube wanted to hear, and over time he became even angrier.

Thabani told me, in one of our many conversations after the massacre, that originally the villagers who lived around the farms were in disbelief of what they heard. They had been so conditioned after centuries of abuse not only by the government, but also the church, that they often had difficulty believing there really were white people who treated black people as equals. He told me that in time the village people started asking, 'What kind of whites are these?' They had never seen anything like this before. When the women would cook big dinners after church for the people in the area, the whites would step right in and help. Everybody helped. Nobody was superior, or received special treatment. 'Everybody was the same, whether black or white,' he said. 'We ate together, we worked together, we did everything together.'

'Everybody was the same, whether black or white,' he said. 'We ate together, we worked together, we did everything together.'

For Thabani, Stephen, Roy, Neville, Nkiwane, Esinath and many others, what they went through that night was unbelievable. They kept trying to wake up from the nightmare but each morning the result was the same. Their 16 family members had suddenly and unexpectedly been stolen from them. Their lives were in absolute chaos as everything they loved had either been killed or burned to the ground. They were uncertain if the dissidents were going to return and kill them and burn their homes down or if the whites were going to retaliate against them. They suddenly felt very alone and scared. In time they would realize that their friends and neighbours in the village and surrounding area were mourning with them. They were assured by the white community that they understood their loss and were welcomed with open arms to mourn with the whole country at this horrible tragedy. No matter how much assurance they received, it still couldn't replace the empty feeling in their hearts that the martyrdom of their friends had created.

How tragic that the dissidents had not taken the time to learn what was going on at the community. As with so many who are blinded by their anger and pain, they were using a political ideology to justify their taking lives. While they were claiming to be liberating their people, they were in fact returning them to the same oppression that they had been set free from by the white people in the community. There were no Africans in any of the villages surrounding the farms who were rejoicing over their deaths. Zimbabwe Home Minister, Enos Nkala said later, 'These were innocent white people engaged in production, talking about peace. They were people we so much valued.'

IN MEMORIAM

NOVEMBER 25TH, 1987

Gerald Keightley	40 yrs
Marian Keightley	39 yrs
Deborah Keightley	16 yrs
Glynis Keightley	14 yrs
Barnabas Keightley	18 mos
Robert Hill	38 yrs
Gaynor Hill	27 yrs
Benjamin Hill	6 wks
David Marais	35 yrs
Kathryn Marais	34 yrs
Ethan Marais	4 yrs
Jean Campbell	56 yrs
Karen Ivesdahl	32 yrs
Penelope Lovatt	28 yrs
David Emerson	35 yrs
Hazel Russell	46 yrs

By Humility and the Fear of the Lord are riches and honor and life.

– PROVERBS 22:4

When he opened the fifth seal, I saw under the altar the souls of those who had been slain because of the word of God and the testimony they had maintained. They called out in a loud voice, 'How long, Sovereign Lord, holy and true, until you judge the inhabitants of the earth and avenge our blood?' Then each of them was given a white robe, and they were told to wait a little longer, until the full number of their fellow servants and brothers were killed just as they had been.

– REVELATION 6:9–11

WOODCUT PRINT BY DAVID POINDEXTER
"IN MEMORIAM" OF
THE COMMUNITY OF RECONCILIATION MARTYRS.

CHAPTER 7

WHEN DEATH BRINGS LIFE

Unless a kernel of wheat falls to the ground and dies, it remains only a single seed. But if it dies, it produces many seeds.

– JOHN 12:24

At midday on Wednesday, 2 December 1987, a huge memorial service was held in the city of Bulawayo to honour the memories of the 16 slain members of The Community of Reconciliation. The service took place in an auditorium located near the City Hall that seated 1 500. Every seat was taken and still people were lined up against walls and out into the hallways. I was told by a local newspaper reporter that the city had never witnessed anything like this. It was the largest integrated gathering of this nature in the city's history.

What made this gathering so unusual was that both communities felt a great sense of loss.

What made this gathering so unusual was that both communities felt a great sense of loss. John and Elaine Russell were well respected in both the white and black communities. People from all over the country and South Africa came *en masse* to support them in their time of grief. With nine of the sixteen people massacred being their family members, it was, as you can imagine, a gut-wrenching time for both of them. John was his typical pillar of strength, holding everything together, while Elaine, as any mother would, wept frequently.

Sadly, neither of the two Americans' (Sharon Ivesdahl of Choteau, Montana and David Emerson of Edmore, North Dakota) families were able to attend. Jean Campbell also had no one present from her family in Scotland. I felt terrible for them and wondered how they were coping with the sense of loss from thousands of miles away. One of the sad ironies of Sharon's death was that her visa had expired earlier that year and she was forced to return home to Montana. Once home, she reapplied for a new visa immediately but was turned down. She pleaded with the Zimbabwean immigration officials to change their mind as they did not seem to want to let her back into the country. In the end, she prevailed and was granted a new visa and returned to finish her work there. She had not been back in Zimbabwe long before she was killed.

Many of the villagers from the small towns surrounding the community spent what little money they had to take the bus into the city to attend the memorial service. I was so deeply touched by the sacrifice they made to be there and their show of support. They wanted everyone in the country and around the world to know how very much the people at the community had meant to them. Each had a story to share. Someone at the community had made a significant difference in their life. They wanted to come and pay their respects and by their presence at the service show their support for the mission of the community.

As you can imagine with something of this magnitude, there were government officials from every strata and department. I was introduced to the US Ambassador to Zimbabwe, James Wilson Rawlings, as well as a host of Zimbabwean officials; the Governors of North and South Matabeleland, Senator Jacob Mudenda, Senator Mark Dube, and the Mayor of Bulawayo, Nick Mabadoko. Some thought that Joshua Nkomo, the leader of the Ndebele people, would attend but we later learned that he was on his way to London.

The service was officiated by the Reverend Peter McKenzie of the Bulawayo Christian Centre, who was not only a close friend of the Keightleys, but of a number of other people living in the community. Both Stephen and Thabani spoke during the service, as did Gary Kroeze. I was impressed with the courage that they displayed in speaking out against this terrible injustice. They drove home the point that the country had lost a great gift from God to bring healing to the nation. They believed that The Community of Reconciliation was showing the way forward out of the ruins of centuries of racial conflict. It took real courage for them to speak up because they had to return to their homes at Olive Tree. There, lying somewhere in the bush, were the dissidents who had threatened that if they ever spoke up, they would die.

I thought that the most powerful moment of the gathering came when Robert Dube spoke. Robert was neither a Christian nor a part of the community. He was the head of the Mzinyathi Council in which the village of Mbezingwe was located. Mbezingwe was adjacent to the Olive Tree land and a place where members of the community frequented, bringing food, clothing and medical supplies. Robert's testimony was that, 'They were just like us and they never saw a difference between the locals and themselves.' Robert went on to tell stories of their humility and compassion for the people of the region.

Thabani told me afterward that Robert had been quite moved by the whole experience of the massacre and when he got up at the memorial service, he wanted to share his heart openly and honestly, even though he was putting his life at risk. What he shared was in direct opposition to what Morgan Sango and the squatters had claimed about the people developing the community. With Morgan and his group of dissidents still loose in the Matopo hill country, Robert was taking a risk by making these very courageous statements.

> *They believed that The Community of Reconciliation was showing the way forward out of the ruins of centuries of racial conflict.*

Robert was well aware that Gerry and the group were continually going into the village to help people with various problems. He witnessed their actions and knew that their hearts were motivated by a genuine love for the people. This impressed him deeply. Robert had visited the community on a number of occasions and he had seen firsthand that the black Africans were treated no differently than the white Africans. He wanted people at the memorial service to know the truth of what was actually going on there and to testify to the fact that the dissidents and squatters had lied. They had tried to make the incident a political issue when in fact the Community was non-political. They were there for one reason and that was to demonstrate the love of God. Robert felt that the deaths of the whites would hurt the black Africans, not liberate them as the dissidents had claimed. He turned out to be prophetic in his assessment.

The Community of Reconciliation was established to promote racial unity and demonstrate the love of God, one toward another.

What was happening in this region had nothing to do with politics, at least, not of any earthly nature. The Community of Reconciliation was established to promote racial unity, to tear down walls that divided people and demonstrate the love of God, one toward another. It was blind to skin colour, political affiliation and ideology. It was about principles that govern the Kingdom of God. Their mentor was Jesus and like Him they laid down their lives for the values and truths He modelled. They were motivated by compassion and built on the principle of justice. They loved their neighbour and gave a drink of water to the stranger. They loved when they were hated and when asked for one they gave two. What they lived and died for was 'Thy Kingdom come on earth as it is in heaven' (Matt 6:10).

By that weekend the crematorium had finally finished processing all of the bodies. John Russell, the family patriarch, decided that even though the Community was the place of their tragic deaths, it was there that they all would have wanted to be buried. Plans were put in place to inter them there and have a burial service among the burnt-out buildings and vehicles.

The day of the service, on the 8th December, was a typically hot Zimbabwean day, with the sun shining brightly from a clear, deep blue sky. One of the family members had collected all the remains of our friends and family from the crematorium chapel early that morning. We then met with everyone who wanted to attend the burial and drove together to the New Adams Farm property.

Not all of the family members decided to be present at the burial ceremony. Some were afraid that there would be more violence; others simply didn't have the stomach to revisit the scene of the massacre. By this point, Elaine Russell was so exhausted that she didn't have the strength to go, and I'm not sure if she ever returned to see the devastation of her home. We were advised by a number of well-meaning people in town that by burying everyone on the Community lands, we might further antagonize the dissidents. They were concerned that we were subjecting ourselves to unnecessary danger by holding the ceremony and burial there. We discussed the situation but John was insistent that this was where they were going to be buried as this was what they would have wanted. I could not have agreed with him more and was willing to take the risk.

The site chosen for the burial crypt was rock hard from years of drought, and I wondered how they were planning on digging there. By the time we had arrived, a number of the Africans who lived in the community had already dug out a six foot by six foot hole. They must have really struggled to get through the first few inches of sun baked soil. They poured a concrete slab floor in the hole and built a 30 cm high wall on the outside edge of the slab surrounding it. John must have arranged everything as the Africans knew exactly where he wanted to bury the remains. He picked a spot that looked down over both farm properties and the valley below where the people they had loved so much had lived.

We arrived and discussed how we were going to do the service and then waited for a few more minutes to make sure that all the guests had arrived. Simon Rhodes, who had relocated to another part of the country and was no longer living on the community, was with us, as was Gerry Keightley's brother and of course John Russell. All the remaining black members of the community were there as well, which I had expected. I also understood that, with all they had been through and the things they were threatened with by the dissidents, it was not a decision without potentially severe consequences. I was deeply touched by their unwavering commitment and faith in God.

As we all turned in unison toward the music, what we saw coming toward us was utterly amazing.

I would say that in all there were approximately 20–25 people present. As we gathered around the gravesite to say a few prayers and lay our friends to rest, we heard the beautiful sound of singing in the distance. For anyone who lives in or has been to Africa, you know that when Africans gather to sing, the sounds they create are amazing. Their rhythms and harmonies seem to reach into the core of your soul and draw you into their community. It is virtually impossible to be a spectator, even if all you can do is stand in one spot clapping your hands and moving your feet. It's infectious.

As this beautiful melody carried through the hot summer breeze and reverberated off the surrounding hills, it settled on us like a fine mist. As we all turned in unison toward the music, what we saw coming toward us was utterly amazing. There, coming over a ridge, were hundreds of Africans dressed in brilliant colours, approaching us and singing together in the most beautiful harmony. It was a deeply moving sight to say the least, and I found myself struggling to hold back tears.

Thabani turned to me and said, 'You have no idea how very significant this is.' On the night of the raid, the dissidents had told the Africans in the village of Mbezingwe that if they had anything further to do with the community or anyone related to the projects, they too would all be put to death. When I realized how much courage it took for them to attend the burial service, it sent a wave of awe-inspired appreciation over me. It was such a strong, and in some ways, defiant statement of how much respect they had for the people who laid down their lives for them. Stephen, who had once lived in the village, greeted them all in Ndebele and shared with them how deeply touched all of us were by their attendance. I looked at John and I could see by the tears in his eyes that he understood what great respect they were paying his family and friends. It was a special moment.

I was asked by John before the ceremony took place to be the one to lay each of their remains to rest in the vault. This for me was such an honour, and when we got to that point in the ceremony my eyes started to water again. I had a hard time navigating over the piles of soil surrounding the vault and tried to not fall. Once I reached the edge of the concrete wall I stepped down into the vault and one by one I was handed my friends' remains.

Being at a burial for a friend is one thing, but being at a burial for 16 friends is quite another story. It was such a deep and moving moment for me. As I was handed the remains of each friend, their names were called out. I was the last person to touch each of them before giving their bodies back to the earth. Sixteen friends being laid to rest one at a time gives you a lot to think about. I decided that it would be a nice gesture to bury the families in groups together. I arranged each of the small wooden boxes carrying their remains in such a way that the parents and children lay side by side. Once I had placed every one, I stood there for a brief moment to take it all in. There I was looking down at my feet surrounded by the remains of sixteen friends. It was surrealistic.

Sixteen friends being laid to rest one at a time gives you a lot to think about.

Gary, Simon, Stephen and even John each took a moment to share some parting thoughts. I remember that Gary was deeply concerned about the psyche of the Africans from the villages. He thanked them for their courage and assured them that they would not be abandoned. After a few more Scripture readings and some singing, the Africans mixed a fresh batch of concrete, which we poured into the vault, covering and sealing their remains. Once the concrete cured, they would build a rock memorial over the vault with a bronze plaque listing each person's name.

As the ceremony concluded, people milled around for a few more minutes and talked amongst themselves while the Africans gave the top of the newly poured concrete its finishing touches. Suddenly, things got really wild. The sky, which up to this point had been clear blue with a blazing hot sun, suddenly turned dark and ominous. Out of nowhere an intense storm front emerged that sent the crowd into a panic. Everyone started running for their vehicles in sheer fright. The Africans made a beeline back down the hill, running as fast as they possibly could. At first I had no idea what all the panic was about. As I stood there taking the whole moment in, I found my mind wandering back to the Gospel accounts that describe the day that Jesus died. After He had passed away the sky became dark. Soon I could feel the drops of water on my face. Within ten minutes the rain had gone from sporadic drops to a torrential downpour. The Africans were scrambling to get a piece of plastic over the fresh concrete so it would not wash away. As I stood there, soaked and still in a state of awe, John Russell grabbed my arm and said 'We've got to go now or we are all going to die.' After what I had been through the last week, those were some sobering words.

> *I wondered if the earth was crying for my friends.*

I ran as fast as I could and jumped into the cab of the truck. John told me on the drive back to Bulawayo that because it had not rained in many years, the ground was as hard as rock. He reminded me that once the rains started, there would be rivers of water rushing down hills everywhere. As we passed over the cattle grid and onto the main road, you could see the other cars already struggling to pass through the various rivers streaming over the roads. Someone with a four-wheel-drive truck followed the whole group to the main highway just in case a vehicle got stuck. I peered out the back window of the truck and watched the water run rapidly over the ground. I could see huge rooster tails of water shooting in the air as vehicle after vehicle scrambled to leave. We hit a couple of low spots in the truck and I could feel the water wanting to take us with it.

Once we arrived safely back in the city, the rain was actually a nice relief from the scorching heat. It seemed to purify the air. I remember the contrast between the horrible smell of death that I had experienced only a few days earlier and the fresh smell of rain on the grass and flowers. I wondered if the earth was crying for my friends. I know that I missed them dearly. I went to sleep that night with the sound of gentle rain striking the tiles on the roof of the house. I thought about happier times when we rode motorcycles together or sat under the stars and talked into the wee morning hours. I remembered the silly things like arguing over whether we add the milk before or after we pour the tea and the beautiful sound of Gaynor playing her guitar.

The next morning after breakfast we decided that since the rains had stopped, a few of us should head to the burial site to see if the concrete vault had stayed intact through that powerful storm. We wanted to ensure that their remains would be protected from any potential vandalism. It was about a 45–50 minute drive back to the farm. As I sat there with my window open, enjoying the cooler temperatures, I was amazed at how quickly so many plants had already turned green. It seemed like we were driving into another world. It was as if they had been waiting for many years to bloom, and now that they had a little water, nature wanted to show off its glory.

Life and Death were dwelling side by side like peaceful neighbours.

After we arrived at the New Adams Farm and parked the truck, I walked around the property to assess the rain's damage. Fortunately, the concrete on the top of the vault had not been damaged at all.

For a moment I just stood there taking in all the sights and smells. It was strange as I found myself looking at such a paradox. On the one hand there was the sight of death and destruction everywhere. Yet, in between all the burnt-out ruins, was green grass, flowers budding and the sound of birds chirping in the trees. Life and Death were dwelling side by side like peaceful neighbours. It was then that the thought hit me: *The weirs! What about the weirs? With all the rain, surely the weirs have captured some of the run-off.*

Death had brought life and I felt so small and frail as I observed these two giant realities of the human experience working out their symbiotic relationship.

I grabbed Thabani and we decided to drive over to the dams to see what, if anything, had happened. As we neared the first one I was absolutely stunned. There, as far as I could see, was water! Lots and lots of wonderfully glorious water. I jumped out of the truck and ran as fast as I could to the dams to get a closer look. I could not believe my eyes. Not only were there two lakes full of water, but the dams were actually overflowing like a waterfall. I came unglued and sat down on the top of the dam and cried and cried. I was so overcome with emotions and the many paradoxes of the moment. Death had brought life and I felt so small and frail as I observed these two giant realities of the human experience working out their symbiotic relationship.

It was as though their blood was shed so that the Africans could have life.

We had all worked so long and hard to get to this place. We had raised funds in the US to get the raw materials. People had moved from the city in order to help with the project. John Russell had called in personal favours and found the heavy equipment needed to move earth. Groups of people from the States went over for weeks or months at a time to do backbreaking work to build these huge dams. Sixteen people had made the ultimate sacrifice and given their lives. Now, there before my eyes, two huge walls of concrete were overflowing with water.

In places like Zimbabwe and all over the world, water is Life. Without it you simply cannot survive. With it you can reclaim the land and feed, house and clothe a city. I was so overwhelmed with the irony of it all. Within days of the dams' completion, their lives were taken. It was as though their blood was shed so that the Africans could have life. The rains that came broke a seven-year drought. As I sat there on that dam and cried, I realized that though I was right in the middle of it all, I really had no idea what God was doing. There were things going on here that were way out of my realm of understanding. I did understand though that I was sitting on Holy ground. The Africans, who were in awe, told us that it rained so hard that 'the trees were drowning'. They were convinced that heaven was talking, as for them water was a clear sign from God that He was pleased.

CHAPTER 8

WHEN DREAMS DIE

Mankind, when left to themselves, are
unfit for their own government.

– GEORGE WASHINGTON

Tragically, when the people of the Community died, so did an authentic working model of reconciliation that could have saved Zimbabwe from ruin in the years ahead. Most of us in the Christian community are familiar with Solomon's proverb, 'Where there is no vision the people perish' (Prov 29:18). This was certainly the case for most, if not all, of the local Africans in and around the Community farms. They lost their livelihood and were suddenly and dramatically forced back into poverty.

In hindsight, I think it could also be said that when the people perish there is no vision. As I look back through the history of how God works with and through men, it seems that when He calls a person, He puts the vision or blueprint in their heart. He also gives them the grace to accomplish the task at hand against all odds. Through the grace that God gives, they then inspire and impart that vision to others, recruiting them to join the cause.

With their deaths it was as though the heart and soul of the project had been ripped out. It felt like something diabolical was at work. The Community was killed in its infancy before it had a chance to survive on its own. Though on the surface it looked to be the death of a few, in reality it was the death of thousands! In hindsight, it seems that the day I laid their remains to rest, I was burying their vision with them. While everything inside me hoped that someone would walk in and take up the cause, no one ever stepped forward who had the same grace that Gerry Keightley and his group from Bulawayo did. It seemed that the grace was gone. The day they were martyred truly was the day the music died.

> *Though on the surface it looked to be the death of a few, in reality it was the death of thousands!*

As things finally settled down after the burial ceremony, I knew there was nothing more for me to do, and it was time to return to Kansas City. Gary and I had a discussion as to what to do for the two American families that had lost loved ones. He asked if I would mind stopping off in North Dakota on the way home to talk with David Emerson's family. At first I was hesitant as I really did not know much about Dave and had never even met his family. After further discussion, I became more comfortable with the idea and scheduled a time to meet with them.

> *The day they were martyred truly was the day the music died.*

After some tearful hugs and good-byes, I climbed aboard my plane and settled in for the long journey home. While the flight over had been filled with grief, anger and frustration, the trip home was simply exhausting. I was mentally, emotionally and physically drained. I was hoping that God would do something to help me on the way back because I was in no shape to meet with Dave's family. I tried to sleep on the flights but it was hard as my mind was so preoccupied not only with all that I had seen in Zimbabwe, but with what awaited me when I returned. I had not seen my family in weeks, nor had I had a chance to talk with any of the church members back in Kansas City. I knew that those who had spent time at the Community would be full of questions as we had not had a chance to talk before I had left. I did not know what mood or frame of mind the church was in or how people had reacted to the news. I had been in another world for the past few weeks and it became clear that it was going to take some time for me to re-acclimatize.

Dave's parents lived in Edmore, North Dakota, and I flew into Grand Forks planning to meet them the next day. As I stood there at the baggage carousel waiting for my backpack I was so exhausted that I was almost dizzy. I felt a strange sensation of being a foreigner in my own country. It was perplexing because I was expecting to feel relief or a sense of 'I'm home'. As I stood there and looked around trying to connect with my surroundings, I realized that I was a changed man. I wasn't the same man who got on that plane weeks before. My confusion was that I had no idea how I had changed and I wasn't sure who it was that was standing there.

> *I felt a strange sensation of being a foreigner in my own country.*

Soon I saw my blue backpack come around. I grabbed it and took the shuttle to the hotel. The first thing I wanted to do was shower, so I threw my pack on the bed and unzipped it. As I peeled back the canvas I was very confused to find my backpack filled with women's clothes! I just stood there and stared. I was so numb and out of it that I thought for a minute I may have been hallucinating. I kept staring at the women's clothes in my backpack but they were not changing. I finally mustered enough nerve to touch the clothes and to my amazement they were in fact real. This was even more perplexing. *How could this be? Everyone else at the baggage carousel had regular luggage. I was the only one with a backpack.*

I called the front desk and explained my dilemma. I needed to go back to the airport right away and find out what happened. They told me that the airport was now closed. My flight had been the last arrival. I called the airlines to see if I could get some help. This of course took forever, as I was transferred from one end of the country to the other. If this situation had happened today, I am sure I would have talked to someone in India as well. Finally, after travelling the country via phone, I was connected with someone in the lost luggage department at the Grand Forks airport! Thankfully they were still there. She started laughing when I told her my story because she had received a call from a young woman just a few minutes before who had found her backpack filled with men's clothes. It was agreed that we would meet at 9 a.m. the next morning to sort this mess out.

I hated calling Dave's parents and asking them if we could postpone our meeting a couple of hours. They had waited for weeks to talk with someone and now, due to a baggage mix-up, they were being put off. I felt terrible. I rose early the next day and showered again. It was so nice to stand in a shower with hot water and decent pressure. I took the shuttle back to the airport and found the lost luggage office. When I walked in, there was a woman a few years younger than I holding the exact same backpack as mine. It was the same brand, model and colour. It was a bit surrealistic. She apologized profusely. She arrived at the baggage carousel before I had and had seen 'her' backpack and grabbed it. She hadn't bothered to look inside as she had never seen another one like hers. We had a good laugh and I told her not to worry about it as in the scheme of things this was a very minor issue.

I hopped back on the shuttle to the hotel where Dave's parents were waiting for me. They were both elderly, and his father, James, was a very distinguished-looking gentleman. I later learned that he was a doctor. They were both very grateful to meet with me, which seemed strange to me because I was so honoured to meet them. I had a few small belongings of David's that had survived the fires, which I gave to them. For the next few hours I sat with them and tried to be as helpful and understanding as I could. I had never been put into this type of situation and had no formal training. I didn't really know what to do or say. I decided to just trust my heart, which naturally tends to be compassionate. I listened to them share about Dave, who was their fifth child and a bit like Huckleberry Finn. Dave was not much for being a part of the 'in crowd' and he was always in search of another adventure. At one time he had lived in an Indian tent called a 'teepee', they told me.

The conversation soon changed to questions about what Dave was actually doing in Zimbabwe. From the little bit of interaction I had had with Dave, I got the impression that he was not much of a communicator. I tried as best I could to fill in the gaps for them and I think it was helpful. While it is never easy losing a child, to know that they died doing something that they believed in certainly helps remove some of the sting. I reassured them that Dave died pursuing a noble cause. Later on, I was pleased to hear from them that Thabani, who was Dave's roommate, wrote to them both to tell them how deeply he missed Dave and how much he had meant to not only him, but the whole black community.

After more teary hugs and good-byes I returned to my hotel room and fell on the bed, absolutely drained. Until the next day, I didn't come out of my room other than to get a meal. I boarded my flight for Kansas City emotionally exhausted and with much anxiety in my soul. When I arrived at the KCI airport I barely remember my family meeting me as I seemed to be in some sort of a daze. I think that my mind finally realized that I was done with this gut-wrenching ordeal for the moment and my body started to react to the exhaustion. I had survived and while my mind and emotions were a wreck, I was home, safe and with my family. It was good to see familiar surroundings and the faces of people I loved, and yet they seemed so far away.

As I looked at my children, I kept thinking about the word 'innocence'. I had lost mine.

I stayed home for the next week to just to play with Kyle and Jessica. It was evident that they were excited to have me home and could not help but climb all over me. Honestly, this had me feeling very conflicted. As their father, I could not get enough hugs and kisses. I loved seeing their cute little round faces and chubby cheeks. Their innocent love and tenderness was the antithesis of the hate and destruction I had just seen. Their joy and happiness was contrasted by the intense pain and sorrow that I had experienced in all those who had lost someone. As I looked at my children, I kept thinking about the word 'innocence'. I had lost mine. They simply wanted to play and be with me. As I interacted with them I couldn't get the images of what I had seen in Zimbabwe out of my head. They would replay on their own like an automated slide show. Suddenly I would smell that horrible fragrance of death even though I was thousands of miles away from it.

There is a cruel side to life as it waits for no one.

What was I to do with all this that my five senses had experienced? How does one talk about this? I had no concept of how to process what I had seen and the only model I knew of how to handle crisis was that of my uncles who had been in World War II. I identified with them. Had only one or two people died it would have been like a car wreck. In this case it was sixteen, and the farms looked like a bombed-out battlefield. In the end I did what my uncles did, which was suck it up and try to move on. I never talked about my feelings to anyone nor did anyone ask. I simply went back to work.

When the images and smells did return I would drift off into another world. I would catch myself in a meeting, lost in Zimbabwe and paying no attention to what was currently being discussed. I was embarrassed by this and never told anyone. For some reason I got it in my head that it was a sign of weakness. The group of men I was with was composed of strong visionaries, and looking back wasn't really in their repertoire. Soon I was back functioning in my role at the church, building the infrastructure so that we could fulfil the mission we were called to. What happened in Zimbabwe, while tragic, faded into the background.

What I was experiencing was similar to the dynamics I had observed at funerals. The person who has lost someone significant is deluged at the funeral by so many well-meaning people who make strong statements about how they are 'there for them', but after the funeral people return to their lives. There are families to raise, careers to pursue and churches to build. Life goes on like huge gears that never stop turning. A cruel side of life is that it waits for no one. Those impacted by tragedy are left to pick up the shattered pieces of their lives. They feel very alone. Most people have no idea how to relate to someone in a state of shock or a great deal of pain and therefore tend to leave them alone or avoid them.

The people at the Community were avid letter writers. They corresponded daily with people all over the world. It typically took two to three weeks for a letter to arrive at its destination. I started hearing stories about people who received a letter from someone at the Community who was dead. It was an eerie feeling, opening a letter from someone who had passed away weeks before. It was like they were speaking from beyond the grave. Many of those letters remain treasured possessions as they were the last thoughts and words from beloved friends and family members.

After being home for a few weeks, someone suggested that we have a Zimbabwe party and get everyone who was connected with the projects together. I thought that 'party' was not exactly the right way to phrase it and suggested the word 'gathering' instead. We set a date and scheduled it after the morning church service. I put together a photo album showing the aftermath of the raid. The Hartleys, Collins, Corums, Reardons, Steadmans and various other friends and well-wishers all stopped by to talk and hear more about all that had happened. While I greatly appreciated all the support and valued all of their friendships, I found myself standing in the middle of everyone feeling all alone.

I found myself standing in the middle of everyone feeling all alone.

I tried as best as I could to answer each and every question and yet, without wanting to be insulting, it all felt so superficial.

In hindsight, I understand that everyone was in pain and trying to deal with it in their own way. The reason that things felt superficial was that I was wearing the experience in every corpuscle of my being, while for them it was more of a sad story that happened far away. While I still smelt the reality of death, these people were reading the magazine. The most precious moment of the gathering was when David Poindexter, an artist, presented me with a woodcut print that he had made. When I saw it, I could not help but get watery eyes as he had captured the moment of their martyrdom in the most incredible way. That print is one of my most prized possessions and has been mounted on my wall everywhere I have lived. I frequently look at it and it reminds me of how fortunate I was to have known such amazing people.

One of the things I soon experienced which further isolated my feelings and drove them deeper into my soul is what I can only call the 'blame game'. As I have come to see over the years, we humans are not very good at dealing with tragedy. When we experience it, one of the first things we want to do is figure out who is to blame. Someone's head must roll. It has to be someone's fault and we have to figure out who that person is and get them.

Humans are not very good at dealing with tragedy.

In the Christian community we are often left to deal with the wreckage of our theology when it derails. For many, including myself, there is a subtle but dangerous assumption that if you do right, only good things will happen to you. When bad things happen to good people we are left scratching our heads. In Jesus' day they would have asked, 'Which of his parents sinned?' Instead of rethinking our assumption, we zero in on the person we have discerned as guilty. It is the Salem witch trials all over again.

In the case of the people who died in Zimbabwe, according to a number of influential people in the church, the blame was squarely on my shoulders. In fact, it was said to me that 'their blood is on your hands.' That was a hard pill to swallow. For me, those were excruciatingly painful words that hit me like piercing arrows at a time when I was already very emotionally vulnerable. I tried to shake loose from them but I could not. I was told that because I had helped raise funds for them, I had encouraged them to stay and that if I hadn't helped they would have become discouraged and left. I knew intellectually that each and every one of those statements was wrong. If you had spent any time with the people there you would have known what was in their hearts. It had nothing to do with anything that I had done to support them. They had set out on this mission long before I was ever involved. They knew what their mission was and were so committed to it that they were ready to die for it. I knew this as did anyone else who had ever been in their presence for any length of time. Even though my head knew that these accusations were preposterous, they still hurt deeply.

Only the stone walls remained, standing like silent eerie pillars against the sky reminding everyone of what had taken place there. It was both horrible and Holy.

Gary Kroeze returned to the devastated Community in 1988 to live on the land for a year with Thabani, and they began the arduous task of cleaning up the aftermath. He was hoping that in some form or fashion the vision for the land could be renewed. Maybe out of the ashes something would rise. The dissidents' fires had destroyed the thatched roofs and almost everything in the buildings. Only the stone walls remained, standing like silent eerie pillars against the sky reminding everyone of what had taken place there. It was both horrible and Holy.

While many talk about laying their lives down for one another, I have found few who are actually ready to do so.

They recruited some of the local Africans from the village to help with the process of cleaning what remained. They decided to re-thatch some of the roofs to make the dwellings habitable again. Gary met with various local church leaders in Bulawayo to see if there was any interest in reviving the project. The black African churches had no financial resources and the white churches were just trying to survive themselves as many of the people in their congregations were fleeing the country. John Russell and Gary became the trustees of the not-for-profit entity that managed the Community land. They tried everything they could to ensure that the African Christian community would be taken care of. They also built a stone memorial over the gravesite with a large bronze plaque listing the names and birthdates of each person who had been martyred.

The church in Kansas City was initially open to participate in the re-building process. After discussing the situation they decided that their investment of finances and personnel was in the people who had the vision for the land. If God was to bring another group with the same sense of commitment, conviction and passion that the original group had, they would have been very supportive. I agreed. I was hopeful that something would happen and was disappointed when nothing did.

It was clear to me that this type of Christian expression was just what Zimbabwe (and Africa as a whole) needed. It was also what many of the local black African politicians of Matabeleland wanted. While it was disappointing that nothing continued, in my lifetime I have met very few people like those at The Community of Reconciliation. While many talk about laying their lives down for one another, I have found few who are actually ready to do so. As time has passed, my appreciation for each of the sixteen martyrs has grown immensely. I have come to see how truly special they were.

The following year the church receptionist rang my office to tell me that someone named Jeremy Russell, who claimed that I knew his family in Zimbabwe, was on the phone. I was stunned as I knew exactly who she was talking about even though I had never met him. I was very pleased to hear from Jeremy. Sure enough, on the other end of the phone there was a distinctly Rhodesian accent that had been flavoured from travels around the world.

John Russell had talked often of Jeremy. He was their youngest and was a year younger than I. He had left Rhodesia in the late 70s and moved to Cape Town, South Africa. In 1980, he set sail with his older brother, Malcolm, and Dave and Kathy Marais to the Canary Islands. He quickly developed his sailing skills and became a Captain. Soon he was running his own voyages around the world and developing lots of friendships along the way.

In 1982, he came to the States to stay for a while and visit the many friends he had met. He ended up working for two of his former clients, one in Connecticut and one in New York. In 1986 he relocated to Florida for a year. It was there at approximately 11 p.m. on the night of November 25th that he received the tragic news of the massacre of nine members of his family. He immediately turned on the TV and within thirty minutes the story had hit the CNN newscast.

I was so relieved to hear his voice as it had bothered me that we did not know his whereabouts when we first heard the news. After we had talked for a few minutes I asked him if he would come to Kansas City as I wanted to make sure he was alright. It bothered me that he had mourned this tragic loss of family virtually alone. Within a few weeks he was on his way and has remained in the city ever since. Jeremy's kind and caring heart made him a favourite of every Junior High and Senior High kid in the church. It was not long before he was a celebrity in his own right. I think God placed a lot of family around him to make up for what he had lost. Thankfully, they loved him because he had a calling in his life, not because of the deaths in his family.

As life went on, Zimbabwe, my martyred friends and John and Elaine Russell were never far from my thoughts. In the spring of 1988, I received further news that would really test my heart. Zimbabwe's leader Robert Mugabe had signed another Peace Accord with his old nemesis Joshua Nkomo. As a part of the agreement, Mugabe announced on April 19th that amnesty was going to be offered to every dissident still on the run in the bush. They had until midnight on May 30th to turn themselves in. One hundred and thirteen rebels in total decided to accept Mugabe's offer of amnesty, including Morgan Sango and his group of dissidents that had killed all my friends.

I know that for the Russells, Marais and the Stewarts (Gaynor's parents) this was devastating news and opened their painful wounds all over again. How could it be that the men who had brutally killed their children were simply going to walk away without suffering any consequences for their hideous actions? It created quite an uproar in Bulawayo, but by this time the white community in Zimbabwe was already marginalized and there was virtually nothing they could do.

In 1990, I relocated to the west coast to begin work with a new Christian community and a completely different ministry team. Their focus was dissimilar from the rugged and violent world of defending the cause of the oppressed poor in Africa. I soon realized that the experiences I had gone through and what I had observed in Africa were considered unsavoury in this new environment. People weren't interested in hearing about it as it made them feel uncomfortable. It was difficult to deal with the fact that what was so precious to me made others uneasy. Once again I was alone.

In 1992, Mike Town returned to Zimbabwe and the village of Mbezingwe to visit the many African friends that he had grown so close to during his time there. He had continued to correspond with them over the past five years and felt a visit was in order to renew old friendships. As you can imagine, it was an emotionally charged experience for him to drive onto the farms, as they were practically deserted and looked like old western ghost towns, complete with tumbleweed blowing through. Having lived there with his family for two years, he'd got used to the constant activity of people coming and going, so the silence was ghostly.

The Africans had kept the gardens going down on Olive Tree as they had plenty of water due to the weirs being full. Rod Capon, a local white pastor from Bulawayo, had agreed to take over working with the Africans. He would periodically drive out to the farms to pick up the produce and sell it on the local markets on their behalf. Thabani had recently married and was living in the Russell's old place up on New Adams. Neville and his wife Janet had settled in at Olive Tree to try and make a go of things there. While Thabani and Neville both wanted to see the farms productive again, they just did not have the strength of soul or the skills to make it happen.

Further complicating matters, the local dissidents who had been a part of the raid and had subsequently accepted the government's amnesty offer, returned to the area and were now living back near the farms. On one occasion Thabani crossed paths with them and they taunted him, saying, 'You had better watch your step. Remember what we did to your friends.' More squatters had settled on the farm properties, which meant the stealing and cattle rustling had started up again. Neither Thabani nor Neville were able to stand up to the situation on their own. Given what had happened in 1987, I think they were both scared, and who could blame them? Neville eventually returned to living in the village and in 1994 Thabani packed up everything and relocated to South Africa were he became an ambulance driver and later a medic. Both of them had such precious hearts, but the pressure of trying to recreate what Gerry and the others had built was ultimately too much. Mike was able to spend some quality time with Esinath and talk more about what had happened on the night of the massacre. It was clear from listening to her heart that, like everyone else who was left alive, the whole incident had left a painful scar in her soul and that she missed her family immensely.

In early 2000, Mugabe tried to change the country's constitution to ensure he could serve more terms. He also wanted to guarantee that his government would not be held accountable for any crimes they had committed while in office. At the time, he was preparing to begin confiscating the few remaining white-owned farms and wanted to be free from any legal backlash. Much to Mugabe's dismay, his referendum was publicly voted down by the people. He could not understand how they could turn on 'the Father of the Revolution'. By April of that year Robert Mugabe had the very same referendum issues pushed through Parliament, but only in the form of an amendment that was then passed by the corrupt party members in his pocket.

In order to win over the people who were angry at him for his power play, he immediately sent out ex-military personnel to seize white-owned farms and 'take them back for the people'. If the white farmers resisted, they were killed on the spot. By 2003, only 500 of the original 6 000 white-owned farms remained in the hands of the white community. This sent the economy into a tailspin. It was a status symbol in the Mugabe government to have been given one of these previously white-owned farms. The Minister of Home Affairs was given five farms, the Minister of Information was given three and Mugabe's latest wife, Grace, was given two. Scores of other party elite members were given at least two farms each, but none of them had any idea how to run a farm. Soon the breadbasket of Africa was in ruins and could not even feed its own people.

In 2000, the New Adams and Olive Tree properties were confiscated by the Mugabe government and made a part of the Mzinyathi Tribal Trust. Not long after this happened, officials from the regional government in Bulawayo came out to the land in search of Neville and the others to try and meet with them. They wanted to inquire about whether the New Adams and Olive Tree Farms could ever be returned to what they were in the 1980s. Even years later, people in the region remembered the profound impact that The Community of Reconciliation had had on the area. Now they were hoping that what worked then could be built again. Even the government was hoping for a resurrection.

Contrary to the Mugabe government that brought so much death, the Community had brought life. I hope that one day people in Zimbabwe will understand that what made the Community so special was who they were! What they did was a result of who they were. God transforms the heart, and from there the catalyst of change is launched. One of the greatest gifts that we as whites can give to our black brothers and sisters in Africa is 'true esteem'. Our actions speak so much louder than our words. Africa is looking for a new kind of white man, one who will give more than he takes. The ones who gave their lives on New Adams and Olive Tree Farms were people like that; they made the ultimate sacrifice on behalf of their black African brothers.

In 2001, Mike Town again returned to Zimbabwe with his friend Graham Beggs for a surprise visit to his old friends in the village. He knew that things were tense in the country with the farm seizures still in progress, but he wanted to come back and help the Africans start up a new chicken enterprise. Back in the 1980s when Mike was living there, he had started up a small company with Neville and Roy that had been quite successful.

With tensions in the rural areas so high, they decided to find a place in Bulawayo to sleep. They inquired if anyone knew a place they could stay while in the area. It was suggested they contact a local black pastor. He agreed to put them up and after getting acquainted, he inquired as to what they were doing in Zimbabwe. When Mike explained that they had come to visit some friends in Mbezingwe and a farm where his friends had been killed, the pastor got very excited. It turned out that the pastor had been John Russell's chief mechanic at Russell Construction for seventeen years. He then told Mike that he had personally carried John Russell's ashes to the farm to be buried there after he had died on October 9th, 1993. Elaine Russell followed John in death nearly six years later on January 29th, 1999.

Robert Mugabe has since continued to destroy Zimbabwe. He won re-election in 2002, but only after having his leading opponent arrested for treason. In 2005, he bulldozed the shacks of 10 000 people in Harare that he had placed there in 1992. Since most of these people supported the opposition party, it was clear that this was politically motivated. The fact that Mugabe's sprawling new mansion was located only a couple of kilometres away from the shacks could also have influenced his actions. Mugabe continued to deflect the blame for the country's decline on drought and former British Prime Minister, Tony Blair's use of chemical weapons to incite droughts and famines in Africa.

The two children who survived that tragic night now both live in South Africa. Laura Russell is married and lives in Cape Town. She works as a therapist for the government at the main hospital there. Matthew Marais was brought up by his aunts and uncles and, after a brief stint in the States, he now works for an insurance firm in Johannesburg. In November 2007 he returned for the first time to the farms where his family had perished. We continue to correspond and in 2008 I received the most amazing email from him that had me crying in front of my computer. God has done such an amazing work in his heart over the years. He now wants to return to Zimbabwe and help the people in the region around the old Community lands. It is my hope and prayer that this book will inspire others to join us as we go back to help the Zimbabweans in this hour of crisis.

CHAPTER 9

THE MARTYRDOM CONUNDRUM

The blood of the martyrs is the seed of the Church.

– TERTULLIAN

A day after landing in Zimbabwe to attend the memorial service in Bulawayo, I was still reeling from the intensity of everything that was going on around me. I do not remember exactly how it happened, but suddenly someone grabbed my arm and I was being ushered into what looked like a chapel. At that point I was told that we were next door to the city's crematorium. What I saw and smelled there has never left me. It was the first time in my life that I had ever been exposed to death before it was all nicely cleaned up. To be honest, I was not sure if my eyes were watering from the tears of seeing sixteen caskets or the wretched smell of death.

There is a sick feeling that develops in your gut when you stand in the presence of your dead friends. Your mind is frantically searching for some way to say this cannot be happening. This is all a bad dream. But your eyes refuse to show you anything else and you are left having to deal with it. I was trying to be stoic, even while my eyes filled with tears. I was actually holding up remarkably well until my glance fell on the small, white caskets of the children lying in the back behind their parents. It was then that I thought my heart would fall to the floor and shatter. I was overcome with such melancholy that these innocent young lives had been taken before they were even allowed to blossom. My heart wept with sorrow at what might have been. Life can be so incredibly unfair.

Lying in one of those caskets was a new baby, the first child of Rob and Gaynor Hill, little Benjamin. In another lay Jerry and Marian's little boy, Barnabas, who had just learned to walk. Then there was blond-haired and blue-eyed Ethan Marais, the youngest son of David and Kathryn Marais, who was so full of life and loved to climb trees and ride bikes. I felt such incredible pain inside. While surviving family members each mourned the loss of their individual loved ones, I seemed to be mourning them all, and the weight of it was crushing. '*Oh martyrdom,*' I thought, '*your glory has faded in the overwhelming sorrow of my soul. The price of martyrdom is not only borne by those who give up their lives, but also those of us that remain behind and daily suffer the profound sense of loss.*'

In the post-modern Western church world, Christian martyrdom is not often discussed. It is rare to hear of someone being killed for his or her faith in either America or Europe. In fact, without organizations like 'The Voice of the Martyrs' keeping this in front of us, most of us would be unaware that people are dying daily for being followers of Jesus. Christianity is illegal in many countries and any proclamation of the 'Good News' message is punishable by death. To be a pastor or to espouse the teachings of Jesus is to live with a death sentence hanging over your head.

> *The price of martyrdom is not only borne by those who give up their lives, but also those of us that remain behind and daily suffer the profound sense of loss.*

The *World Christian Encyclopedia* suggests that there have been nearly seventy million Christian martyrs throughout the past 2 000 years. It also states that 45 million have died in the twentieth century.[1] That is an astounding statistic. To put it in perspective, the number of people who have died for their faith in the twentieth century equals the total population of America's fifty largest cities combined. Currently, it costs Westerners very little to become a Christian. In fact for most, they are converted under a Gospel message that promises to bring them personal benefit and blessing. This is in contrast to the life and message of German theologian Dietrich Bonhoeffer, who was hanged by the Nazis for his faith. He said, 'When Christ calls a man, He bids him come and die.'

> *It costs Westerners very little to become a Christian.*

Researchers tell us that there is an unequivocal correlation between persecution, martyrdom and church growth. Paul Marshall, senior fellow at the Centre for Religious Freedom and author of *Their Blood Cries Out,* stated, 'It was estimated in 1980 there were one million Chinese Christians and by 1999 that figure had grown to fifty million.' He went on to say, 'Eighty per cent of the church lives outside the West. Africa will soon be the continent, if not already, with the greatest number of Christians. Christians in the world are more likely to be Chinese or Nigerian or Sudanese than Westerners.'[2]

While the American church may be the most prosperous and best organized, we are no longer the fastest growing. Those with much less materially are making a greater impact spiritually. Why? There is much food for thought here. Can you imagine a church growth seminar in the West promoting poverty, persecution and martyrdom as tried and tested strategies for church growth? That is a strategy we won't see implemented any time soon, and yet Tertullian was right when he wrote in 197 AD that, 'The blood of the martyrs is the seed of the Church.'

> *Those with much less materially are making a greater impact spiritually. Why?*

After burying my friends and returning from Zimbabwe, I soon learned that people in the American Christian community were very uncomfortable with the subject. Other than a few close friends, no one wanted to talk about it. It is often seen as an unsavoury topic and, for some, a sign of defeat. Given the current world geopolitical environment, martyrdom is seen by many as the fanatical expression of extreme Jihadists. Countless people in the West view martyrdom as the archaic act of uncivilized people living in the Dark Ages. They see no honour in it, only a delusional act of madmen. Yet, whether we like the subject or not, almost daily there are people who are laying down their lives for the sake of the Kingdom of God. Someone somewhere is making the ultimate sacrifice.

Watching my fellow brothers' and sisters' blood run between my feet was a sobering wake-up call to the reality of what was at stake.

After having been impacted by the death of my friends for the sake of the Kingdom of God, I am a changed man. It affects how I view and respond to so many things. I live in a constant paradox between two very real worlds. In one, my friends died violently, sacrificing their lives for the sake of others. In the other, I see a tranquil Sunday morning world where people attend church for what they get out of it. These worlds co-exist but are diametrically opposite in nature. I hope that none of you will ever have to experience the pain, sense of loss or disillusionment I went through. Yet on the other hand, I wish that all of you had experienced it, as it would indelibly reshape so much of your thinking and priorities and challenge the depth of your commitment to the values of The Kingdom of God.

While most all of us would agree that one of the realities of our faith is spiritual warfare, most of us have never been in a significantly violent, physical battle. Unless you are a part of the military, a policeman, a firefighter or work in the emergency room at a hospital, violence is something that you experience via TV or the Internet. There are times when I find myself sitting in church listening to people talk about the principles of spiritual warfare, and I struggle. I wonder whether it's real to them or simply theory. At times it feels like they are playing a spiritual video game. While the content of their message is graphically excellent and the sound quality superb, it lacks the credibility of real world experience. It feels more like a science fiction novel. I must confess that until November 26, 1987, I too was a spiritual video game player. I had no idea how very real and violent the battle was between the two kingdoms. I thought I knew; I learned I had no idea. Standing there on the Olive Tree property at The Community of Reconciliation and watching my brothers' and sisters' blood run between my feet was a sobering wake-up call to the reality of what was at stake.

I didn't really know what 'martyrdom' was until I first heard about it in Bible School in the mid-70s. Over the course of our studies during my first semester, I discovered various accounts of how the early Christians had been killed in the most brutal ways by Nero and other despotic Roman Emperors. First century Christianity was certainly very different from the Christianity I had been converted into.

I had come to the Christian faith with my Halloween basket ready to hold all the goodies. A few years later, I was introduced to John Foxe's *The Book of Martyrs*. There I was surprised to read that Christians had been dying for the faith for hundreds of years. In fact, some of the very first 16th century church reformers, called the 'Anabaptists', had been killed for the simple act of pouring water over each other's heads in a form of re-baptism. I was equally stunned to learn that these Anabaptists had been persecuted and killed by their fellow Christians who also considered themselves reformers! It took some time for me to get my head around that. Martyrdom at the hands of the enemies of the faith was understandable; martyrdom at the hands of your own brothers was unnerving.

First century Christianity was certainly very different from the Christianity I had been converted into.

Until the massacres in Zimbabwe I had never met anyone who had experienced the martyrdom of a friend or colleague. Neither had I met anyone who knew someone who had died that way. My only point of reference was what little I had researched while at school. One thing that was consistent all the way through these stories was that the authors believed it was a celebrated way to die. In fact, it was believed that martyrdom was the highest and most glorious way to die and that martyrs would stand before God with the highest distinction and have a special place in eternity.

While reading these texts at Bible School, I was so inspired that I started thinking that that was the way I wanted to die. I decided, *'If I'm gonna go, I might as well go out in a blaze of glory.'* To die in obscurity seemed such a waste. As a young Christian full of more smoke than substance, I vividly remember how my friends and I had stayed up late one night talking about how we wanted to die for God. We went around sharing our aspirations, each story more elaborate and sensational. I, of course, was going to die rebuking the Antichrist on national TV as my head was being cut off. I must confess that my experience in Zimbabwe brought my naïve, self-serving fantasies crashing back to earth with a sobering reality.

As a little boy growing up in Greendale, Wisconsin, my favourite magazine was *National Geographic*. OK, I was a little strange, but I did have a life. I remember the excitement of seeing that brown-paper-wrapped periodical sitting on the counter and the excitement of slipping off the packaging to see what adventures awaited me in that month's issue. As I thumbed through each edition, looking at all the exotic places, I remember thinking, *'Someday when I get big I am going to be a photographer for National Geographic'*. I was always fascinated by the variety of animal species in Africa and how differently people in the world lived. It was my dream to someday go for myself and see it first-hand.

On my first trip to Africa in 1984, I had a whole day's layover in Nairobi, Kenya and noticed that there was a large game park not too far from the Jomo Kenyatta International Airport. I decided to take a safari tour and see if I could get some *National Geographic* quality photos. I was pumped and I had my camera gear all prepared to capture some amazing animal shots. After about 20 minutes into the tour, a humorous thought crossed my mind about role reversal. All my life, in order to see amazing and exotic creatures, I had to go to a zoo and see them in a cage. It dawned on me, as we were driving along locked in our Land Rover, that I was now the one in the cage. I wondered how these animals viewed me as I trespassed through their world.

About an hour into the tour, the guide got very excited and headed off the road through the bush. He had spotted a lion kill and it was very rare to get a photo of one. As we got closer to our destination I could see the vultures circling above. I worked furiously to get my camera ready as this was a once in a lifetime opportunity. As the guide pulled near the carcass, I noticed that a lioness (typically the hunters) was lying next to her prize kill, guarding it. I was so excited I spun around and lowered the window so I could get a better shot. As I did, I was hit with the disgusting smell of rotting flesh and the sight of flies all over the dead animal. In fact, my eyes started watering so heavily I could barely focus my camera. After sucking it up and getting some shots, I quickly closed the window. While attempting to find some fresh, clean air to breathe, it suddenly dawned on me; I was not exposed to this putrid smell when I looked at photos in *National Geographic*. I had seen but not smelt those moments. I had only been exposed to the 'scrubbed' version. I had played the 'video game', as it were. While those were real photos in the magazine, there was so much more going on than a photo could ever communicate.

> *While those who remained suffered an overwhelming sense of loss, those who were martyred died in a glorious fashion.*

In hindsight, I wonder if that isn't the case with martyrdom. While the books tell of glorious deaths, I have a feeling that for those who were there, forced to observe it, it was not so glorious. Mary watched her son

Jesus get beaten to the point of being unrecognizable, have his hands and feet pierced through with nails and be left hanging to die. It must have been a gut-wrenching experience to behold. I am sure that if asked Laura Russell, who was one of only two children to survive the massacres, how glorious it was, she would be hard-pressed to say that it was anything but terrifying. The same could be said for Thabani, Esinath or Stephen as they watched their friends put to death at the Community.

But, here again we are faced with one of the many paradoxes of living in two realities. While those who remained suffered an overwhelming sense of loss, those who were martyred died in a glorious fashion. As Stephen, who witnessed each and every death said, 'Those that died did have a noticeably different composure and faced their deaths in the most peaceful state of mind. No one cried, screamed or was in a state of panic. In fact they were gently singing and praying for their killers as they were being put to death.'

Terrible and wonderful shared the same moment.

Once they had given up their lives, someone or something in the form of a white light came to welcome them and guide them home. Terrible and wonderful shared the same moment.

While I was attending to things in Bulawayo, back home in Kansas City many of the folks were still in shock. For them this situation was as catastrophic as the unexpected death of Christian singer/songwriter Keith Green five years earlier. They were reeling with the news and for many it was a blow to their assumptions of how God operated. The events in Zimbabwe unsettled people. They suddenly felt vulnerable and uncertain about the future. For some, it was easier to ignore and detach themselves by rationalizing that it was an event unique to violent and primitive Africa. It made others angry and they felt that somehow I was to blame. If only I hadn't rallied people to support them, they would have packed up, gone home and this would never have happened. And then there were those who simply had no idea what to make of any of it. They had that proverbial 'deer in the headlights' look.

One of my colleagues at the church back home was Dr. J. Wesley Adams, a theology professor. 'Wes' as we called him was the co-editor of the *Life in the Spirit Study Bible* and a man with an impeccable theological mind. He was also one of the Directors of *Grace Training Center*, which was affiliated with our church. Wes was quick to discern that people were struggling with how to process this whole scenario. Feeling the need to bring clarity to the situation, he gave an enlightening teaching, 'The New Testament Perspective of Martyrdom'. Wes shared that, by definition, a martyr is 'a believer who has proved the strength and genuineness of his faith in Christ by undergoing a violent death rather than compromising or giving up his faith, mission or witness for Christ'.

> *A martyr is 'a believer who has proved the strength and genuineness of his faith in Christ by undergoing a violent death rather than compromising or giving up his faith, mission or witness for Christ.'*

He reminded people that the first Christians were well aware that their commitment to follow Jesus and be obedient to his purposes meant that they would suffer. The Apostle Peter wrote to the Christian community to remind them, 'Dear friends, do not be surprised at the fiery ordeal that has come on you to test you, as though something strange were happening to you' (1 Pet 4:12). Suffering for your faith was not an unusual occurrence for those first saints as they laboured to establish the Kingdom of God in pagan cultures.

> *I would have thought that the beauty of their lifestyle would have been seen and celebrated, but that was not the case.*

Not long after the initial euphoria of the powerful day of Pentecost, the established Jewish religious hierarchy pushed back hard. We read that,

'The high priest and all his associates, who were members of the party of the Sadducees, were filled with jealousy. They arrested the apostles and put them in the public jail' (Acts 5:17–18). This attitude of jealousy by local leaders was not altogether different from what The Community of Reconciliation experienced. As the power of God was being shown through them daily by their love for God and each other, some of the local socialist party leaders became increasingly jealous. I would have thought that the beauty of their lifestyle would have been seen and celebrated, but that was not the case. As with the early church in Jerusalem, their values and way of life were a threat to the established system. The potential loss of influence over the general populace enraged those in power.

> *Those in the political, business or religious communities responded with violence to the potential loss of influence.*

Soon after the Apostles were jailed, things escalated to the point that the religious establishment brought in a young zealot named Saul to deal with these 'Christians' by jailing or killing them. He was the enforcer for the religious mafia. One of the first recorded incidents of his bloody purge was the martyrdom of a young evangelist by the name of Stephen (Acts 6 & 7). It is interesting to note that all through the history of the early church, whenever there was a display of God's power through someone in the Christian community, there was a corresponding backlash from those in various positions of power. Those in the political, business or religious communities responded with violence to the potential loss of influence. Someone was always beaten, thrown in jail or killed. I often wonder how many of us would desire the 'power gifts' if we knew that we might be beaten, thrown into jail or killed. It is a sobering thought.

Dying for your faith was not unexpected by the early Christians and it was a price they were ready to pay for the sake of spreading the Gospel. Years later, after having a traumatic encounter with God, Saul, now re-named Paul, addressed the believers in the city of Rome. He wrote,

156

'For we do not live to ourselves alone and we do not die to ourselves alone. If we live, we live to the Lord; and if we die, we die to the Lord. So, whether we live or die, we belong to the Lord. For this very reason, Christ died and returned to life so that he might be the Lord of both the dead and the living.'

– ROMANS 14:7–8

To the community in Philippi he wrote, 'For to me, to live is Christ and to die is gain' (Phil 1:21). While staying in Ephesus he said, 'However, I consider my life worth nothing to me; my only aim is to finish the race and complete the task the Lord Jesus has given me, the task of testifying to the good news of God's grace' (Acts 20:24).

This was not a video game and these were not merely theoretical words to Paul. Soon he would back them up by his actions, much to the confusion and dismay of his friends. In the twenty-first chapter of Acts, Paul and his friends have an interesting encounter with a prophet named Agabus. In order to add visual effects to his message, Agabus tied Paul's hands and feet together with his own belt and prophesied over him. 'The Holy Spirit says, "In this way the Jews of Jerusalem will bind the owner of this belt and will hand him over to the Gentiles"' (Acts 21:11). Upon hearing this, Paul's associates concluded that this was a warning from God and pleaded with Paul to avoid Jerusalem. However, Paul disagreed and said, 'Why are you weeping and breaking my heart? I am ready not only to be bound, but also to die in Jerusalem for the name of the Lord Jesus' (Acts 21:12–13). Why did Paul disagree with their counsel and proceed to Jerusalem? He did not disagree with the prophecy, he embraced it. I think that where others saw danger, Paul saw opportunity.

Where others saw danger, Paul saw opportunity.

As we later learn, as a result of what happened in Jerusalem, Paul was arrested and subsequently had opportunity as a prisoner to preach the Gospel in court hearings and before Roman rulers throughout the region.

This was something that most likely would not have happened under any other circumstance. In time, he used his Roman citizenship to appeal for a fair hearing in Rome (Acts 22:23–29; 23:11; 25:11). Knowing that he would have to be shipped there for his court proceedings, he saw an opportunity. There were 30 000 Jewish refugees living in Rome at the time. He also knew that the Christian community in Rome was growing more rapidly than in virtually any other city. Paul was prepared to lay his life down for the opportunity to share his faith with those being influenced daily by a pagan culture. The fact that it might cost him his life was merely a secondary concern to him. Paul was a man who lived his life with his eyes always on eternity.

There is a profound truth in this story that will shake most of our modern paradigms of how we discern God's will. Most people's paradigms only equate something good with God's will. Anything that could bring bodily harm or require us to give up something precious, like our freedom, would immediately be cast down as heresy. This story and Paul's subsequent decision should inspire all of us to take a second look at our priorities and recalibrate our paradigms. For the past two thousand years, millions of believers around the world have been giving their earthly lives so that others could find their spiritual ones. This was certainly the case with those who established The Community of Reconciliation.

I remember that on my second trip to visit them in 1986, I had one of the most sobering discussions of my entire life. It was just a few days before we were scheduled to head back home when Gerry Keightley and Dave Marais (two of the Community leaders) asked if they could take us kudu hunting that night. Kudu are large antelope, the size of an elk. There had been a few spotted in the area recently and they thought that it might be a fun experience for us. While I knew absolutely nothing about hunting, the thought of being a 'big game hunter' certainly did appeal to my male ego.

Once the sun went down, a few of us jumped on the back of the truck, while the guys from the farms drove. They had a powerful high beam light which they shone into the darkness as we drove through part of the

45 000 hectares. They told us to look for a set of illuminated eyes peering back at us through the night. We drove around for a couple of hours without spotting anything taller than some hares. It was almost midnight so we headed back to the New Adams community centre. Once there, we drank some water and decided to climb a few hundred yards to a hilltop. It was a great place to get a view of not only the valley below but the stars above. Being so far away from the city lights, the sky was covered from one end to the other with more stars than I could count. We sat there in the darkness for the next hour or so and talked about where the Community should go from here.

It soon turned into a very tender and intimate time as we each shared all the things that our hearts hoped for through the myriad of projects we had going. We were so thankful for all that God had done in such a short period of time, and yet we knew that there was so much more work to be done. As the night started to draw to an end, I had a very delicate question I wanted to ask but was unsure exactly how to broach the subject. I finally decided to just go for it and bluntly asked Gerry and Dave if they were aware how dangerous their situation was.

I still had memories of the armed guards and barbed wire fences at Boetie York's farm where we first went to look at weirs. The openness and lack of protection on the community properties had me concerned for their safety. I was curious to hear their thoughts as the spirit of the place was peaceful and there wasn't a sense of fear anywhere.

Both Gerry and Dave were very thoughtful and slow to answer. It was clear they had given this issue a lot of consideration. Gerry shared that they felt that three-metre-high fences with motion activated lights and around the clock guards would send the wrong message, not only to the people living in the community, but also to the whole region. He did not want the people living there to feel like they were imprisoned. He also did not want to send an unintentional message to the local Africans that they did not trust them. While I understood, I also knew that this left them vulnerable to possible attacks which had happened in other parts of the country.

The discussion shifted to the whole issue of martyrdom. It is one thing to read and theorize about it but a whole other issue when you actually face it. In their situation it was a very real possibility. Dave said that they had, as a community, discussed the issue openly and frankly several times. Over the course of the past few years, a number of families had spent time at the communities and just did not have the grace for it. They eventually decided that it was too risky and returned to the city. Dave assured me that all of those who remained, each and every one, had soberly thought through the issue and were ready to lay down their lives for the sake of the Kingdom of God and what He was doing here.

I had never been around people who were committed to the point of being willing to lose their very lives for the sake of fulfilling God's purpose.

I was so deeply moved by their sense of commitment that, for a moment, I was speechless. I had never been around people who were committed to the point of being willing to lose their very lives for the sake of fulfilling God's purpose. It was a Holy moment for me. I knew at that point that I had some extraordinary friends.

To make sure I had heard them correctly, or perhaps just out of nervousness, I asked the question again in an even more straightforward manner: 'So you expect to lose some people?' Gerry replied carefully and soberly, 'Yes, we think there is a very real possibility that one or two could die, and we are prepared for that eventuality.' I was again speechless. What do you say to that? Everything I could think of seemed so trite and shallow. Jesus said, 'There is no greater love than to lay your life down for your brother' (John 15:13). These people had a depth of love that I could only dream about.

For the next few minutes as we sat under the stars together, there was total silence. We all pondered the significance and depth of what had been shared. Little did I know that that moment was to be the last time I would see these ordinary but extraordinary people alive. They are for me, true heroes of the faith … martyrs.

If you are anything like me, the burning question that you are left with after reading the story up to this point is, 'Why? Why did this happen?' Honestly, I can't answer that definitively as I'm sure there is much I do not understand. I have my suspicions and perspective but that's all it is. One thing that life and age have taught me, is that time brings perspective. It's taken me 20 years to get to a point where I can have a somewhat healthy point of view about the massacre of my friends and the destruction of everything they worked so hard to build. At first glance you might conclude that it was an exercise in futility. Only recently have I begun to understand that the story isn't finished, the book isn't closed and God isn't done. There are more chapters to be written. God has a plan for the people of Zimbabwe.

CHAPTER 9 ENDNOTES

1. *World Christian Encyclopedia* (2nd edition). David Barrett, George Kurian and Todd Johnson. New York: Oxford University Press, 2001. 2 vols.

2. Evangelical Press News Service, 1999 Mennonite Brethren Herald, report on a town hall meeting on the persecuted church held at Southwestern Baptist Theological Seminary, Fort Worth, TX.

PHOTOGRAPHS

The New Adams Farm Community Centre

New Adams Dining Room

L-R Noel Alexander, Bob Scott, Gary Kroeze, Robert McGeorge

John Russell with one of his prize citrus trees

African huts in the Matupo Hills near the village of Mbezingwe

Dave Marais and sons eating Sadza together with the Africans

They died like martyrs

AXED TO DEATH ... missionary's daughters Glynis (left) and Deborah Keightley were among those massacred. Deborah was 16 and Glynis 14 when they were killed.

Matabeleland massacre victims prayed silently before the slaughter

Peter Wellman

ESIGODENI — The missionaries hacked to death in Matabeleland this week lived as Christians and died as martyrs, — silently, and without a fight.

In the eerie silence only the sounds of machetes hacking at flesh was heard, and the short-lived screams of the two babies among the seven women, five children and four men cut down.

The adults and the teenagers uttered no word and made no protest.

Farm 40 km south of Bulawayo on the Beitbridge Road on Wednesday night.

The farm was owned and run by the Community of Reconciliation, a group of born-again Christians who cut loose from the establishment churches in 1982 to come to this tough drought country and be at one with the locals.

They refused to use the security fencing, agric-alert radio or to have local militia protect them from dissidents — which most farmers in Matabeleland

Matabeleland is dissident as well as drought country.

Dissidents have killed more than 70 whites and hundreds of blacks in Matabeleland and the Midlands since the attacks began in 1982.

The New Adams massacre was the biggest and most sadistic of all the brutal slayings, which include 13 missionaries slaughtered at Elim Mission on the eastern border in 1978.

Only two children survived the New Adams massacre. Laura Russell, 13, saw her

a Johannesburg businessman, who does not share the community's evangelical beliefs, said she was "numbed but calm" and would return to Johannesburg with him after the funerals on Wednesday.

Six-year old Matthew Marais, whose mother, father and teenage brother Ethan died, survived by climbing through a window and hiding in the bushes until the next day.

Mrs Dube told me the dissidents first killed eight people in one house, slaughtering them in

Sunday Star, 29 November 1987

Newsweek
THE INTERNATIONAL NEWSMAGAZINE

A Massacre's Message: Get Out or Die

Other white farmers in southern Zimbabwe post guards with automatic weapons against the rebels. At Olive Tree Farm and neighboring New Adam's Farm, the Pentecostal ministers simply trusted in God. One night last week an armed gang seized the missionaries and their children from their beds, bound them in barbed wire and methodically butchered them with axes. After three hours of mutilation and murder, the attackers torched the houses. They threw the bodies of their victims into the flames and departed.

Five were children; one was only six weeks old. One of the two survivors, Laura Russell, 13, was given a written message for "all people from Western or capitalist coun-

Bloody feud: *Two of the victims*

tries" living in Zimbabwe: get out or die. "We are prepared for our last man to face their last man," the letter warned. The dead included two Americans and a Scotswoman.

Last week's attack in the Matabeleland region was the bloodiest massacre of whites since Zimbabwe won independence from Great Britain in 1980. The immediate cause seems to have been a confrontation two weeks ago. A group of black squatters, driven by drought to find new pasture for their cattle, had moved onto the whites' land. The whites ordered them off. "You

ed blacks. Zimbabwean officials say the squatters then sought help from a local gang.

The group was one of Matabeleland's many loosely organized rebel bands, known as dissidents, that oppose the rule of Prime Minister Robert Mugabe. (Mugabe's old foe, opposition leader Joshua Nkomo, denies any connection with the dissidents.) Since 1982 the rebels have waged a campaign of terror against the whites who have title to much of the best farmland. Last week's massacre brought the campaign's toll to 66. "These were innocent missionaries," mourned Home Minister Enos Nkala. "Engaged in production, talk-

Newsweek, 7 December 1987

Gerry & Marian Keightley – With the Lord

David Emerson
– With the Lord

Karen 'Sharon' Ivesdal – With the Lord

Glynis Keightley
– With the Lord

Gary Kroeze

Penny 'Sarah' Lovatt
– With the Lord

Seth Town
– Montana

Francy Town & son, Judah – With the Lord

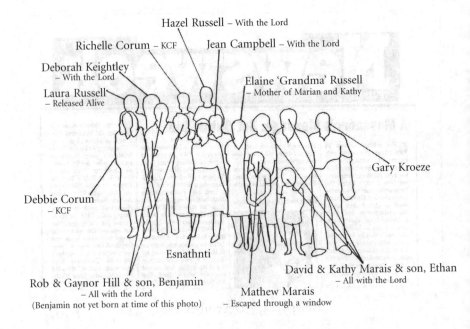

Hazel Russell – With the Lord

Richelle Corum – KCF

Jean Campbell – With the Lord

Deborah Keightley
– With the Lord

Elaine 'Grandma' Russell
– Mother of Marian and Kathy

Laura Russell
– Released Alive

Gary Kroeze

Debbie Corum
– KCF

Esnathnti

David & Kathy Marais & son, Ethan
– All with the Lord

Rob & Gaynor Hill & son, Benjamin
– All with the Lord
(Benjamin not yet born at time of this photo)

Mathew Marais
– Escaped through a window

168

Memorial Service in Bulawayo on 2 December 1987

Sixteen caskets lying in silence at the Chapel

Burnt-out New Adams Community Centre

Burnt-out vehicles on New Adams

Baby carriage frame with strange image on the wall behind

Destroyed New Adams Kitchen

Inside view of the burnt-out New Adams Community Centre

Eight people were killed in this building on New Adams Farm

Eight people were killed in this building on Olive Tree Farm

This weir was completed just weeks before the masacre

Burial Ceremony at New Adams Farm

Water running over the weirs after the rain

FACING ZIMBABWE'S PAST

History is the sum total of the things
that could have been avoided.

– KONRAD ADENAUER

I n the next couple of chapters I would like to offer some context for the 'why' questions. Why did my friends' killers so misunderstand what they were doing? Why did they think they were liberating the black Africans by killing the white Africans? I think it is important to understand the mistakes of the past if we are ever to change the future.

I would like to give you a brief overview of the history of the continent of Africa, the country of Zimbabwe and the role of the church. It is a fascinating journey into how humanity can be so easily blinded by its selfish ambitions. The biblical writer, James, wrote thousands of years ago, 'For where you have envy and selfish ambition, there you find disorder and every evil practice' (Jas 3:16). Church pioneer, the apostle Paul, later exhorted the Christian community, 'Do nothing out of selfish ambition or vain conceit, but in humility consider others better than yourselves' (Phil 2:3). Had those words been heeded by the explorers, administrators and missionaries who settled and evangelized the continent, the current state of Africa would be a very different one, in fact, profoundly different. Instead, it reached the point where one group of people would kill another group of people who were actually trying to help them. What a train wreck! It seems so counterproductive and downright foolish, yet this has been the recurring narrative from one end of the African continent to the other. As with most man-made catastrophes, one need only look at the heart to find the motivation which drives men to make such foolish and self-destructive choices.

If we are ever to change the future we must understand the mistakes of the past.

Simple words can sum up what is behind Africa's failure to find peace and prosperity. Arrogance and greed followed by resentment and anger have all fuelled the fire that has repeatedly burned down the African dream. When the European settlers came to her shores at the end of the nineteenth century to further the expansion of their empires, it lit a fuse that has not stopped burning. That fuse still smouldered 100 years later in The Community of Reconciliation massacre, where in one volatile moment, the past destroyed the future and everyone lost because of it.

I was not born or raised in the Kansas City area. When I first moved here in 1982, I knew virtually nothing about the region or its history. After being in the city for a few months, I noticed that there was an interesting rivalry that simmered under the surface between the neighbouring populations of Kansas and Missouri.

They were divided by an invisible line that ran right down the middle of State Line Road, but I sensed that something more divided them. On the surface, the people living on either side of this invisible line looked exactly the same. Underneath, however, something seemed to separate them. I noticed that, depending on the subject matter, this attitude that lurked just beneath the surface would raise its head.

Besides bi-state tax issues, this rivalry would reach peak hysteria during sporting events between the University of Kansas Jayhawks and the University of Missouri Tigers. The term 'Border War' was used frequently to describe these sporting contests. It was intense. Families were divided. People would stake tribal flags in their front yards in direct view of their neighbours. By the time the contest began, things had reached fever pitch.

It seemed to me that there was a lot of extra passion surrounding the term 'Border War', so I decided to find out its history. The term goes back to 1854 when Kansas was opened for settlement. Those leading Kansas took a strong stance on being an anti-slavery state, and with Missouri being a pro-slavery state, it was a time of great conflict. Raiding parties on both sides of the state line attacked each other and many people were killed, the most fa-

One need only look at the heart to find the motivation which drives men to make such foolish and self-destructive choices.

mous being John Brown. This went on for many years and over time became known as 'The Border War'.

I found the history fascinating and the long-term residual psychological and sociological effects on the people very interesting. One hundred and fifty years later, there is a significantly more civilized and subtle continuation of the original Border War.

In order to understand who we are, we need to know where we've come from. To accurately put into context any current social or geopolitical developments, one has to have a grasp of history. To understand

In order to understand who we are, we need to know where we've come from.

what was happening in Zimbabwe in 1987, you have to be aware of the journey its people took to reach that tragic moment.

Zimbabwe is a country of approximately 12 million inhabitants. They are landlocked by Zambia to the north, Mozambique to the east, South Africa to the south and Botswana to the west. It has the same approximate land mass as the US state of Montana. Like most of the nations on the African continent, it has had a violent and tumultuous history.

In the nation's recent history, there are two primary indigenous people groups that comprise 95% of the country's population. The Shona tribe, which settled predominantly in the northern part of the country, makes up about 63% of the population. The southern part of the country has been settled by the Ndebele tribe, who make up approximately 30%, and 2% of the people come from minor tribes, namely Tonga, Kalanga, Chewa, Sena, Hlengwe, Venda, Lemba and Sotho. The other 5% are predominately European, most of who have immigrated to the country.

This expansion later called 'Imperialism' or 'Colonialism' was at the root of almost all conflict on the continent.

Looking back at Zimbabwe's ancient history, we know that around the third century AD, Bantu tribes living in northern Africa migrated south. By the tenth century they had settled in the region, establishing a communal structure they brought with them. There is an amazing archaeological site located in the south-eastern part of the country near the town of Masvingo. The site called 'Great Zimbabwe' ('Zimba Ramabwe' in Shona) reveals that there was a large and sophisticated culture that ruled that region between 1250 and 1450 AD.

Late in the 15th century, European explorers were beginning to venture to uncharted lands, looking for wealth and expanding the rule or influence of their host countries. This expansion was later called 'Imperialism' or 'Colonialism' and would be at the root of almost all conflict on the continent. As we will see, it inflamed the embers of racism which resulted in a simmering anger that boiled over in the 1960s.

The Portuguese were the first Europeans to make contact with the indigenous peoples living in the region. From the little history that survives, it seems that the region was fairly stable and the Portuguese had an amicable relationship with all the tribes. It was in the 1830s that the area became a hotbed of conflict with the migration north of the Ndebele tribe. 'Ndebele' means 'the people of the long shields' which is a reference to the Ndebele warriors' use of the Zulu shield and assegai.

The first Ndebele tribe to come north from South Africa was lead by Mzilikazi who had been a general in the Zulu nation under the rule of King Shaka. Shaka is considered by many historians to be the greatest of all the Zulu rulers. He was responsible for uniting many of the indigenous tribes in what is now South Africa, and forming them into a single nation. He was a military genius who moulded his armies into a fierce fighting unit. Shaka developed new weapons and military tactics that gave his armies a significant tactical advantage over the other tribes in the region. His warriors were responsible for the deaths of nearly two million people as they conquered tribes and put down revolts.

King Shaka and Mzilikazi got into a conflict in 1823, but before Shaka could gather his armies to kill him, Mzilikazi fled north with a few hundred people who were loyal to him. Along the journey they gathered other tribes, and those that resisted were conquered and assimilated into this new Ndebele clan. As their numbers grew, Mzilikazi shaped them into a fighting force that rivalled Shaka's Zulu warriors. By the time they reached what is now southern Zimbabwe in the 1830s, they were ready to conquer the original Shona tribes that had settled there, whose populations were now in the thousands. The local tribes were no match for this well-trained and fierce army. It wasn't long before Mzilikazi had subdued the whole area and established his permanent kingdom.

In his autobiography, missionary doctor David Livingstone referred to Mzilikazi as the second most impressive leader whom he had encountered on the African continent after Shaka. It was Mzilikazi who established the raiding party mindset that has been a historical characteristic of the Ndebele people for hundreds of years.

King Mzilikazi died in September 1868 and the leadership mantle fell to his 23-year-old son, Lobengula. He was a large man, weighing almost 130 kilograms, but he ruled with a soft voice. While he was not as militant as his father, he was a great warrior in his own right. In the early days of his reign, Europeans were rarely sighted in the region. Unless they were missionaries, Lobengula didn't have any significant interaction with them until Cecil John Rhodes arrived on the scene in 1888.

At the core of Imperialism is the fundamental belief that, 'We can do it better and the world will be a better place if they do it our way.'

Rhodes, a British mining magnate from South Africa, wanted the rights to excavate for minerals on the Ndebele lands. He sent a negotiating team to meet with 55-year-old Lobengula to see if something could be worked out. Lobengula was suspicious of the Europeans and negotiations dragged on for months. Rhodes finally secured the help of Dr. Leander Starr Jameson who had treated Lobengula for gout in the past and was one of the few whites he trusted. Jameson was able to negotiate for money and weapons with the understanding that the British would be living and working on Ndebele land with limited access.

Cecil John Rhodes (who later established the 'Rhodes Scholarship') was born in 1853, in England, to an Anglican vicar. He was asthmatic as a teenager and was sent to live in South Africa's drier climate in hopes of clearing up the asthma. He returned to England for college and was deeply impacted by the then prevailing nationalist philosophy of British Imperialism. At the core of Imperialism is the fundamental belief that, 'We can do it better and the world will be a better place if they do it our way.' In fact, in his last will and testament, Rhodes said of the British, 'I contend that we are the finest race in the world and that the more of the world we inhabit the better it is for the human race.'[1] It is essential to understand that this was one of the significant motivating factors in how the British and their European counterparts approached and interacted with the indigenous peoples on the African continent. Sadly, this 'enlightened' philosophy masked another deeper, diabolical motivating factor, which was greed.

The British were only one of a number of European nations to have big aspirations in Africa. In the late nineteenth century, all across Europe, meetings were taking place in Berlin, Paris and London on how to divide the continent's land amongst these self-proclaimed enlightened ones. Sadly, in most cases, those who did the dividing had never set foot in Africa and were working with inaccurate and outdated maps. Lord Salisbury told an audience in London, 'We have been giving away mountains and rivers and lakes to each other, only hindered by the small impediment that we never knew exactly where they were.'

They carved up the land for themselves without taking into account any of the continent's history, existing chiefdoms, or people groups. In their arrogance, they believed that these were insignificant issues as the people of Africa were merely 'uneducated savages'. The result was that over 190 cultures were suddenly ripped apart and hundreds of others that had no common ground were thrown together under a form of government they knew nothing about. As author Martin Meredith stated in his book, *The Fate of Africa*: 'By the time the scramble for Africa was over, some 10 000 African polities (the aspect of society that is oriented to politics and government[2]) had been merged into forty European colonies and protectorates.'[3] The Europeans toyed with the lives of the African people as though they were simply pieces on a game board. They signed treaties, bought lands, sold and traded and the Africans had very little voice in any of it; they were deemed insignificant. The message that was communicated loud and clear was that they were inferior to their more enlightened European masters who would deliver them from themselves.

> This 'enlightened' philosophy masked another deeper, diabolical motivating factor, which was greed.

In 1880 Rhodes, along with his partner Charles Rudd, founded the DeBeers Mining Company which we know today as DeBeers Diamonds. They were adept at developing strategic relationships within the British Government under the guise of expanding the British Empire. This allowed their mining investments to be protected by the military and also meant that they had the support of the British authorities to expand the Empire into new territories. In order to expand their interests, however,

This received the seal of approval from the church which agreed that the British way of life was in fact 'God's way'.

they had to use deception and deceit.

Sadly, the Christian missionaries played a significant role in this unseemly exercise as they too were caught up in the aura of British Imperialism. They saw themselves as expanding the Kingdom of God by expanding the kingdom of Britain. Rhodes believed that, just like in South Africa, riches of gold and diamonds laid untapped further north in Ndebele lands. Rhodes convinced John Moffat, who was the son of renowned missionary Robert Moffat, to help him secure more concessions from Ndebele King Lobengula.

Robert Moffat had earned Lobengula's trust and so, when his son John approached the King about signing a treaty with England, he agreed. Francis Thompson, who was Rhodes' agent at the negotiations, promised the King that there would be no more than 10 white men mining on Ndebele lands at any one time. This verbal promise was deceptively left off the final document that everyone signed, which was called 'The Rudd Concession'.

Later, when the King discovered the deceit and that he had agreed to allow the British to do anything they needed to maintain the mines, he tried to back out of the agreement. Of course, the British refused to let him and felt it was now within their rights to use force if necessary to protect their interests. By the following year, Rhodes had secured the charter he needed from the British Government to form the British South Africa Company (BSAC). He and his team used the same deceptive tactics on other chiefs to secure mineral rights for regions surrounding the Ndebele land.

As the resentment grew among the African tribes, hostilities increased between the two people groups. This, astonishingly, caught the British completely off guard. This was of course due to their strongly held core belief that their way of life was superior to every other. Married to that thinking was the assumption that everyone would see the obvious brilliance of their superior culture and desire to adopt it. This received the seal of approval from the church which agreed that the British way of life was in fact 'God's way'. While the Ndebele people had always been warriors, the real surprise was that the Shona people also started to rebel against British authority.

The relationship between the Shona and the Ndebele tribes had never been good. When Mzilikazi had first made his foray into the region, the Shona had already been settled there for hundreds of years. They were the indigenous tribe in the region. Mzilikazi's war machine had raided and pillaged hundreds of villages, taking the Shona people as slaves. In 1893, just before the Ndebele War, Rutherford Harris, the BSAC's secretary, told the London office that it was estimated that the Ndebele had killed 100 000 Shona during the previous 70 years. There were whole villages standing desolate that the Ndebele had raided, killed or enslaved.

One of the great misnomers in the modern west is that slavery or racism is a matter of skin colour. Nothing could be further from the truth. Tragically, people have been enslaving each other from the dawn of time. Historically, slavery has been considered the right of conquerors, and those they enslaved were considered their property to do what they pleased with. Sometimes I remind myself that many of the great ancient monuments that I admire were built on the backs of slaves. The formation of my own country, the United States, which established some groundbreaking freedoms for the individual, was slow to abolish slavery.

People have become more aware of other cultures; they have learned that while we may do it differently, we all want the same basic things.

While the founding fathers wrestled with the morality of the issue, the economic frailty of the country ended up being the determining factor that allowed slavery to continue another 100 years. The Civil War tore our country apart and millions of men died, but it was another 100 years before a black man could vote. For all of our enlightenment, it sure took us a long time to get it right, and even now racism continues in the hearts of some.

Fortunately for me, I learned as a young man that racism wasn't always a skin colour issue. My German grandfather Joseph Kammer was born in 1900 in Chicago. His grandparents, like so many other Germans, had emigrated from Europe to America to get away from the many regional conflicts that embattled that continent.

I remember many stories about the ethnic boroughs of Chicago and how dangerous it was if you got caught out of the neighbourhood boundaries. He often told the story of having to draw straws to see who was going to retrieve the baseball that had just cleared the fence and gone into another ethnic neighbourhood. You had to be nimble on your feet in order to retrieve the ball, because if you weren't, the boys on the other side would catch you and give you a beating.

As a child of the 60s, I remember how most ethnic groups had a negative slang name that we all used. Archie Bunker, a TV character, was the stereotypical white racist who couldn't put a sentence together without inserting a racial slur, and we all laughed with him. It seems that over the years and through technology, the world has become a smaller place. I think that TV and the internet have done much to introduce the global community to each other. People have become more aware of other cultures; they have learned that while we may do it differently, we all want the same basic things. Mothers all over the world want their children to be loved, healthy and safe. Fathers want an opportunity to provide the same things for their families. While tolerance for cultural distinctiveness has increased, there is still a lot of ignorance, which breeds fear and the tendency to want to isolate.

Unfortunately for the characters in this unfolding drama in 19th century Southern Africa, it would be many, many years before they woke up to realize the foolish arrogance and counter productiveness of their thinking. They justified their place of superiority based on the belief that they were doing a 'higher good'. By humiliating the indigenous people and de-valuing their cultures, they created a deep resentment that, in the end, led to the demise of everything they hoped to build.

When you strip a man of his dignity, he only has one of two options. Either he allows himself to be less of a man and become a slave, or he dies fighting to regain his dignity. The British didn't seem to understand this and were utterly shocked when the Shona started to push back. As the Shona uprising started in the west central region, the Magistrate Marshall Hole wrote:

This sudden departure on the part of the Mashona tribes has caused the greatest surprise to those who from long residence in the country thought they understood the character of these savages and to none more than to the Native Commissioners themselves ... With true killer deceit they have beguiled us into the idea that they were content with our administration of the country and wanted nothing more than to work for and trade with us and become civilized; but at a given signal they have cast aside all pretence and simultaneously set in motion the whole of the machinery which they have been preparing.[4]

> By humiliating the indigenous people and devaluing their cultures, they created a deep resentment that, in the end, led to the demise of everything they hoped to build.

The British had barged into the region being guided by their overconfidence and the assumption that they knew better. 'Wiri' Edwards, the first Native Commissioner of Mrewa in central Mashonaland confessed:

We had underrated the Mashonas, we knew nothing of their past history, who they were, where they came from and although many of the Native Commissioners had a working knowledge of their language, none of us really understood the people or could follow their line of thought. We were inclined to look on them as a downtrodden race that was grateful to the white man for protection.[5]

To add insult to injury, they saw it happening on what they believed was land that had been stolen from them.

They believed that the Shona people would not rebel because they supposed that the Shona had no roots, no sense of history, no sense of religion, and the feeblest of political institutions; in short, no way of life worth fighting and dying for. They also believed that the Ndebele would not rebel because they thought that Ndebele society, no matter how centralized and effective it had been in the past, had also been so arbitrary and oppressive that it had been abhorrent to most of those involved in it.

The British believed that the Shona welcomed British rule as a protection against the Ndebele, and that the accumulation of the Ndebele people welcomed British rule as a protection against their own oppressive institutions. They could not have been further from the truth. In 1893, the region erupted again as Lobengula realized that he had been deceived by Rhodes and his associates. Warfare broke out between Lobengula's warriors and the men of the BSAC. The BSAC had purchased and imported the recently invented Maxim gun which was the first self-powered machine gun. The Shona and Ndebele tribes stood no chance against this high-powered weapon and it was not long before most of their leaders were either imprisoned or killed. By 1895, the white colonists had subdued the whole region and Matabeleland no longer existed. It was subsequently renamed Rhodesia in honour of Cecil John Rhodes, the founder of the BSAC.

During the next 60 years, armed conflicts between the black Africans and white Europeans continued sporadically. In 1923, with the white population near 30 000, Rhodesia became a self-governing colony of the British Empire. More Europeans (primarily from England) immigrated to the country and land was needed to support them. With their knowledge of agriculture, they found and settled the soil-rich lands best suited for crop production. Rhodesia, it turned out, didn't have the rich gold and diamond deposits like South Africa. Most people, even miners, had to turn to agriculture as a way of life.

The British passed laws guaranteeing more rights to the whites and stripping them from blacks. Land was redistributed to white farmers, which fed the growing resentment in the black communities. By 1931, 50% of Rhodesia's land was owned by 2 500 white farmers. Soon there was a burgeoning economy as the white farmers transformed the land and built an agricultural industry that was unsurpassed in Africa. The blacks were, by and large, excluded from this newfound prosperity as they didn't have the financial resources to compete. In the end they worked on the white farms for very small wages. This added to the mounting hostility. They saw the white farmers prospering and living in luxury while they toiled under the hot African sun, for minimal wages, living in squalor. To add insult to injury, they saw it happening on what they believed was land that had been stolen from them.

In 1941, a significant event took place that would be the catalyst for change across Africa and the beginning of the end of European colonial rule. US President Franklin Roosevelt and British Prime Minister Winston Churchill held a secret meeting off the coast of Newfoundland to work on a document they called *The Atlantic Charter*. One of the key tenets of the charter was that all people should have the right to choose their own government. While Roosevelt believed that this pertained to all people across the globe, Churchill felt that the British colonies were excluded. Roosevelt further agitated the situation in 1943 when, in Casablanca for a meeting, he told the Sultan of Morocco that under the tenets of The Atlantic Charter, it was justifiable for him to declare independence from France. As you can imagine, this infuriated the French government. In 1945, there were only four independent governments in the whole of the African continent!

In 1957, the African National Congress (ANC) was launched in Zimbabwe. Joshua Nkomo was selected to be its leader as he was considered a moderate and had a good reputation within the white community. Nkomo, who was born in 1917, was the son of missionary teachers in the southern region of the country called Matabeleland. He was educated in South Africa, where he met Nelson Mandela, who had a huge impact on him. Nkomo was also a lay preacher within the British Methodist Church.

In 1959 the Rhodesian government outlawed the ANC, fearing that it would incite rebellion amongst the black African population. In 1961 a new nationalist party was formed called the *Zimbabwe African Peoples Union* (ZAPU). Membership consisted of black Africans frustrated by what seemed like a hopelessly slow political progress and wanting to accelerate the process by using violence to bring change. White-owned farms, schools and churches all came under attack in hopes that Britain would notice and want to get more involved in the affairs of the country.

Attitudes in England had changed significantly over the years, and the British now wanted to rid themselves of their colonies and see the black Africans brought into the political process with hopes that one day they would self-govern. Nkomo travelled around the world attempting to gain support from other nations, hoping that they would put pressure on the white leadership to grant the Africans a greater say in the government. This resulted in the white Rhodesian leadership digging their heels in deeper. ZAPU was outlawed and all their leaders were thrown into prison.

In 1963 the nationalist movement split into two groups and the Zimbabwe African National Union (ZANU) was formed. While the two parties wanted the same thing, the ZANU leadership was unhappy with Nkomo's progress and felt that things weren't moving fast enough. The Secretary-General of the party at that time was a young radical by the name of Robert Mugabe. Mugabe, who was Shona, and Nkomo, who was Ndebele, never did get along. Even years later when they finally won everything they had fought so hard for, Mugabe saw Nkomo as a rival and tried to eliminate him.

Mugabe was born in 1924, and was educated in Jesuit schools as a young boy. Later he received a degree in economics from the University of London. In time he would earn five more degrees from the University of South Africa. Mugabe entered the political fray in 1960. Four years later, both he and Joshua Nkomo were thrown into prison for ten years for making speeches seen as subversive to the government. Mugabe was released in 1974. He had been elected President of the ZANU party while still in prison. Mugabe had grown angrier and more militant because his four-year-old son had died while he was imprisoned and he was refused the right to attend the funeral. This painful and degrading experience only further fuelled the fire of hatred and anger that was already burning in his soul toward the white population.

In 1972 the two African parties established military wings that began sporadic operations against the white government's security forces and also against the white farm operators. In the country of Zambia, adjacent to Zimbabwe's northern border, they established ZAPU and east of the country in Mozambique was ZANU. This armed conflict, called the Bush War or the Zimbabwe Liberation Struggle, lasted for approximately seven years.

Ian Smith, the contentious Prime Minister of the country, had declared independence from British rule on November 11, 1965. This set off a long series of condemnations from the international community that ultimately led to sanctions against Rhodesia. Over the next few years as the countries surrounding Rhodesia were transitioning to black-run governments, the white government in Rhodesia became increasingly isolated, other than some initial help from South Africa. While the government had superior firepower, they were significantly outnumbered and in the end had to ask for a peace settlement with the two black parties and their military wings.

In May of 1979, under intense international pressure, Ian Smith's government returned power to the British government in hopes that they could negotiate a settlement. British negotiators set to work to find a path to peace and invited Nkomo and Mugabe to London for talks. While Nkomo was ready to negotiate, Mugabe was still extremely angry and at first refused to attend the meetings. Mugabe had his heart set on a military victory and felt he was being robbed. He wanted to crush the white minority in order to eliminate any negotiating position they might have. Both the bordering nations of Zambia and Mozambique had suffered tremendously as a result of the war. Presidents Kenneth Kaunda and Samora Machel told Mugabe, in no uncertain terms, that they would withdraw their support if he refused to attend the London meetings and negotiate a settlement. This further angered Mugabe and he considered them 'sell-outs to the cause'. Though fuming and frustrated, both he and Nkomo signed 'The Lancaster Agreement' on December 21, 1979. The agreement ended biracial rule in the nation and established a roadmap to black rule and the establishment of the independent nation of Zimbabwe.

The British managed the transitional government for the next months. On March 4, 1980, new national elections were held. Robert Mugabe was swept into power by the overwhelming population advantage of the Shona people. Despite his overwhelming advantage, Mugabe still resorted to intimidation and violence to secure his victory. There was great speculation that Mugabe rigged the elections with the help of the British. Nkomo accused him of being a 'terrorist' during the campaign.

Nkomo finished second to Mugabe in the polls and there was a lot of debate as to what to do with such an influential and revered figure. Mugabe's problem was that he deeply disliked and distrusted Nkomo. Finally, they decided that he would accept a cabinet position within the Mugabe government. Nkomo was appointed Minister of Home affairs in charge of the police.

The new nation of Zimbabwe, like The Community of Reconciliation, started out with such hope and promise. In 1980, as the country's first black President was getting ready to assume office, the general mood was one of optimism. While there was anxiety within the minority white community as to what lay ahead, Mugabe went out of his way to assure them that they had a significant role in Zimbabwe's future. This was his attitude for the next two years. To reinforce his stance, he appointed two white ministers to cabinet posts in his administration. Even more shocking, he struck up a cordial relationship with his old nemesis, Ian Smith.

At the time he seemed to understand that good relationships with the country's white farmers were crucial for economic stability. There were nearly 6 000 white farmers who owned and operated 40% of the productive agricultural land. Their holdings consisted of over two-thirds of the country's most fertile soil. Zimbabwe was known as the 'breadbasket of Africa' as her productivity was so high that she was exporting maize and wheat across the continent.

The new nation of Zimbabwe, like The Community of Reconciliation, started out with such hope and promise.

Mugabe's initial relationship with the white community was so good that they called him 'Good old Bob' or 'Uncle Bob'. With the country's resources no longer being drained to finance a war, and an adequate rainfall, the economy soared and the white community prospered in an unprecedented manner. Life after independence changed little for them. Most of the high-paying, skilled positions in the country were filled by whites and the *status quo* remained for the next few years.

As a part of his political campaign, Mugabe promised the Africans significant land reform. The land had been disproportionately divided with 95% of the black population living on 60% of the land. To make matters worse, it was land that was prone to drought, resulting in sporadic productivity. At the time, one-third of the population was living on overcrowded tribal trust lands which are similar to the Indian Reservations seen in the US.

During the governmental transition negotiated by Britain, Mugabe had made a commitment that he would not embark on any radical land reform for at least ten years after Independence. While he did start relocating some families to new land, it was farmland that had been abandoned by white farmers during the war. All other land transactions were done under a British sponsored programme called 'willing buyer-willing seller'. The British even funded the programme, providing 44 million pounds to allow Africans access to the funding needed to purchase the farms from their white owners.

One of the many sad ironies of Mugabe's tenure as President was that while he was cosying up to the white community, he was beginning military operations against his own people! In 1982 he began reprisals against ex-Zipra soldiers who had fought in the war of Independence alongside his ZANU forces but were more closely aligned with Joshua Nkomo's ZAPU party. Hundreds fled into the bush and became known as 'dissidents', running for their lives from Mugabe's troops. They survived by robbing and pillaging anywhere they could find supplies.

Nkomo was falsely accused by Mugabe of plotting a coup supported by the South African government. In his 28 years of ruling, Mugabe has accused all the opposition leaders of illegally attempting to overthrow him.

Double agents in Zimbabwe's Central Intelligence Organization were working with South Africa to undermine Mugabe's effort to form a one-party socialist system. They felt that a one-party system would leave too much power in one man's control. In fact, by the end of the 1980s not a single African head of state in three decades had allowed himself to be voted out of office! In an effort to cause distrust between ZAPU and ZANU and preserve the multiparty system, they planted arms on ZAPU-owned farms and tipped Mugabe off as to their existence. This gave Mugabe the excuse he needed to eliminate his rival and launch what he called 'The Gukurahundi' which in Shona means 'the early rain which washes away the chaff before the spring rains'. In other words, 'it is time to wash away the garbage'.

What followed was a series of politically-motivated mass murders, or genocide against Nkomo's Ndebele people. This occurred predominantly in the southern part of the country in Matabeleland. Mugabe hired the North Koreans to come to Zimbabwe and train a special army unit called 'The Fifth Brigade' that reported directly to him. Mugabe placed his cousin Perence Shiri in charge and they killed suspected members and supporters of the ZAPU. It is estimated that 20 000 to 60 000 civilians were murdered during this time. They dug mass graves to hide the atrocities while others were thrown down deep mine shafts. The Ndebele people who survived were refused medical and food supplies, which resulted in massive starvation and death. They were also forced to speak Shona so they could survive.

There was more going on under the surface than most people understood. History played a role in what was now was unfolding. For hundreds of years the Shona people had been raped, pillaged and forced into slavery by the stronger Ndebele tribes. In their mind it was time for payback, and they did it with a vengeance.

The church leadership began to speak out about what was going on, but Mugabe angrily responded that the church needed to stay out of politics. It was in the midst of this genocide and injustice that The Community of Reconciliation was established.

As Mugabe increasingly turned to anger and violence and turning the Africans against each other, the white community became disillusioned and began to emigrate out of the country *en masse*. By the end of 1987, when my friends were killed, Mugabe had, for all practical purposes, removed his chief rival Joshua Nkomo and declared himself head of state and head of the military with sweeping powers to do pretty much whatever he wanted. To solidify his position, he began the process of installing loyal friends and allies, no matter their qualifications, in key government posts. This resulted in him having virtually complete control over every aspect of the government.

In time, Mugabe's policies would continue to destroy the country's economy until he had taken it from being one of Africa's most prosperous nations and reduced it to one of the poorest. His socialist political agenda was an abysmal failure. As he started to lose his power and influence over the people, he would give some high profile speech blaming the 'Western Imperialists' for all the country's problems.

I have often wondered if he actually believed what he was saying or if it was a cover up. Under the guise of returning Africa to its rightful owners, he simply took farms and land away from those who had made them productive, and gave them as political favours to those who had no idea how to manage them. Within a few more years, the country's economy had bottomed out and hyperinflation set in, which has produced even more poverty and hardship.

In 1990, in an effort to win another election, Mugabe decided to stir up the masses by announcing more land reform. He planned to redistribute 5,2 million hectares to peasant farmers, half of which was still in white hands. His cronies in the parliament pushed legislation through that allowed him to confiscate land and pay a price of his discretion. The landowners were stripped of any recourse they might have had in the courts. The great injustice was that more than half the white landowners had purchased their lands after independence and with government approval. Now the government was turning on them and they appealed to the world for help. Britain, the United States and the World Bank all spoke out on not only how unethical it was, but the long-term damaging affect it would have to the country's economy.

> *When men with weak character are given power and influence, the result is always corruption.*

Mugabe had worked the population into a frenzy of revenge, and reason was thrown out the window. He claimed that his decision was a reckoning between the land-hungry majority and the 'greedy bunch of racist usurpers determined to thwart the popular will'. As with most things done in anger and reaction, the results were a disaster, and Mugabe eventually had to tone down his racist comments. Nonetheless, he continued with his land redistribution plans, which eventually became engulfed in scandal.

As history has shown, when men with weak character are given power and influence, the result is always corruption. The good of the country and the needs of people are drowned out by the lust for power and possessions. Mugabe's corrupt officials began the secret process of stripping the country clean of its farms and businesses. It soon came to light that his ministers had defrauded the British government's funding for the land programme and used the money for themselves. The British immediately cancelled the programme.

While Mugabe got the loyalty he wanted, the people of Zimbabwe ended up far worse off under his regime than before independence. His officials were not only corrupt but inept. They mismanaged the businesses, the government agencies and ultimately the whole agricultural sector. With agriculture employing a majority of the population, unemployment began to rise as more and more farms failed. Not only were people out of work, the land was lying fallow and therefore not producing the food that was needed to feed the nation.

The disease swept through the country with such virulence that Zimbabwe ended up with the highest per capita infection rate anywhere in the world!

By the end of the 1990s, 50% of the population was unemployed and 70% lived in abject poverty. Inflation hit 60% and those who did have jobs worked harder and had less to spend. Almost all schools and hospitals fell into great disrepair and when the AIDS crisis hit, they had absolutely no resources or ability to respond. The result was that the disease swept through the country with such virulence that Zimbabwe ended up with the highest *per capita* infection rate anywhere in the world!

In 2000, veterans of Zimbabwe's war for independence began squatting on land owned by white farmers in an effort to reclaim land taken under British colonization. In August of 2002, Robert Mugabe ordered almost all white commercial farmers to leave their land without compensation. Once heralded as a champion of the anti-colonial movement, Mugabe is now viewed by much of the international community as a despotic ruler responsible for egregious human rights abuses and for running the economy of his country into the ground.

In March 2002 Mugabe was re-elected president for another six years in a blatantly rigged election whose results were enforced by the president's militia. In 2003, inflation hit 300%, the country faced severe food shortages, and the farming system had nearly been destroyed. Parliamentary elections held in March 2005 were judged by international monitors

The presidential election did take place, but it was neither free nor fair.

to be seriously flawed and, in all likelihood, rigged.

Zimbabweans, clearly fed up with the economic collapse and the lack of available necessities, expressed their anger at the polls in the March 2008 presidential and parliamentary elections. The opposition party, the Movement for Democratic Change (MDC) won a majority of the seats in Parliament, a remarkable defeat for Mugabe's ZANU-PF party. Four days after the vote, Morgan Tsvangirai, the leader of the MDC, declared himself the winner by a slim margin. Mugabe refused to concede until the vote count was complete. More than a month after the election, however, the vote was still not yet finalized. Zimbabwe's High Court dismissed the opposition's request for the release of election results. Many observers speculated that Mugabe ordered the delay to either intimidate election officials or to rig the results in his favour. Indeed, in April, police raided the offices of the opposition and election monitors and detained dozens of people for questioning. After the raid, supporters of Mugabe began a brutal campaign of violence against the opposition that left more than 30 people dead and hundreds wounded. Tsvangirai fled the country, fearing assassination attempts. He returned to Zimbabwe in late May.

The people in the nation are on the verge of a catastrophic humanitarian crisis.

On May 2nd, election officials finally released the results of the vote, with Tsvangirai defeating President Robert Mugabe, 47,9% to 43,2%. A runoff election, scheduled for June 27, was necessary because neither candidate won more than 50%. In the lead up to the runoff election, police intensified their crackdown on Tsvangirai and members of the MDC. At least 85 supporters of his party were killed in government-backed violence. Officials banned rallies and repeatedly detained Tsvangirai for attempting to hold them.

In June, Mugabe barred humanitarian groups from providing aid in the country. This was a drastic move which aid organizations estimated would deny about two million people much needed assistance. On June 22, Tsvangirai withdrew from the race, saying he could not subject his supporters to any more violence and intimidation. He then took refuge in the Dutch Embassy. The United Nations issued a statement condemning the violence that had plagued Zimbabwe and said it would be 'impossible for a free and fair election to take place'. However, the presidential election did take place, but it was neither free nor fair. Nevertheless, Mugabe was elected to a sixth term, taking 85% of the vote. US President Bush joined the chorus of world leaders who condemned the election and the government-sponsored crackdown on the opposition. After intense international pressure, Mugabe finally agreed to meet with Tsvangirai to negotiate a transitional joint government.

Over the later part of 2008, Mugabe's ZANU-PF party officials and Tsvangirai's MDC team have attempted to iron out a power sharing agreement in order to form a new government. After some initial hopeful signs, the talks have stalemated and left the country spiralling out of control. Mugabe refuses to relinquish control of the military and the police which allow him to use force to maintain power. While Mugabe spends his time scheming to maintain control, the people in the nation are on the verge of a catastrophic humanitarian crisis. Most of the country's infrastructure has ground to a halt. Hospitals have closed and there is no medicine to combat the AIDS epidemic. Water treatment facilities have shut down and there is a cholera outbreak that has the potential to kill tens of thousands. Inflation is in the millions of percent with a simple

> *History testifies that when leaders gain power with bitterness, resentment and unresolved conflict in their souls, they become destructive.*

doughnut costing Z$15 000 000. With the government's land distribution policies such an abysmal failure, few crops are being planted and the nation stands on the precipice of massive starvation in 2009.

Robert Mugabe's dream of a new world quickly turned into a nightmare for the people of Zimbabwe. What happened? Where did things go wrong? Mugabe, like so many others, started out with noble but naive aspirations. An extremely intelligent man with six university degrees, he genuinely wanted to make a difference and improve the plight of his people. What he underestimated (as we all do) is the wickedness that lies within the human heart, including his own.

When one is suddenly handed the reins of a whole nation and given such power and authority, it's too intoxicating to handle. Men change. Brilliant men become stupid. History testifies that when leaders gain power with bitterness, resentment and unresolved conflict in their souls, they become destructive. Revenge becomes their obsession at the cost of everything else. Mugabe fell prey to what was hidden in his heart. The truth always has a way of coming into the light and revealing itself. Mugabe was in fact 'the Emperor with no clothes'.

When one has power, it unfetters the greed and lust hidden in one's soul. Like Mugabe, you lavish yourself with a massive new palace and bulldoze thousands of people's homes (that you put there) to 'clean up' the neighbourhood. Once you have power you become paranoid about losing it. In order to preserve your power, you gather around you family and friends that you trust and put them in key positions in your government. In order to maintain their loyalty you grant them special privileges and wealth, which in turn corrupts them. Over the course of time, instead of having a truly socialist government where everyone is equal and cared for, you have a few at the top who control the wealth, while the masses are still enslaved to poverty. This corruption trickles down until you have a totally dysfunctional family under the guise of a government. Whether Imperialism or Socialism, the result is the same for the little guy who has no power; he remains poor.

CHAPTER 10 ENDNOTES

1. Flint, John (November 1974). *Cecil Rhodes.* Little Brown and Company.

2. *Encarta Dictionary: English* (North America).

3. Meredith, Martin (2005). *The Fate of Africa.* Public Affairs, Perseus Book Group.

4. Acting C.N.C. to Acting Administrator, March 30th, 1896, A 10/1/1 report by Marshall Hole, Oct. 29th 1896.

5. Reminiscences of 'Wiri' Edwards, ED 6/1/1.

Chapter 11

Who Speaks For God?

Watch out for false prophets. They come to you in sheep's
clothing, but inwardly they are ferocious wolves. By
their fruit you will recognize them.

– Matthew 7:15–16

The history of the church in Zimbabwe, and of the whole continent of Africa, is one of great victories and humiliating defeats. In the early days of the faith, the Christian influences shone brightly from northern African cities, among them Alexandria in Egypt. Thinkers and writers like Origen, Tertullian and Augustine greatly impacted the expression of 2nd century Christianity. At the same time, Sub-Saharan Africa remained largely untouched by the message of Christianity until the 1500s when European missionaries explored its uncharted lands.

The history of the church in Zimbabwe, and of the whole continent of Africa, is one of great victories and humiliating defeats.

The great wave of colonial evangelism that swept over Africa's shores in the late 1800s tragically left a deep scar on the soul of its indigenous people. It has only recently started to heal. It has taken time and tragedy for the western church to come to a place where it can objectively re-evaluate its methodology and attitudes. In hindsight, much could have been done differently, but that is just wishful thinking. The mindset of the period deeply affected the way in which those who evangelized approached their task.

To the African people, Christianity came hand-in-hand with the Imperialistic philosophy of the white Europeans as they conquered and divided Africa for themselves. Christianity ended up being viewed as the white man's religion and as the deceiving means used to colonize people. While many missionaries landed on Africa's shores with a sincere motivation to convert the lost from the Kingdom of Darkness to the Kingdom of Light, they also ended up leading them away from their African way of life to a more 'enlightened' way. This, as we've previously discussed, was based on the assumption that the British or European lifestyle was not only superior, but also God's way. This created a lot of confusion, shame and duplicity within the African communities.

> *The great wave of colonial evangelism that swept over Africa's shores in the late 1800s tragically left a deep scar on the soul of its indigenous people.*

> *To the African people, Christianity came hand in hand with the Imperialistic philosophy of the white Europeans as they conquered and divided Africa for themselves.*

Other missionaries, once they saw the opportunity to prosper, ignored the Gospel message to serve and minister to the poor. Instead, by aligning themselves with men like Cecil John Rhodes, they selfishly grabbed resources, including land, from both the Shona and Ndebele people. Many missionaries became very wealthy. Later, as black consciousness grew and African nationalists took up arms against the Colonialists, some church leaders continued to support colonial rule and the 'apartheid' or segregationist philosophy so prevalent in South Africa. Three decades ago, Zimbabwean statesman and Methodist preacher Joshua Nkomo addressed a rally in what was then Rhodesia:

> *The Christian churches have failed. Ministers have preached to people that they are the same in the eyes of God; at the same time they have*

supported a social system that divides these people into groups of un-equals. It is here where Christian churches have lacked moral courage. The Christian philosophy is good, but the men preaching it are bad.[1]

This was quite an indictment, given that Nkomo's father, Thomas, was also a preacher and worked for the London Missionary Society. Nkomo was brought up in a deeply Christian family and all through his education attended Christian schools. It was there that he was daily exposed to the hypocrisy of the racial double standard. While God was interested in his soul, it seemed that the colour of his skin relegated him to a subservient role behind the 'far superior' white people. As they became educated, the conflict that arose for many Africans was that the Jesus of the New Testament certainly didn't seem to see things in quite the same way as some of their religious brethren.

In 1998, in a formal address to the World Council of Churches assembly on his analysis of the role of Christianity in Southern Africa, President Robert Mugabe said that Churches had played midwife to colonialism, 'succumbing or voluntarily surrendering God to the racism of colonial structures.'[2] These are hard words to hear but they are in fact the heartfelt truth of how many Africans feel about the influence of the western church in their society. It's a sad story but one that needs to be told so future generations can learn from these mistakes and not repeat them.

The first recorded missionary who journeyed to that region of Africa was the Portuguese Jesuit, Father Goncalo da Silveira, who set up his mission near the present border with Mozambique in 1560. His time in the area was short-lived as he was martyred on March 16, 1561. The Portuguese had settlements in Mozambique, on the coast of Africa, as they had established a colony there. Following Father da Silveira was an influx of Dominican Fathers who established themselves south of the great Zambezi River, in the northern region of present day Zimbabwe. They remained there until 1775. The Dominicans tried very hard to influence King

Munhumutapa to covert to Catholicism, but in the end they only suc-
ceeded in convincing the King to let them take some of his sons. His three
boys, Miguel, Constancio and Joao, all became priests and later died in
Goa, India and Brazil.

While the Dominican priests had unfettered access to the kingdom of Munhumutapa, they had very little success in
converting any of the people. After 1775,
all Catholic missionary work ceased in
Zimbabwe for over a hundred years, until
1879 when Catholic priests once again entered the region.

The white missionaries
didn't believe that the
Shona people had any
comprehension of
religion.

This time they came north. Father
Prestage travelled from Grahamstown, South Africa. They journeyed five
or six months with four ox-drawn wagons until they arrived in Bulawayo.
It was a trip of nearly 1 600 kilometres to reach the interior. Disease
devastated their ranks.

Father Prestage was granted by King Lobengula the right to establish
a mission in Empandeni (south-west of Bulawayo) in 1887. The English
Jesuit Fathers and the Dominican Sisters from King William's Town in
South Africa returned, along with the 'Pioneer Column'. The Pioneer Col-
umn was a private mercenary military force that Cecil Rhodes' British
South Africa Company had raised to subdue the Shona and Ndebele
tribes. They also established the Chishawasha Mission in 1891, east of
Harare, and the Dominican Convent School in 1892 in Harare.

The white missionaries didn't believe that the Shona people had any
comprehension of religion. 'Among the Mashona (also known as Shona)
there are only very faint traces of religion,' observed Jesuit missionary,
Father Hartmann, in 1894. 'They have hardly any idea of a supreme being ...
the Mashonas are united as a commonwealth by nothing except the unity
of their language.'[3]

The Jesuit fathers at Chishawasha believed the Shona to be so far from
religious understanding that they thought it necessary to first instruct

206

them in natural 'religion' before broaching the great truths of Christianity. There wasn't much difference of opinion about the Shona people whether you were a settler or a missionary, as all the Europeans disliked them and held the whole tribe in contempt. A Bulawayo diarist summed up the general white attitudes of the time when he noted in June 1896: 'No one likes the Mashonas, dirty, cowardly lot, Matabele bloodthirsty devils but a fine type.'[4]

> *They believed their western 'Christian' culture to be far superior to anything in Africa and that it was God's ordained plan that they should rebuild the continent in their own image.*

As incredible as it sounds, the missionaries held the Shona in such low regard that Lord Grey wrote this from Chishawasha in January 1897: 'Father Biehler is so convinced of the hopelessness of regenerating the Mashonas, whom he regards as the most hopeless of mankind ... that he states that the only chance for the future of the race is to exterminate the whole people, both male and female, over the age of 14.'[5]

Unbelievably, this was not an attitude unique to the region or even the African continent. Wherever the British and Europeans settled to extend their imperialistic empires, a significant portion of the church leadership reinforced their right to take lands from the indigenous people and do whatever it took to subdue the local population. Across the centuries the cry was heard from Crusaders and missionaries alike: 'Convert or die by the sword.' They believed their western 'Christian' culture to be far superior to anything in Africa and that it was God's ordained plan that they should rebuild the continent in their own image.

The reason the missionaries didn't see the Shona as having a religion is that they never took the time to listen and learn. In their arrogance, they saw themselves as superior in every way and what little they might have gleaned from talking with the Shona as insignificant. As the white settlers took their lands and shoved their form of Christianity down their throats, the Shona, to the surprise of the Europeans, stood up and rebelled against it all.

What they failed to understand was that the Shona had been resisting this self-serving form of Christianity for hundreds of years as it was shamefully colonial and completely demeaning. For centuries the Portuguese power and ideas had been thrust on the eastern and central Shona peoples. Portuguese dominance had been successfully turned back by the military strength of the 'Razwi Confederation', an alliance of various tribes that banded together to fight the Portuguese. Their ideas had fared no better. A Jesuit historian, describing the fate of the Portuguese missionary effort amongst the Shona said, 'What was the result of these hundred years of devoted effort, almost nothing. It was one of the most complete failures of missionary history.'[6]

Their inept effort to convert the Ndebele should have led to some serious soul searching.

In three year's work prior to the establishment of the Roman Catholic mission at Chishawasha, they could record only two baptisms. A close acquaintance with the Shona confessed to a Jesuit missionary in 1897: 'It shows at all events that they have but little willingness to become Christians.' He put it down to 'their depraved habits and their low intelligence'.[7] By 1896 the Shonas' anger had reached the tipping point and they launched an armed attack upon the missions and their few converts as well as upon the white settlers.

The Shona were not the only tribe to incur the wrath and hatred of the church. While the Shona were despised, the Ndebele people were hated as they were seen as too self-sufficient, too arrogant and too brutal. The Ndebele didn't believe that they needed the military, political or economic systems the Europeans were offering. 'I abhor the Matabele,'[8] wrote the great game hunter Fredrick Selous in a letter to his mother. He was expressing the common feeling of almost all the hunters, traders and prospectors. This hatred was shared by the missionaries who had been working among the Ndebele for 30 years. They called it 'The Thirty Year Quarantine'. 'Their lack of success,' writes one historian of the missionaries, 'made them natural, if qualified, supporters of (Cecil John) Rhodes.'[9] Their inept effort to convert the Ndebele should have led to some serious soul-searching. Instead, their arrogance and self-righteousness prevented them from looking at their own lives as the possible source of failure.

In the mid-1850s, Robert Moffat, the famed Scottish missionary for the London Missionary Society, had ventured into Matabeleland for some time from his South African post. Moffat's oldest daughter Mary had married the famed medical missionary David Livingstone, in 1845. Robert Moffat, in his short time in Matabeleland, had developed a trusted relationship with King Lobengula.

In 1888 Cecil Rhodes convinced Moffat's son, John, to help him secure more concessions from King Lobengula by using his father's relationship with the King. Whether Moffat was aware of everything that transpired is unknown, but Rhodes' men dealt dishonestly with the King and it stained John Moffat's reputation among the Ndebele people. From the perspective of the Ndebele people, Moffat's Christianity was no different from Rhodes' Imperialistic ambitions. In their eyes God was taking away their land and they were being relegated to a subservient role in his Kingdom.

In their eyes God was taking away their land and they were being relegated to a subservient role in his Kingdom.

The missionaries had come to believe that Ndebele society presented no opportunities for development toward commerce and civilization, let alone Christianity. They saw the Ndebele as a people whose military system and caste tradition prevented the hope of their ever being brought, as a whole, into the circle of civilized nations. Thus they frankly welcomed the arrival of white power in Mashonaland. 'We are very thankful for the result,' wrote Elliot and Carnegie of the London Missionary Society's Matabeleland Mission, congratulating Rhodes on the successful occupation of Mashonaland. 'The hateful Matabele rule is doomed. We as missionaries, with our 30 years' history ... have little to bind our sympathies to the Matabele people, neither can we pity the fall of their power, but

The missionaries' refusal to integrate the Africans' cultural expression into their faith resulted in a religious form of faith instead of a more spiritual, heartfelt expression.

we earnestly rejoice in the deliverance of the Mashona.'[10]

For years, the missionaries had hoped that the Ndebele leadership would be overthrown by British military power. Their attitudes are recorded in a report by Captain Lendy of the British South Africa Company after a visit to Bulawayo. Lendy, in reporting his conversations with missionary David Carnegie in January 1893, said, 'It is amusing to hear the missionaries talk. Regular fire-brands, they admit that the sword alone will Christianize the natives.'[11]

Carnegie and his colleagues therefore supported the invasion of Matabeleland, which came later in 1893, and rejoiced in the overthrow and death of Lobengula. Lobengula's grave was never found and legend has it that he disappeared. The Ndebele believe he did not die, but just vanished. 'We expect great things,' wrote Carnegie, 'Now is the grand opportunity of Christianizing the Matabele.'[12]

Once the Ndebele had been defeated, the missionaries set out to transform the cultures of the two tribes. Along with the burgeoning new mission field of white settlers, the missionaries set up schools, training centres and churches across the region. Sadly, they kept everything segregated even though the two races lived side by side. They believed that this was 'the order of things'. They condemned the African custom of polygamy and this created tremendous pressure for women as they had no means of supporting themselves or their children. Africans were forbidden to partake in any of their social customs and were encouraged to move out of the villages and onto mission farms. This turned out to be a disaster as many Africans moved not because of a conversion, but because of the economic benefits of living there. The missionaries' refusal to integrate the Africans' cultural expression into their faith created a huge conflict that resulted in the Africans living a rather duplicitous lifestyle that bred a religious form of faith instead of a more spiritual, heartfelt expression.

As the Africans found themselves caught between their traditional culture and being converted to a western-style Christian culture, at times it simply became unpalatable. For all its virtues, western-style Christianity wasn't an African expression.

There is an Old Testament story that sheds some light on this situation. In I Samuel 17, the Philistines were waging war against Israel. Their champion was a giant named Goliath who challenged the Israelites to a fight every day, but no one would accept his challenge because they were all scared of him. One day a boy named David brought his brothers some food and overheard the soldiers talking about Goliath. David decided to accept the challenge and was subsequently rushed to King Saul. Saul saw that he was a just a boy and laughed out loud. Once he realized that David was serious, Saul decided to let him have a go at it. Since it was customary that a warrior wear all the correct battle gear, Saul began to adorn him with all his personal armour.

Then Saul dressed David in his own tunic. He put a coat of armour on him and a bronze helmet on his head. David fastened on his sword over the tunic and tried walking around, because he was not used to them. 'I cannot go in these,' he said to Saul, 'because I am not used to them.' So he took them off. Then he took his staff in his hand, chose five smooth stones from the stream, put them in the pouch of his shepherd's bag and, with his sling in his hand, approached the Philistine.

– 1 SAMUAL 17:38–40

This is exactly how many Africans felt trying to 'fit in' to the armour of western-style Christianity. Because racism had crept into the traditional church structures, many Africans departed from the mainline denominations and formed churches of their own with a uniquely African flavour. This movement has been labelled by historians as the African Initiated (or Independent) Churches (AIC). Because they tended to be poor and rural, there was very little written history. In recent years the church missiologists (researchers) have discovered that, contrary to the long held perceptions, it has actually been the impact of these AIC churches that has given rise to the rapid expansion of Christianity in Africa. While books were published by the European denominations praising their great successes, it was the Africans that were taking the message of the Gospel to the 'highways and byways' of rural Africa.

While books were published by the European denominations praising their great successes, it was the Africans that were taking the message of the Gospel to the 'highways and byways' of rural Africa.

Because African culture was by nature a very spiritual one, everyday life was seen as being affected by events and entities with a spiritual origin. Their expression of Christianity was far less focused on proper church structure and hierarchy and much more on the supernatural aspects of their faith. The AIC churches instinctively looked to the power of God to rescue them from the oppression of evil spirits and heal the sick. They saw life as a daily spiritual battle between the forces of good and evil. The Shona understood that there was Mwari (God) called Musika Vanhu (Creator of men) and that the way to get to him was through their dead ancestors.

The Shona prophet John of the Wilderness (Johane Masowe) in recounting his reasons for breaking away from the traditional churches, said:

When we were in these synagogues [churches] we used to read about the works of Jesus Christ ... cripples were made to walk and the dead were brought to life ... evil spirits driven out ... That was what was being done in Jerusalem. We Africans, however, who were being instructed by white people, never did anything like that ... We were taught to read the Bible, but we ourselves never did what the people of the Bible used to do.[13]

For many of the Africans, the expression of Christianity that they needed was one that was practical, tangible and made a difference in their everyday lives. The Africans were culturally a communal society as far back as they could recall. The extended family was relevant to their way of thinking. The European way of life and its form of Christianity was foreign and unnatural to them. They actually had more in common with their Christian brothers and sisters whose simple expression of faith for the first 300 years of Christianity was also more communal and without all the ecclesiastical baggage that was added over the subsequent years.

As with all institutional religion, the heart and compassion are relegated to a virtually nonexistent role, and the use of the Bible to justify one's personal ambitious goals becomes the sad expression of Christianity. As history has shown repeatedly, at this point the religious church climbs into bed with the secular government for a marriage of convenience. The church becomes the false prophet, proclaiming the government's divine right to do as it pleases and the government, in turn, finances and upholds the church's role as God's spokesman. In this insidious relationship the innocent end up becoming the oppressed poor as both the church and the government plunder them.

> *As with all institutional religion, the heart and compassion are relegated to a virtually nonexistent role, and the use of the Bible to justify one's personal ambitious goals becomes the sad expression of Christianity.*

It is through this reality that the Shona and Ndebele people developed a deep-seated distrust of the missionaries and any work that they attempted. Over the years, some Shona and Ndebele young men brought up on mission farms and educated in seminaries took leadership roles in the various denominations. By and large these appointments were over black-only congregations as whites had their own churches and leaders. This was an awkward arrangement and by the 1960s there was a deep divide within the various church institutions in Zimbabwe between the black ministers and white ministers. The white ministers refused to support the humanitarian efforts of both the ZAPU and ZANU parties while at the same time wanted funding for chaplains for the Rhodesian Security Forces. Instead of being a unifying force and preventing the country from sliding into civil war, the racial divisions within the church became part of the problem.

Instead of being a unifying force and preventing the country from sliding into civil war, the racial divisions within the church became part of the problem.

In the 1960s a significant event happened which would have consequences for Africa and in particular, Zimbabwe. Meeting in Rome in 1968 at the Roman Catholic Vatican II Council, church leaders took the issue of racism head on. The church realized that it had a deplorable racist history across the continent and that things needed to radically change if it was going to make any significant impact. The Vatican decided to accelerate the development of black African clergy and, within a decade, African Catholicism was dominated by Africans. In fact, the church sent Africans to minister around the world into a variety of cultures.

In the 1970s Rhodesia, the Catholic Church and the World Council of Churches challenged the white government on its blatantly racist policies. Many white priests and ministers wanted the *status quo* and remained sided with the white government. However, more and more white church leaders were being challenged by a crisis of faith. The issue of racial equality and justice was tearing at their consciences.

In November of 1971, a group of white priests, sisters and laity set up 'The Justice and Peace Commission'. By publishing a newspaper, they addressed the issues of social injustice in the country. As you can imagine, this infuriated the government leaders and three years later they banned the organization. Not to be deterred, the priests and sisters found a new outlet in the United Kingdom through the 'Catholic Institute for International Relations'. From there they reported more boldly on the struggle and the horrible treatment that the Africans received from the government. Their voice brought a lot of international attention which resulted in greater scrutiny of Ian Smith's government.

In 1978 the World Council of Churches gave $85 000 to the African nationalist movement under the auspices of helping them combat racism. This caused a lot of consternation across the Christian community as these Marxist revolutionary organizations had recently killed both Catholic and Pentecostal missionaries in the country. The church was being torn apart as again, the past was at war with the future.

> *The church was being torn apart as again, the past was at war with the future.*

In the midst of all this conflict, in 1980, a few ordinary people from Bulawayo decided that they couldn't stand by and let the country tear itself apart. If Jesus' teachings were true, then it was possible for former enemies to live in peace. God's power could transform a man's heart from hatred to love.

Luke records that Jesus proclaimed: 'Love the Lord your God with all your heart and with all your soul and with all your strength and with your entire mind; and, love your neighbour as yourself' (Luke 10:27). When He was finished, a legal expert asked Him 'Who then is my neighbour?' Jesus' answer is amazing and thought-provoking. He told the parable of 'The Good Samaritan' (Luke 10:27–37). What makes this scenario so incredible is that the Samaritans were despised by the Jews! It was very clear where Jesus stood on the issues of non-discrimination and interracial harmony.

The apostle Paul reinforced this years later when he wrote to the church in Galatia: 'So in Christ Jesus you are all children of God through faith, for all of you who were baptized into Christ have clothed yourselves with Christ. There is neither Jew nor Gentile, neither slave nor free, neither male nor female, for you are all one in Christ Jesus' (Gal 3:26–28). The people of the Community set out on a perilous journey to discover exactly how to live out that message daily with their African brothers and sisters.

CHAPTER 11 ENDNOTES

1. Southern African News; 'Role of Religion in Southern Africa' by Diana Mavunduse, Jan. 13th 1999.

2. Mugabe Accuses the Church Of Double Standards In Africa, By Lewis Machipisa, IPS, 8 December 1998.

3. Reports on the Administration of Rhodesia, 1892–4 p.82.

4, 5 Grey to Lady Grey, Jan. 23rd 1897, GR 1/1/1; diary of F.R. de Bartodano entry for June 21st 1896 BE3/2.

6, 7 W.F. Rea S.J., 'The Missionary Factor in Southern Rhodesia,' *Historical Association of Rhodesia and Nyasland*, Local series, 7, 1962.

8. Selous, to his mother April 30th 1890.

9. R. Brown, 'Aspects of the Scramble for Matabeleland' in *The Zambesian Past*, eds. E.T. Stokes and R. Brown, Manchester 1966.

10. Elliot and Carnegie to Rhodes, Dec. 2nd 1890, Rhodes House, Mss. Afr. s. 288, Vol. C. 3A.

11, 12 Lendy Report, Jan 25th 1893, LO 5/2/26; Carnegie, op cit.

13. 'A History of Christianity' Elizabeth Isichei, Erdmanns Publishing Company.

PART TWO:
THE ROAD AHEAD

'For tomorrow belongs to the people who prepare for it today.'
– AFRICAN PROVERB

CHAPTER 12

A NATION OF DESTINY

Our mouths were filled with laughter,
Our tongues with songs of joy,
Then it was said among the nations,
The LORD has done great things for them.

– PSALM 126:2

I n the next few chapters I'd like to gaze into the future and look at what Zimbabwe could become as a nation. I'd also like to offer a few suggestions for the road ahead to help her reach her God-ordained destiny. I need to say up front that I am not an expert on macro-economics nor trained in the skills to understand all the nuances of geopolitics. I will leave the nation building to those much more experienced than I.

Having said that, one thing that has become evident over my lifetime, and observed throughout human history, is how often the 'experts' get it wrong. I believe this is due to their gross misunderstanding and underestimation of the power of the human heart and its penchant for evil. After years of working with people and cultures, one thing I can say with confidence is that I do understand the human soul and its motivations. I know unequivocally that having the best education, experience and economic plan does not guarantee success. Unless those bricks

I know unequivocally that having the best education, experience and economic plan does not guarantee success.

are laid on the foundation of a humble and teachable heart, which has been rid of selfishness, they will fail every time.

For those of you reading this who may not be followers of the teachings of Jesus, nor have that spiritual paradigm, I am asking that you have an open mind about what I am trying to communicate. I have witnessed, over many decades, how our overconfidence in what we think we know has been repeatedly humbled. The history books record one failure after another by well-intentioned governments and international organizations trying to make the world a better place. Why is that? I believe that no matter how noble the cause, when the human heart has not been brought under control, corruption sweeps in like a flood, destroying our noblest of intentions.

Jesus knew the human heart better than anyone. He spent his short lifetime exposing its hidden motives and teaching mankind how to purify it. One day he said:

> 'Those who come to me and hear my words and put them into practice, I will show you what they are like. They are like a man building a house, who dug down deep and laid the foundation on rock. When a flood came, the torrent struck that house but could not shake it, because it was well built. But those who hear my words and do not put them into practice are like a man who built a house on the ground without a foundation. The moment the torrent struck that house, it collapsed and its destruction was complete.'
>
> – LUKE 6:47–49

With hindsight, history has borne witness that Jesus' words were in fact not only true, but equally wise. Those who refused to listen to his counsel (because He exposed their impure motives) found that in time all they had built was swept away just as he had warned. Their legacy lay in ruins and they became a footnote in history. Those who chose the road of humility changed the world and history granted them a place of honour.

There is very little that you could get former United States President

George W. Bush and current President Barack Obama to agree on. Yet one thing that they both have come to understand is that faith-based humanitarian initiatives are far more effective than government-run programmes. Why is that? Because those who run Christian faith-based relief organizations typically aren't motivated by the money but by compassion and principles built on integrity. They have a conviction that their cause is just and that God is on their side. They also see themselves as a hands-on extension of God's heart and values and therefore accountable to Him for everything they do.

Those who run Christian faith-based relief organizations typically aren't motivated by the money but by compassion and principles built on integrity.

The first President of the United States, George Washington, once said, 'It is impossible to rightly govern a nation without God and the Bible.' Washington understood that unless the human heart has been brought under the influence of a higher power, held to a higher standard, and ultimately is accountable to God, the wickedness hidden in our hearts would run wild. Power and money are two keys that can unlock the selfish beast within. Only the grace of God can subdue it or slay it.

For those of us who have watched from afar and who care deeply about the country of Zimbabwe and its people, it's been a long, painful and tragic story. Once again, history has repeated itself and the innocent and powerless are its victims. King Solomon, who was also a philosopher, lamented this sad state of affairs thousands of years before Zimbabwe's woes began:

'Again I looked and saw all the oppression that was taking place under the sun: I saw the tears of the oppressed – and they have no comforter; power was on the side of their oppressors – and they have no comforter.'

– ECCLESIASTES 4:1

Mankind's lust for power and wealth blinds him to the truth. We in the West set this terrible African tragedy in motion by our own arrogance and greed. We created the demeaning and oppressive environment that fuelled the anger that Robert Mugabe and many of his revolutionary friends fed on. Arrogance and greed are no respecters of skin colour. Sadly, now the liberators are the oppressors as they furiously fight to hang on to their power. They cannot fathom why the people of Zimbabwe want change, because they are delusional in their self-importance. They are blinded by their ideology, which has become their god. They are willing to sacrifice their own people to it and in their madness believe that the people should gladly embrace it for the good of the cause. What is so painfully clear to objective observers is that their ideology masks a deeper, more diabolical evil. Ideology is not the real issue, power is.

Washington understood that unless the human heart has been brought under the influence of a higher power, held to a higher standard, and ultimately is accountable to God, the wickedness hidden in our hearts would run wild.

The situation in Zimbabwe today is not altogether different from one in Israel 3 000 years ago. The historical record in 1 Samuel 8:4–17 states:

'All the elders of Israel gathered together and came to Samuel at Ramah. They said to him, "You are old, and your sons do not follow your ways; now appoint a king to lead us, such as all the other nations have." But when they said, "Give us a king to lead us," this displeased Samuel; so he prayed to the LORD. And the LORD told him: "Listen to all that the people are saying to you; it is not you they have rejected, but they have rejected me as their king. As they have done from the day I brought them up out of Egypt until this day, forsaking me and serving other gods, so they are doing to you. Now listen to them; but warn them solemnly and let them know what the king who will reign over them will claim as his rights." Samuel told all the words of the*

LORD to the people who were asking him for a king. He said, "This is what the king who will reign over you will claim as his rights: He will take your sons and make them serve with his chariots and horses, and they will run in front of his chariots. Some he will assign to be commanders of thousands and commanders of fifties, and others to plough his ground and reap his harvest, and still others to make weapons of war and equipment for his chariots. He will take your daughters to be perfumers and cooks and bakers. He will take the best of your fields and vineyards and olive groves and give them to his attendants. He will take a tenth of your grain and of your vintage and give it to his officials and attendants. Your male and female servants and the best of your cattle and donkeys he will take for his own use. He will take a tenth of your flocks, and you yourselves will become his slaves."'

This scenario has repeated itself all through Africa over the past 40 years. While African leaders were elected to the democratic office of President, they quickly disassembled governments run by the will of the people, to governments ruled by kings and tribal chiefs. Few stood in their way, and in most cases the people supported them as they too wanted a king. Just as Samuel had predicted thousands of years ago, the kings turned their people into poor slaves. Saul was first chosen as king, then David, then his son Solomon. Two generations after Saul, Solomon wrote, 'A ruler who oppresses the poor is like a driving rain that leaves no crops' (Prov 28:3).

> *Arrogance and greed are no respecters of skin colour. Sadly, now the liberators are the oppressors as they furiously fight to hang on to their power.*

The people of Zimbabwe understand the realities of this type of oppression all too well. They cry out daily to God for deliverance as they watch their country deteriorate into chaos due to corrupt mismanagement. All across the land they have seen the fruit of this madness, and they desire radical change. They have come to see that their leaders care about only one thing, and that is themselves.

While it's true that the nation is in its darkest hour, I sincerely believe that there is hope. I believe that God's heart breaks over Zimbabwe and the plight of its inhabitants. Everything inside Him wants to bring redemption to the people as it's his nature and it's his land.

I believe that God's heart breaks over Zimbabwe and the plight of its inhabitants.

'Because the poor are plundered and the needy groan, I will now arise,' says the LORD. 'I will protect them from those who malign them' (Ps 12:5). God's heart is motivated by justice and He is ready to fight on behalf of any people who truly want Him and are willing to walk in his ways. God looks at the heart and if what He sees there has a pure motive, He will move heaven and earth for them. Deliverance and redemption are not new to Him; in fact He has shown these powerful aspects of Himself to mankind all through history.

The Israelites in Egypt were in circumstances not altogether different from the people of Zimbabwe today. Listen to their testimony:

'But the Egyptians mistreated us and made us suffer, subjecting us to harsh labour. Then we cried out to the LORD, the God of our ancestors, and the LORD heard our voice and saw our misery, toil and oppression. So the LORD brought us out of Egypt with a mighty hand and an outstretched arm, with great terror and with signs and wonders. He brought us to this place and gave us this land, a land flowing with milk and honey.'

– DEUTERONOMY 26:6-9

For years it has been my conviction that God has a unique destiny for the people of Zimbabwe. In a manner of speaking, when they got the deliverance they badly wanted 30 years ago, they made a horrible mistake and chose a false god/king. They have had to live with this choice for a generation. That god has consumed all their land, their food and their children and left them poor and barren. Many have come to see that they were deceived, but the question of the moment is, are they willing, as a nation, to humble themselves before God? Are they willing to pursue a new course and build a nation on the values of the Kingdom of Heaven? If so, they have a promise from God:

> *'If my people, who are called by my name, will humble themselves and pray and seek my face and turn from their wicked ways, then I will hear from heaven, and I will forgive their sin and will heal their land.'*
>
> – 2 CHRONICLES 7:14

Zimbabwe is standing at the crossroads of destiny; the choices her people make now will determine their fate for another generation or more. Their choices are not, as Mr Mugabe states, between black independence and white imperialism. Their choices are between those values that Jesus taught which establish the Kingdom of God in the heart of men, and the values that rule this world: pride, greed, jealousy and selfish ambition. One brings peace and prosperity; the other brings death and destruction.

Zimbabwe is standing at the crossroads of destiny; the choices her people make now will determine their fate for another generation or more.

At first glance it would seem ludicrous to try to tackle a subject so fraught with political, racial and religious sensitivities, and I am sure some of you are wondering if I have lost my mind. I assure you that I am keenly aware of the extremely volatile nature of this topic and the rawness of emotions that I am trying to navigate through. I have absolutely no desire to rub salt into old wounds. It is my heart's desire to bring healing, restoration and fullness of joy. Frankly, I can't help but pour my heart out in the words of this book; it's what is in my soul. I love the Zimbabwean people, the nation and the continent of Africa.

One thing that actually has given me the confidence to write so transparently on this sensitive topic, is that when I look into my own heart I know I am not a racist. In fact it's quite the opposite; I believe that there is strength in diversity. At times I wish that I had become a sociologist. I believe that all cultures must be celebrated as they reflect the many-faceted aspects of God's personality. When I look across the table at my many African friends, I see men and women who want the very same things I do. They want health, security and the opportunity to provide for their families. They want to live in peace and grow old with their children and grandchildren. While we look quite different on the outside, on the inside we are identical.

I am convinced that the principle of 'diversity in harmony' is one of the most powerful foundation stones that the Kingdom of God is built on.

I am convinced that the principle of 'diversity in harmony' is one of the most powerful foundation stones that the Kingdom of God is built on. For that matter, I also believe that it's the key to peace in any nation. First century church planter Paul wrote to the Christian community in Colossae exhorting them to:

'Put on the new self, which is being renewed in knowledge in the image of its Creator. Here there is no Gentile or Jew, circumcised or uncircumcised, barbarian, Scythian, slave or free, but Christ is all, and is in all. Therefore, as God's chosen people, holy and dearly loved, clothe yourselves with compassion, kindness, humility, gentleness and patience. Bear with each other and forgive one another if any of you has a grievance against someone. Forgive as the Lord forgave you. And over all these virtues put on love, which binds them all together in perfect unity.'

– COLOSSIANS 3:10–14

Paul understood the power of diversity in harmony. The early church was built on it. This simple but profound truth was at the root of why a group of people with no money, organization or political power could turn the world upside down within a few hundred years. All hell seemed to be threatened by this powerful expression of unity, because everywhere it sprung up, someone tried to kill it. As we discussed in Chapter 9, 'The blood of the martyrs is the seed of the Church.' Unity is a powerful force. Gandhi overthrew an established world power with great military might and never fired a shot. Martin Luther King forced a nation to deal with its racism to change course, and he too never resorted to violence. They brought about national change by understanding the power of unity.

So to ensure that you fully understand where I'm coming from; I do not represent any government, political party or religious denomination. I do not want or need anything from Zimbabwe. I have no desire to gain wealth from her resources. My heart is only motivated by a love for her people and the God they want to serve. If I represent anything, it would be the values of the Kingdom of God through Jesus Christ. I believe in the truth that it is built upon and the myriad of people who have died laying their lives down to see it established.

My friends who died at The Community of Reconciliation believed in the destiny of Zimbabwe. They put their lives on the line for it. Whether black or white, I'm asking you, the people of Zimbabwe, not to let my friends' blood have been shed in vain. They believed in you and the destiny that God has for you.

Like they did, I believe with all my heart that Africa, and Zimbabwe in particular, can blossom like a rose and that her best days lie ahead. It is my hope that you will give me the benefit of the doubt as far as my motivation is concerned. I believe that God has a divine plan for Zimbabwe that she must discover for herself. I want to see her find it and prosper under the grace of God. To realize this destiny will not be easy, but it is attainable. In order for her to do so, all of us who love her must be willing to take the journey

I believe with all my heart that Africa, and Zimbabwe in particular, can blossom like a rose and that her best days lie ahead.

together down the pathway of truth, no matter where it leads. We know from Jesus' teachings that it is the truth alone that can set her free. We need understanding. As King Solomon exhorted us,

> '... *turning your ear to wisdom and applying your heart to under-standing, and if you call out for insight and cry aloud for understanding, and if you look for it as for silver and search for it as for hidden treasure, then you will understand the fear of the* LORD *and find the knowledge of God. For the* LORD *gives wisdom, and from his mouth come knowledge and understanding.'*
>
> – PROVERBS 2:2–6

If we are to turn Zimbabwe around and align her on the path of divine destiny, we must, together, ask probing questions without fear of what we may discover. We must humble ourselves before heaven and each other. We must be more concerned with 'what' is right than 'who' is right. We must check our egos at the door and be less concerned with what we get out of this journey and more concerned with what the people and God get out of this. This is the attitude of heart that God is looking for. This is humility. The men or women who can embrace this pureness of heart will see the Kingdom of God on earth in Zimbabwe. As Jesus said, 'Blessed are the meek, for they will inherit the earth' (Matt 5:5).

We will never find the correct answers if we are unwilling to ask the right questions. It has been my experience that often fear keeps most of us from closely examining things. To step out of the shadows and into the light can be a frightening experience. We could be exposed to a new perspective that forces us to make difficult decisions. We may have to shift our paradigm, which often results in us changing our attitudes and perceptions of others. This can initially be a difficult transition, but in time it produces great joy as there is freedom and power in the truth. There are many who wonder if Zimbabwe can ever be saved. How can a country with such a violent history and in such economic ruin ever find peace? Can she ever heal from her many deep wounds inflicted over the generations?

I believe that Africa and Zimbabwe have a destiny and that its lands have been the battleground for an intense spiritual struggle that has played itself out in the lives of her people. I do believe that Zimbabwe can be saved. The real question is: *Will* Zimbabwe be saved? I believe the answer falls squarely on the shoulders of the country's leadership. Are they tired of seeing failure and do they want to transform the country's present state? Is the current political leadership willing to let go of the past, look forward and think in terms of what is best for the nation over what is best for them personally? Will the Church leadership rise up and fulfil its God-ordained role and guide the nation toward the destiny that God has for it? Is it willing to stand and speak for God and God alone?

> *We will never find the correct answers if we are unwilling to ask the right questions.*

I know that there are many international governmental organizations doing their best to try and bring a lasting peace. Their relief efforts are keeping people alive and avoiding a catastrophe of enormous magnitude. I appreciate all that the United Nations is trying to do for Zimbabwe, but I do not believe that it can ultimately save her. I am grateful for the efforts of the World Bank, but I do not believe that it can save Zimbabwe either. In fact, each one of these organizations suffers from the same malady that has infected Zimbabwe's leadership … corruption.

> *I do believe that Zimbabwe can be saved. The real question is: Will Zimbabwe be saved?*

No matter how well-intentioned their vision is, or how sound their investment plans are, when men with corrupt hearts are given access to enormous resources they can't control their urges. What's hidden inside always comes to the surface!

For Zimbabwe to be truly and tangibly saved and change course, the

God of Heaven is going to have to transform the hearts of her leaders first, and from there, the hearts of her people. I believe that it is God's desire for the Christian community in Zimbabwe to play a significant role in this, but only after putting its own duplicitous house in order. The church leadership has to stop speaking on behalf of political parties and start speaking on behalf of God. God is not for hire to the highest bidder, nor does He care about party affiliation. Zimbabwe's primary problem is not political, economic or racial; it is spiritual. It is her heart and what motivates her that first needs to change. This is the role of the Christian community; to be the moral compass for the nation.

True change starts from within. If external behaviour changes without a true change of heart, it quickly becomes religion or institutional Christianity. It cannot last, or even worse, it will turn into legalism, which is all about law enforcement. In fact, it is this very type of religion that Jesus was in conflict with during his whole earthly ministry. He understood that its fruit or ultimate goal was to enslave or control people. He knew that, in the end, it would only produce death and destruction, and history has borne this out. Political leaders have used religion as a justification for conquest and, in the name of God, have killed millions. The last thing Zimbabwe needs is more religion. It needs a changed heart produced by an impartation of the Spirit of God.

This being the case, one has to ask a very hard question. What originally came to Zimbabwe: Oppressive religion or life-giving spirituality? I think that its fruit speaks for itself. The religion that came and enslaved people was in direct opposition to everything Jesus was about. Jesus was about Life. Is the Zimbabwean Church about life?

> *Zimbabwe's primary problem is not political, economic or racial; it is spiritual.*

I would like to share a very simple but profound saying that is filled with truth. It is the key to unlocking Zimbabwe's destiny and changing her present course. I hope that you will take some time to ponder this statement:

'TRANSFORMATION OF THE SOUL IS THE SOUL OF TRANSFORMATION.'

The key to Zimbabwe's outward transformation starts with her people's souls first being transformed inwardly. I have read volumes of material by the leading experts of our generation. They all agree that Africa and Zimbabwe have all the land, water and mineral resources she needs to be prosperous. In fact, she has so much natural resource that she can feed her own people and have enough left over to export to other nations.

Based on all the scientific and statistical data, there should not be a starving person on the continent, and yet it is the poorest region on the globe. Fifty percent of her children will not reach their fifth birthday. Her adult population is being ravaged by HIV/AIDS. It is wiping out a whole generation, leaving only grandparents and children as the future hope. Then, if it's not disease killing people, they are killing each other in armed conflicts and acts of genocide. This demands that we ask another hard question. Why? Why, if there is so much potential in Africa, has it not been realized? Why, if she is rich, does she live in such poverty?

The last thing Zimbabwe needs is more religion. It needs a changed heart produced by an impartation of the Spirit of God.

Africa is a continent that has been a slave to the spirit of death and destruction for hundreds of years. Its fires have been fuelled by racism, anger, hatred, jealousy, arrogance and corruption. It seems as though hell itself has loosed untold legions of demonic warriors to besiege this land. Their sole purpose is to destroy her and her people. Why? Why are they so focused on this continent? Could it be that they are scared of her true potential? What destiny might God have for her that all hell is so determined to kill her before she reaches adulthood?

This same tactic was used nearly 2 000 years ago when hell whispered into the ear of King Herod and suggested that he kill all the boy children in the area, thereby wiping out any threat to his throne and the mysterious

Messiah who had just been born (Matt 2:16–18). Destroying things in their infancy has long been a strategy used by the Kingdom of Darkness to thwart God's plans.

Jesus, in preparing his students to go into the world and share his life-giving wisdom, warned them about the heart of humanity and how potentially deceitful it can be when influenced by evil. He also encouraged them that, conversely, when the heart is influenced by good, it is wonderfully truthful and liberating. He wanted to prepare them to tell the difference between what is good and what is evil; between his Kingdom of Heaven and the Kingdom of Darkness. He said to them:

'Watch out for false prophets. They come to you in sheep's clothing, but inwardly they are ferocious wolves. By their fruit you will recognize them. Do people pick grapes from thorn bushes, or figs from thistles? Likewise, every good tree bears good fruit, but a bad tree bears bad fruit. A good tree cannot bear bad fruit, and a bad tree cannot bear good fruit. Every tree that does not bear good fruit is cut down and thrown into the fire. Thus, by their fruit you will recognize them.'

– MATTHEW 7:15–20

Jesus made it very clear that talk is cheap and costs men little. People can be frivolous with words. Men will stand before large crowds and blatantly and unashamedly tell lies and misrepresent the facts for their own gain. They are false prophets, false proclaimers and false leaders. They will deceive and lead people to their own destruction because they are motivated by their own selfish desires and hidden agendas.

Jesus warned his students not to listen exclusively to men's words but to look at the 'fruit' or the results of their life's work. In other words, look at their walk, not just their talk, and from what they do you will know if they are good or evil. To discern a man's fruit is the responsibility of all those who consider themselves followers of Jesus. Even more so, it is the responsibility of those in Christian leadership. But, He warns them too that they must make sure their own hearts are clean. They must not fall into the trap of the religious leaders of Jesus' day, of whom Jesus said, 'Woe to you, teachers of the law and Pharisees, you hypocrites! You clean the outside of the cup and dish, but inside they are full of greed and self-indulgence' (Matt 23:25).

Years later, Jesus' most accomplished student, Paul, in writing to a group of followers in the city of Galatia, defined in more detail what the fruit of these men with evil hearts would look like so that there could be no confusion:

> 'The acts of the sinful nature are obvious: sexual immorality, impurity and debauchery; idolatry and witchcraft; hatred, discord, jealousy, fits of rage, selfish ambition, dissensions, factions and envy; drunkenness, orgies, and the like.'
>
> – GALATIANS 5:19–21

He went on to describe the fruit, or characteristics, that a man with a good heart would have. 'But the fruit of the Spirit is love, joy, peace, patience, kindness, goodness, faithfulness, gentleness and self-control' (Gal 5:22–23).

We need to ask ourselves a hard and direct question. Which of these two groups of fruits describes Zimbabwe's secular and sacred leaders today? One only has to look at the fruit to see clearly whether they are good or evil. Paul, writing to a group of followers in the city of Ephesus, said:

> 'For you were once darkness, but now you are light in the Lord. Live as children of light (for the fruit of the light consists in all goodness, righteousness and truth) and find out what pleases the Lord. Have nothing to do with the fruitless deeds of darkness, but rather expose them.'
>
> – EPHESIANS 5: 8–11

I love the phrase 'children of light'. I think it would be a great name for a school. Can the church in Zimbabwe honestly declare before God that they have been and are children of light? Is this the fruit or testimony of their individual and community life? Do they have a daily expression of their faith that is genuine and tangible, or is it merely empty words? What expression of Christianity in the country has people's attention and respect? Where do the people see the light? Are they moving toward anything?

Has the Zimbabwean church led the way to goodness, righteousness and truth? Has it exposed the 'deeds of darkness'? Have they boldly declared God's way and lifted the light of truth so high into the darkness that the people of Zimbabwe know there is hope? Like the pillar of fire that led the children of Israel out of the desert to the Promised Land, has the leadership of the Zimbabwean church become such a significant light that they are leading the country to their Promised Land?

Jesus characterized or defined His own earthly ministry by service to the poor, the outcasts, and the downtrodden, thereby establishing justice. Early in his public ministry, Jesus entered the synagogue in his home town and in front of his family and friends, quoted from the prophet Isaiah to describe and declare his ministry:

> 'The Spirit of the Lord is upon me, because he has anointed me to bring good news to the poor. He has sent me to proclaim release to the captives and recovery of sight to the blind, to let the oppressed go free, to proclaim the year of the Lord's favour.'
>
> – Luke 4:18–19

Is this the ministry of the African church today? Has it led the people out of darkness and into the light? Has it exposed the darkness for what it is – evil? Has it held its leaders accountable? Are the oppressed really free or have they just become enslaved again by another master?

James, another student of Jesus, wrote years later that, 'the wisdom that comes from heaven is first of all pure; then peace-loving, considerate, submissive, full of mercy and good fruit, impartial and sincere. Peacemakers who sow in peace reap a harvest of righteousness' (Jas 3:17–18). James beautifully expands on Paul's list of the characteristics of 'good fruit' that clearly lays out for us a road map to Heaven on Earth. The continent of Africa, which historians have too often called the 'dark continent', can be transformed into the 'continent of light'. So too can Zimbabwe. In order for it to happen, the Christian community must bring forth a transformation of the heart in her people and her leadership so that God can work a transformation of her lands.

My heart longs for God to say of Zimbabwe what He spoke over Jerusalem in the coming millennial Kingdom:

'I will rejoice over Jerusalem [Zimbabwe] and take delight in my people; the sound of weeping and of crying will be heard in it no more. Never again will there be in it infants who live but a few days, or older people who do not live out their years; those who die at a hundred will be thought mere youths; those who fail to reach a hundred will be considered accursed.

They will build houses and dwell in them; they will plant vineyards and eat their fruit. No longer will they build houses and others live in them, or plant and others eat. For as the days of a tree, so will be the days of my people; my chosen ones will long enjoy the work of their hands. They will not labour in vain, nor will they bear children doomed to misfortune; for they will be a people blessed by the LORD, they and their descendants with them.

Before they call I will answer; while they are still speaking I will hear. The wolf and the lamb will feed together, and the lion will eat straw like the ox, but dust will be the serpent's food. They will neither harm nor destroy on all My holy mountain,' says the LORD.

– ISAIAH 65:19–25 (AUTHOR'S INCLUSION)

Chapter 13

Transformation

'We can easily forgive a child who is afraid of the dark.
The real tragedy of life is when men
are afraid of the light.'

– Plato

As we move forward on this road we must ask ourselves another difficult and probing question. How and where does this process of transforming the heart of Zimbabwe start, and where does it need to go? I humbly
submit to you my perspective on the issue. The following are key points that
hopefully will stimulate thinking and discussion and ultimately result in
action which bears good fruit.

Transformation of
the Church Leadership

It is my opinion that transformation must start first with the Christian
community and its leadership. We need to get our house in order first
before we ask others to join us. The history of the Church in Zimbabwe
is a tragic one. We Europeans and Americans have had a significant role
in laying a tragically flawed foundation on which the current Zimbabwean church now stands. For this I am truly sorry and feel a deep sense of
sadness and disappointment. We should have done better. This damaged
foundation must be repaired at all cost, and soon, or Zimbabwe will never

see the transformation she so desperately needs. No matter how much work is done, no matter how many people come to build, without a solid foundation their efforts will not last and the church will again crumble under outside pressure.

As we have discussed earlier, when we (Europeans and Americans) began our foray into Africa to evangelize its many people, we did it not as spokesmen for God alone, but often as spokesmen for the imperialist nations that we originated from, or those that sponsored us. We mixed our 'Good News' message with a political message so that not only was our God superior, but also our political system and way of life.

We completely dismissed and devalued the people and the cultures of Africa as irrelevant and, in worst case scenarios, as downright wrong. The effect was a long-lasting and deep-seated resentment among the Africans that hardened many of their hearts against our message. The more they resisted, the harder we pushed, to the point that missionaries were encouraging military force to subdue the heathen by the gun. Our 'convert or die by the sword' mentality was driven by institutional religion and not by the Spirit of Life.

The Church failed miserably. Many missionaries became nothing more than spokesmen for imperialistic governments that participated in unscrupulous business dealings with tribal leaders. They prospered financially with land grants from the governments they served, and operated under their protection. This marriage of convenience had deadly long-term consequences in that not only did it set a precedent that the black African church leaders later followed, but it also created the same anger and resentment within the African church community as it did in the political community.

In the 1950s and 60s when the black African people had finally had enough of being looked down upon, they fought back violently, fuelled by the rage that had been building over many years of oppression. All across Africa, freedom fighters and revolutionaries rallied men to fight back against the oppression that they had suffered over the past few hundred years. Bit by bit, Europe's colonial territorial possessions were reclaimed by the Africans and reformatted back into African nations with African names.

As did their white predecessors before them, many of the leaders of the black African church sided with the political ideologies of these revolutionaries and became their spokesmen. Liberation theology (which emphasized the Christian mission to bring justice to the poor and oppressed, particularly through political activism from a socialist perspective) became the philosophy of the day. Bolstered by the church leaders, these freedom fighters used the name of God to justify their conflicts and their methodologies while the church leaders looked the other way.

In the same way that the hypocrisy of the white missionaries was eventually exposed, the duplicity of the black church leadership has come to light. Further complicating the situation today, religious leaders have taken sides in the conflict between political parties. Now we have church leaders holding prayer meetings asking God to judge, and in some cases, kill their brothers in the 'other party'. I'm sorry, but this is wrong – very wrong! Thousands of years ago as the Israelites were preparing for battle against Jericho, God appeared to Joshua:

'*Now when Joshua was near Jericho, he looked up and saw a man standing in front of him with a drawn sword in his hand. Joshua went up to him and asked, "Are you for us or for our enemies?" "Neither,"* *he replied, "but as commander of the army of the* Lord *I have now come." Then Joshua fell face down to the ground in reverence ...*'

– Joshua 5:13–14

Zimbabwe's church leaders need to take the posture of Joshua and hit the ground on their knees in reverence to God. Being forced to choose a political side by church leaders has created a terrible dilemma for the innocent people of Zimbabwe as they do not know who they can trust since 'all have sinned and fallen short'. The Zimbabwean church needs to focus its energy on its higher calling, which is to transform the hearts of the nation's people. The nation needs a spiritual awakening to turn its heart back to God. I suspect that as long as our enemy can keep the church leadership preoccupied down in the trenches with politics, he will keep them from the true power to bring change. The church leadership needs to wake up and realize that it is being led astray. The real power is not in politics but in the Spirit of God.

Jesus had great compassion for the poor and innocent of his day. It's interesting to note that He was often more inclined to defend the poor from the oppressive religious leaders of his day than from the oppressive civil authority of Rome. He believed that the religious leaders were more to blame because they were supposed to be the spiritually enlightened ones. Instead of 'setting the poor captive free', they further enslaved them by religion. Then to make matters worse, we later discover that while the religious leaders publicly proclaimed their loyalty to God first, they were secretly in bed with the Romans. Jesus had finally had enough of their hypocrisy and one day let them have it:

> 'Woe to you, teachers of the law and Pharisees, you hypocrites! You give a tenth of your spices – mint, dill and cumin. But you have neglected the more important matters of the law – justice, mercy and faithfulness. You should have practised the latter, without neglecting the former. You blind guides! You strain out a gnat but swallow a camel. Woe to you, teachers of the law and Pharisees, you hypocrites! You clean the outside of the cup and dish, but inside they are full of greed and self-indulgence. Blind Pharisee! First clean the inside of the cup and dish, and then the outside also will be clean.'
>
> – Matthew 23:23–26

I submit to you that if Zimbabwe is ever to be transformed, the church leadership across all colour spectrums must repent and humble themselves before God and cry out for his mercy and grace. The heart of Zimbabwe must be transformed, but it has to start with her church leaders. They have to disavow their earthly political loyalties and renew their commitment and loyalty to the Kingdom of God first and foremost. They must cry out for God to purify their hearts so that they can lead, based on the principles and values of God's Kingdom and by his Spirit alone. There should be no more religious leaders living like kings while their people live in poverty.

From my perspective, we in the West have set before the world a horrible example as to the way a pastor or church leader should live. I cannot find a single example in the New Testament of Jesus or his disciples living like kings! Neither do I see Paul or any of those who worked side-by-side with him living like kings. In fact, the foundation of the church was built on those who lived as though their 'treasure was in heaven' (Matt 6:19–24).

Just as Jesus did at the Last Supper, the church leadership needs to be washing the feet of its people, not the other way around (John 13:1–17). Leadership is about serving and losing one's life, not gaining power and wealth. The people must see church leaders emerge who can be trusted because they know that their hearts are governed by integrity and truth and that they are beholden to no one other than their Lord and Master Jesus Christ.

The Gospel writer Matthew records a story that gives us great insight as to Jesus' perspective on how He viewed leadership in his Kingdom:

> 'Then the mother of Zebedee's sons came to Jesus with her sons and, kneeling down, asked a favour of him. "What is it you want?" he asked. She said, "Grant that one of these two sons of mine may sit at your right and the other at your left in your kingdom." "You don't know what you are asking," Jesus said to them. "Can you drink the cup I am going to drink?" "We can," they answered. Jesus said to them, "You will indeed drink from my cup, but to sit at my right or left is not for me to grant. These places belong to those for whom they have been prepared by my Father." When the ten heard about this, they were indignant with the two brothers. Jesus called them together and said, "You know that the rulers of the Gentiles lord it over them, and their high officials exercise authority over them. Not so with you. Instead,

whoever wants to become great among you must be your servant, and
whoever wants to be first must be your slave – just as the Son of Man
did not come to be served, but to serve, and to give his life as a ransom
for many."'

– MATTHEW 20:20–28

Later when Paul was addressing the Christian community in Philippi he
reiterated Jesus' philosophy on leadership when he said,

'Do nothing out of selfish ambition or vain conceit. Rather, in humil-
ity value others above yourselves, not looking to your own interests
but each of you to the interests of the others. In your relationships
with one another, have the same attitude of mind Christ Jesus had:
Who, being in very nature God, did not consider equality with God
something to be used to his own advantage; rather, he made himself
nothing by taking the very nature of a servant.'

– PHILIPPIANS 2:3–7

When the Son of God can remove his robes and bind himself with the
loincloth of a humble servant and then get on his knees to wash the feet
of his brothers, how much more should today's church leadership be doing the same thing. If one sees a church leader living like a king, then
that is exactly what he is, and not a true servant of God. In reality, he has
hijacked the true purpose of church and made it all about him and not
the Kingdom of God. Remember, we must evaluate the true motives of
the heart by the fruit that is born. The true spiritual leader is a servant
before all else and his humility of heart will be evident to all.

An old colleague once told me, after a death experience he had, that
when we stand before God, the first thing He will look at is how much
of the image of his dear son Jesus we bear. I ask the church leaders of
Zimbabwe, when the people see you do they see Jesus? Are you their light
shining in the darkness? Are you the moral and ethical voice in the nation? When you speak do they believe that you speak for God because

you have a life that has produced good fruit? Zimbabwe needs transformed church leadership.

TRANSFORMATION OF THE
POLITICAL LEADERSHIP

I realize that I am treading on very dangerous ground here, but as a servant of the Kingdom of God I am under an obligation to speak the truth in love. My observations are not based on any personal, arbitrary or flippant standards but on the specific teachings of Jesus that have historically been shown to be wise. As I have written earlier, there are some very distinct guidelines given us for discerning whether something is good or evil. Again it has nothing to do with words and everything to do with the fruit of one's life.

Given that this is the plumb-line that I suggest we all use, I believe it is only fair to say that Zimbabwe's past and current political leadership has been lacking, and in most cases, severely lacking. This evaluation is not limited to just white European leaders but black African leaders as well. The blame for this is shared with the church leaders who in many cases have not spoken up and made sure that Africa's political leaders have feared or respected God's ways. Zimbabwe's political leadership will be held accountable to God. One day soon they will have to answer for their actions. I believe that God will have plenty to say and do to those who oppress the poor. As we will discuss soon, He has great energy when it comes to injustice. While it may appear that these leaders are in control, ultimately God is in control and in a moment's time He can bring them down. The great Middle Eastern King David understood this and warned political leaders to remember,

> Therefore, you kings, be wise; be warned, you rulers of the earth. Serve the LORD with fear and rejoice with trembling. Kiss the Son, lest he be angry and you be destroyed in your way, for his wrath can flare up in a moment. Blessed are all who take refuge in him.
> – PSALM 2:10–12

When the learned men of the world all agree that Africa has all the natural resources to not just sustain itself, but also prosper, it causes us to ask the question: Why then so much poverty and suffering? Africa can in fact feed itself; it has half the population of India which is self-sufficient when it comes to food on one-twelfth of the land area. Wise King Solomon gave us a very concise answer to that question in his writings on the subject of wisdom, 'When the righteous thrive, the people rejoice; when the wicked rule, the people groan' (Prov 29:2). He also stated, 'By justice a king gives a country stability, but those who are greedy for bribes tear it down' (Prov 29:4).

While Africa's leaders have proclaimed 'freedom for all', it has, in reality, only been 'freedom for some'.

While poverty may be a problem affecting the masses of humanity in Africa and Zimbabwe, its people are really starving because of the corruption of their political leaders. Corruption is the evil in men's hearts and poverty is its bad fruit. What is so painfully sad for the Zimbabwean people is that the very leadership that led them out of the tyranny of one system has enslaved them under another.

The Nobel Prize-winning economist Amartya Sen of Trinity College in Cambridge, England has famously argued that no functioning democracy has ever suffered a famine, because democratic governments 'have to win elections and face public criticism, and have strong incentive to undertake measures to avert famines and other catastrophes.'[1] While Africa's leaders have proclaimed 'freedom for all', it has, in reality, only been 'freedom for some'. That 'some' has been the elite few who have been corrupted by the trappings of power and have no fear of God, and who plunder and steal from the people for their own personal wealth.

The funds that should be going to build infrastructure and develop agriculture to help feed the people are going into the lavish lifestyles of the elite few. They are starving their own people while deceitfully lying to them about all that they are doing on their behalf. This is not unique to Zimbabwe; it was the same scenario the world discovered when the Iron Curtain fell in 1989. Socialist leaders were exposed as not truly burdened for the welfare of their people but only interested in their own prosperity.

Zimbabwe needs a political leadership whose hearts have been transformed from an 'it's all about me' attitude, to one that believes they are servants of both God and the people. Zimbabwe needs leaders who understand that principles like integrity, justice, compassion and selflessness are what lasting governments are built on. Zimbabwe needs leaders with a vision for a new future; one based on transforming it and setting into motion a new course that will allow her, as a nation, to realize her divine destiny.

The nations of the earth would then line up to help a truly righteous ruler who could be trusted. What Africa needs is men like Jesus, Gandhi and Mandela who never took, made nor accumulated personal wealth as leaders. The people loved them because they knew that they could be trusted. They were men who carried themselves in humility and therefore they had great power. They were men who considered others before themselves and were greatly loved for it. They were men of principle and conviction and thus had great influence. God cannot help but smile on a man like that and grant him favour. He would open up the storehouses of heaven and rain peace and prosperity on the land.

> *What is so painfully sad for the Zimbabwean people is that the very leadership that led them out of the tyranny of one system has enslaved them under another.*

TRANSFORMATION THROUGH FORGIVENESS

When we cannot find forgiveness for others, it keeps us hostage to our past. It creates a bitterness and anger in our soul that festers like an infected wound. If we are honest about the situation in Zimbabwe, we have all sinned against each other and, more importantly, against God. There is no one in Zimbabwe with clean hands or without blame in this long and tragic story.

The next question we need to ask is how long do we all want to live in this state of not forgiving each other? How long do we want to be slaves to the sins of our fathers and our foolish pride? If we are ever to see Zimbabwe transform and fulfil her destiny, we must forgive others and look to the future with hope in the grace of God. We must let go of the shameful attitudes and actions of the past. We must forgive the wrongs done to us and love those that hurt us. This is never more poignant than in the case of those of us who have lost dear friends due to hatred and racism. I have often wondered how I would respond if I had to face those who killed my friends. Unless I have something hidden in my heart that I am unaware of, I believe that I could embrace them, for I have forgiven them.

When we cannot find forgiveness for others, it keeps us hostage to our past.

It would be easy to say the issue of forgiveness is strictly limited to blacks and whites, but that would be disingenuous. Again, if we are to be truthful at all costs, the peoples of Africa have their own forgiving to do among each other. Slavery, oppression and genocide have not been restricted to Europeans and Americans only. Black Africa must face her own internal past, whether it's the Tutsi and Hutu tribes of Rwanda, the Kikuyu and Luo tribes of Kenya or the Shona and Ndebele tribes of Zimbabwe. They have not lived in peace with each other, nor have they treated each other with honour and respect. They have sinned against their own brothers. Racism, slavery and genocide are not skin colour issues, they are the issues of a heart that needs transformation.

Again I ask the question, where is the Church? Where is the Christian community in leading the way to forgiveness and the fruit of forgiveness, reconciliation?

In August of 2007, Arab Pastor Anis Barhoum invited Jewish Pastor Avi Mizrachi to his Christian community of Shfaram, which is located in the Galilee region in northern Israel. The Adonai Roi congregation, which is located in Tel Aviv, boarded buses and travelled north to spend the day with their Arab brothers and sisters. They sang, shared meals and prayed for each other with genuine heartfelt love and concern. They left the gathering blessing each other and wishing the best on their newfound friends.

Now, if people who have been in conflict with each other for thousands of years can move past the sins of the past and find peace, so can we. How did this happen? Was it a government or academic sponsored event? No, it was the Christian community showing the way by being the Children of Light. They showed their fellow countrymen that transformation of the soul is the soul of transformation. They demonstrated that God's way was a higher way that transcended all earthly governments, political affiliations and enslavement to a bitter history.

At the time of Jesus there were conflicts everywhere. The Jewish people were being occupied and governed by imperialist Rome, which had headquarters in Caesarea. They were also in conflict with Greek settlers who had taken up residence in Samaria in the middle of the country.

Racism, slavery and genocide are not skin colour issues, they are the issues of a heart that needs transformation.

To compound things, they were in conflict with each other due to the various religious sects that had formed since their return to the land. Simply said, it was a land filled with emotionally charged animosity. There was offence on every side. Jesus was approached by his student, Peter, and asked a very relevant question: What about forgiveness? 'Lord, how many times shall I forgive someone who sins against me? Up to seven times?' Jesus answered, 'I tell you, not seven times, but seventy-seven times' (Matt 18:21–22).

I am sure this must have taken Peter aback as this was just not the attitude of the day. This was a region that fed off their unwillingness to forgive each other. It fuelled the fires of nationalism and it kept them crying out for a military Messiah who would come and deliver them from their oppression. Jesus went on to tell a story:

'Therefore, the kingdom of heaven is like a king who wanted to settle accounts with his servants. As he began the settlement, a man who owed him ten thousand bags of gold was brought to him. Since he was not able to pay, the master ordered that he and his wife and his children and all that he had be sold to repay the debt. The servant fell on his knees before him. "Be patient with me," he begged, "and I will pay back everything." The servant's master took pity on him, cancelled the debt and let him go.

But when that servant went out, he found one of his fellow servants who owed him a hundred silver coins. He grabbed him and began to choke him. "Pay back what you owe me!" he demanded. His fellow servant fell to his knees and begged him, "Be patient with me, and I will pay you back." But he refused. Instead, he went off and had the man thrown into prison until he could pay the debt.

When the other servants saw what had happened, they were greatly distressed and went and told their master everything that had happened. Then the master called the servant in. "You wicked servant," he said, "I cancelled all that debt of yours because you begged me to. Shouldn't you have had mercy on your fellow servant just as I had on you?"

In anger his master handed him over to the jailers to be tortured, until he should pay back all he owed. This is how my heavenly Father will treat each of you unless you forgive a brother or sister from your heart.'

– MATTHEW 18:23-35

I get the distinct impression from reading this parable that Jesus is not neutral on the issues of forgiveness and restoration. It is not an option unless you want bad things to happen to you. Given that the message here is straightforward and obvious, again we need to ask a direct question. Where is the Zimbabwean church in leading the way to forgiveness and reconciliation between all races and people groups? Are we leading the way? Are we the driving force? This should be one of the defining characteristics of our community. We should all be the peacemakers. As James wrote, 'But the wisdom that comes from heaven is first of all pure; then peace-loving, considerate, submissive, full of mercy and good fruit, impartial and sincere. Peacemakers who sow in peace reap a harvest of righteousness' (Jas 3:17–18).

TRANSFORMATION THROUGH TAKING PERSONAL RESPONSIBILITY

The issue of personal responsibility is a foundational concept of life that was instituted by God at the very beginning of creation. The concept incorporates two aspects, both seen in the first few chapters of the Book of Genesis.

1. Personal Responsibility to take care of ourselves; and
2. Personal Responsibility to be accountable for our actions or inactions.

It is the responsibility of each human being to use and manage the natural resources of the earth to sustain life for themselves and the lives of their family. When God first created Adam He *did not* say, 'Let Us create man in our image and make him *co-dependent* on Us for his every need.' What He did say is recorded in Genesis: 'Then God said, 'Let us make man in our image, in our likeness, and *let them rule over* the fish of the sea and the birds of the air, over the livestock, over all the earth, and over all the creatures that move along the ground'(Gen 1:26). The record also states that, 'The LORD God took the man and put him in the Garden of Eden to *work it* and *take care of it*' (Gen 2:15). In other words, rule over the livestock and work and take care of the land. It is actually very simple and quite straightforward. It wasn't going to happen on its own, nor was God going to do it for them. Adam was personally responsible for his own well-being.

One really nice thing that God did for Adam in the beginning was create a helpmate. She was to be someone to share life experiences with and to be a partner in expanding his family. Sadly, it was through an experience that they had together that we see the very first bad fruits of sin. When held accountable for their actions, they did not take any personal responsibility and shifted the blame to someone else.

After they had been in the Garden for some time, Eve had an encounter with a serpent that convinced her that the reason God didn't want them to eat from a certain tree was that it would make them like God. In other words, he used the same tactic on her as he does on us today. This is to tell us that 'the reason we don't have something is because someone else is keeping us from having it because they are afraid that if we had it, we would be just like them!' He appeals to our jealous nature.

Once Eve, and then Adam, had eaten the forbidden fruit, God appeared. When He confronted Adam as to why he was disobedient, Adam's first response was to refuse responsibility for his actions and shift the blame to Eve. 'The woman you put here with me, she gave me some fruit from the tree, and I ate it' (Gen 3:12). Eve did exactly the same thing and shifted the blame to the serpent: 'Then the LORD God said to the woman, "What is this you have done?" The woman said, "The serpent deceived me, and I ate"' (Gen 3:13).

While this issue of not wanting to be personally responsible for our actions is thousands of years old, in the past century there has been a concerted effort by many in the academic community across the globe to make it acceptable by intellectualizing it. They want us to believe that we are helpless victims of our circumstances. They want us to accept that our imperfections are due to our flawed parents or the faulty genetic inheritance that we are presented with at birth. This is done to absolve us of any personal responsibility or accountability. This is such an easy concept to sell as we all want to believe it is true. We have a disposition in our hearts that wants to blame others and now we have an academic justification for doing just that. The truth is that as difficult as our circumstances may be, they do not relieve us of accountability for our actions or our inactions.

Again we have to ask a very difficult question: Has Zimbabwe's leadership used this 'false teaching' to manipulate the masses for its own selfish gain? Have they played the 'blame game'? Where has the Church stood? Have they repudiated this 'false teaching'? Are they 'false prophets' telling the people what they want to hear versus what they need to hear? If they have, then they have again perpetuated their enslavement and sent them down a path that can only lead to ruin. Again we must remember it is the truth and only the truth that can set us free (John 8:32). Anything but the truth is a return to bondage. Has Zimbabwe's church leadership loved its people enough to tell them the truth? Or do they want them to remain victims so that they can control them by their constant need of them?

At the time of Jesus and Paul, the world was primarily an agrarian culture, much like Africa is today. Most of their teachings were done in stories or parables that were based on agricultural principles that everyone could understand. One of the most important principles that they shared with people was the concept of 'Sowing and Reaping'. It is a principle that is part of the genetic code of life and incorporates the concept of personal responsibility. Paul reminded the Christian community in Galatia:

> 'Do not be deceived: God cannot be mocked. People reap what they sow. Those who sow to please their sinful nature, from that nature will reap destruction; those who sow to please the Spirit, from the Spirit will reap eternal life. Let us not become weary in doing good, for at the proper time we will reap a harvest if we do not give up. Therefore, as we have opportunity, let us do good to all people, especially to those who belong to the family of believers.'
>
> – GALATIANS 6:7–10

Africa can be transformed by the Christian community taking the lead in teaching personal responsibility and the principle that they will reap what they sow. In the natural world, if you sow life (seed) into the ground and nurture it with life (water) you will reap life; this applies in the same way in the spiritual world.

TRANSFORMATION THROUGH THE
CELEBRATION OF DIVERSITY

Something that I have observed in studying human history is that there is strength in diversity. The prosperity of America with all her flaws is a testament to this truth. People from every nation under the sun have come there to 'sow and reap' and make a life for themselves.

I think that nature bears out the fact that there is strength in diversity. One of the most fascinating edible plants in North America is called 'Indian corn'. It has grown in the wild for thousands of years, enduring vast changes in the weather, drought and every form of pestilence. It has survived on its own with no help from humanity. The corn is short, stubby and its kernels are a variety of colours. While it has fed thousands of people over the centuries, you won't find it on the shelves of the grocery store. Now you will only find large, yellow corn that all looks the same. Why? Because it is easier to produce and manage.

A number of years ago the United States had a corn leaf blight that within three months almost wiped out the entire corn crop from one end of the country to the other. The big mystery was how the disease moved so fast. It turned out that the corn that was planted had been genetically engineered and that the blight took advantage of its 'genetic window' and raced through the crop unimpeded. Amazingly, it didn't affect the Indian corn. Why? Because science had left it alone and it had retained its genetic diversity, which enabled it to be strong enough to weather the blight.

Despite the obvious benefits of the strength of diversity, humans are often afraid of it. Selfishly motivated political leaders are terrified of its strength and will do almost anything to eliminate it. The average person is often scared of it as we tend to fear what we don't know. Despite what creation teaches us, we fight against it so that we can control it. To travel through one of Africa's game reserves and observe the diversity of her animals is a sight to behold. Animals in every size, shape and colour roam the landscape. Marine life has its own unique and colourful spectacle to behold. God celebrates diversity everywhere. He shows it off in his creation.

What about mankind? Did God stop there? No; the world is full of a vast array of cultures that each have a unique way of expressing themselves. Yet at the core of their hearts they all want the same thing; food to eat, clothes to wear, a warm place to sleep, good health, family and peace with their neighbours. Mankind was created to bear the image of God, and in order to do so God needed a world of diversity to reveal Himself. In

God celebrates diversity everywhere. He shows it off in his creation.

order for Zimbabwe to be transformed, she must understand that God loves diversity and that it must be celebrated, not destroyed.

I have spent many years in the world of music and have a great love for the sounds of Africa. I have seen the power of music and how it can transcend culture and bring people together. Music notes are a universal language of their own that we all seem to understand. I believe that in music, God again reveals the truth that there is strength in diversity. When I first came to Africa and heard the singing, I was taken aback by the quality. I was sure that every African had a beautiful voice and that they could all be soloists. I was very surprised when I walked around and listened to individual voices, that that wasn't the case. What made the singing so profoundly beautiful was the harmonies they created together.

Religion is one of the worst culprits in trying to destroy the beauty of diversity. In fact, hundreds of millions of people have died in the name of God as one group has waged war on another to force them to worship exactly as they do. The European missionaries made this same mistake by trying to force the whole continent of Africa to conform to their particular form or expression of worship. They did not celebrate diversity; they opposed it on every front.

If the African church will bring transformation of the soul through forgiveness and by each person taking personal responsibility, the path ahead to the celebration of diversity will be much clearer. When we are secure in who we are, and know what God has called us to do, we are less threatened by others. The focus of our efforts at that point is not on what

I need to feel good about myself, but how I can use what I'm good at to contribute to the greater good? If men's hearts can be transformed, they will no longer be threatened by the strengths of others, but celebrate them.

When we are secure in who we are, and know what God has called us to do, we are less threatened by others.

If Africa can let go of her past through forgiveness and forge a new path of mutual respect and honour, she will prosper. Men must no longer be judged by skin colour, but by character and skill sets. The church should be leading the way. We are God's prism; when his light shines through us, we should manifest a vast array of colours, all in harmony. As Paul exhorted, 'Live in harmony with one another. Do not be proud, but be willing to associate with people of low position. Do not think you are superior' (Rom 12:16).

Earlier in his letter to the Roman church, Paul asked the question, 'Who shall separate us from God's love?'

'Who shall separate us from the love of Christ? Shall trouble or hardship or persecution or famine or nakedness or danger or sword? As it is written: "For your sake we face death all day long; we are considered as sheep to be slaughtered." No, in all these things we are more than conquerors through him who loved us. For I am convinced that neither death nor life, neither angels nor demons, neither the present nor the future, nor any powers, neither height nor depth, nor anything else in all creation, will be able to separate us from the love of God that is in Christ Jesus our Lord.'

— ROMANS 8:35–39

If none of these things can separate us from the love of God, should we allow them to separate us one from another?

Remember ...

Transformation of the Soul is the Soul of Transformation.

Chapter 13 Endnotes

1. Amartya Sen 'Democracy as Freedom' (Anchor, 1999).

CHAPTER 14

LESSONS FROM HISTORY

*What experience and history teach is this – that people and
governments never have learned anything from history,
or acted on principles deduced from it.*

— GWF HEGEL

The people of Zimbabwe have a fascinating historical link to the people of Israel that, until recently, remained largely unknown outside of a small region of the country. In the early 1990s, Dr. Tudor Parfitt, a British Professor of Modern Jewish Studies at the University of London, heard a story while lecturing in South Africa about an African tribe claiming to have descended from Jewish priests fleeing Israel thousands of years ago. The Lemba people, who populate southern Zimbabwe and northern South Africa, have a rich oral history that tells their ancestors' accounts. They also have many customs that are distinctly Jewish and totally unique from the neighbouring tribes that surround them. They practise circumcision and refuse to eat pork, rabbit, carrion and scale-less fish as is laid down in Leviticus 11 in the Old Testament. When they do eat meat, they always use the 'kosher' manner by bleeding the animal first.

These distinct customs intrigued Dr. Parfitt enough to begin an indepth research project to uncover the true origins of the Lemba people. What he soon discovered was intriguing. As the Babylonians were getting ready to invade Jerusalem around 586 BC, a group of temple priests fled south and settled in what is modern day Yemen. There they established a Jewish community near a town called Sena. At some point there was an agricultural disaster, possibly due to the destruction of a dam, and the community had to move again.

Lemba tradition says that a group of Jewish priestly males headed south by boat along the eastern coast of Africa. On the journey they encountered a violent storm and while half the group was lost at sea, the survivors landed on the beach and headed inland. Once there they set up a new community and intermarried with the Africans.

The Lemba believe that Zimbabwe's greatest archaeological treasure, a large stone city called *Great Zimbabwe*, was first engineered by these priests in the 11th century AD. What makes their story so compelling is that the stonework is similar to that found in ancient Jerusalem. Their oral history claims that together, the Africans and their new Jewish family members, built a huge city that continued to grow until the 15th century, when it reached its zenith at approximately 18 000 inhabitants.

As DNA testing became available, Dr. Tudor decided to return to Zimbabwe with DNA experts to test the Lemba men's Y chromosome. This one chromosome would reveal the true biological ancestry of the Lemba and prove, once and for all, whether their story was true. Much to everyone's excitement, the test results authenticated the Lembas' assertion that they were descendants of Israel! Lemba men carry a DNA sequence that is distinctive to the 'Cohanim', a hereditary set of Jewish priests. The oldest of the twelve Lemba clans, the Buba, have the highest concentration of the Cohanim gene.

This amazing discovery means that the people of Zimbabwe have a unique historical connection to the ancient people of Israel and are a part of its history as well. Fortunately for later generations, the ancient Hebrews valued written history. Their scribes recorded the account of their journey to share with future generations. I have always appreciated the honesty of their writings as they avoid the temptation to gloss over the record. They tell a story of how mankind has interacted with God over many centuries. They are painfully honest about the frailty of humanity. They are transparent about their people's successes and failures and warn those that come after them of life's many potential pitfalls.

For those who are currently in some form of leadership or aspire to be, the lessons recorded in the Bible are invaluable. While our cultures have evolved and our lifestyles changed dramatically, the human soul has remained the same. The Bible is like a mirror, timelessly reflecting the best and worst of the human race.

While our cultures have evolved and our lifestyles changed dramatically, the human soul has remained the same.

What does history teach us? What can Zimbabwe and her leaders learn from looking back over the ages at the rise and fall of another nation to which they have a connection? A wise man searches for understanding from those leaders that have gone before him in order to avoid the same mistakes. I believe that there is a period of history around 1000 BC that has a number of great lessons to be gleaned for leaders of today.

The story starts in the Middle East with a young shepherd boy named David who ultimately becomes a mighty warrior king. His people had come out of Egypt in slavery 300 years earlier, in the form of a dozen individual tribes, and had settled across a whole region on the eastern side of the Mediterranean. His predecessor, the first king, Saul, had had moderate success in uniting the tribes, but it was under King David that they became a unified nation. He was able to take their diverse tribal cultures and bring them together as a distinct people. He unified the leadership of each tribe under the banner of a single nation called Israel. Years later, his son Solomon would build upon his father's work and form this fledgling nation into a wealthy world power. How did they transform a nomadic culture of sheep herders, who had spent hundreds of years as slaves, into such a vibrant and successful nation?

It started with David who had a profound understanding of the supremacy of God over all aspects of life. His journey had brought him to the place where he had developed a deep respect for the divine intervention of God in the affairs of men. He had started out life inconspicuously as the seventh son of a man named Jesse. He spent most of his youth herding sheep around the arid desert, trying to find foliage for them to graze. One day, the prophet Samuel arrived at the family compound asking to look at Jesse's sons to anoint one of them as the next king. After looking over the oldest six boys, he hadn't found what he was looking for. At that point God spoke to Samuel and gave him a profound lesson in how God sees and evaluates humanity.

> 'But the LORD said to Samuel, "Do not consider his appearance or his height, for I have rejected him. The LORD does not look at the things human beings look at. People look at the outward appearance, but the LORD looks at the heart.'
>
> – 1 SAMUEL 16:7

While mankind is busy looking good, God sees through the facade and straight into the heart. While Samuel was impressed with David's older brothers, God saw something else. Once Samuel realized that none of the six boys he had looked at were God's choice, he turned to Jesse and asked if he might have another son. Jesse told Samuel that he had a younger son, but he was out back tending the sheep. As small, ruddy David stood before Samuel, God spoke through him, saying, 'This is the one that will be king.' I'm sure that Samuel must have thought, 'Are you kidding me?'

David could not possibly have understood in that moment what was about to transpire in his life. The journey that he was about to embark on would be one far different from the serene life of tending sheep. God was about to teach him, in the most dramatic ways, that He can take the most obscure person and turn him into a mighty leader. Those lessons were not lost on David.

As he matured, he came to the understanding that there was one reason he was King and that was because God had chosen him. He understood that he was accountable to a higher authority. One day he would have to answer to God for his stewardship as king and leader of a nation. David left no doubt about his deep-seated beliefs:

'God reigns over the nations; God is seated on his holy throne. The nobles of the nations assemble as the people of the God of Abraham, for the kings of the earth belong to God; he is greatly exalted.'

– PSALM 47:8-9

One of the first acts of David's administration was to bring the Ark of the Covenant, where God's presence dwelt, and the Tabernacle, where the tribes worshipped, to Jerusalem, the new national capital of this fledgling nation. He made 'the house of God' the focal point of the whole country. Besides being a unifying force, it also established a national precedent that under his administration, God would be at the centre of everything he did as a leader and what they did as a nation. It also established the fact that 'the law of God' would be the standard by which he would govern and the people would live their lives. No longer was it going to be every man being ruled by whatever was 'good in his own eyes', but life in the nation was going to be lived in light of accountability to God first and then with each man being responsible for his brother.

Because of David's understanding that he was responsible for the welfare of his people and accountable to God for them, he ruled fairly and justly among the twelve tribes, never showing favouritism. He also understood that each citizen carried a responsibility to care for his neighbour. He was a man of great compassion for the orphan and widow, and defended the cause of the oppressed. He taught these ways to his son Solomon, who was not a man of war like his father, but a man of peace.

Solomon was a man with a humble heart by virtue of the fact that he was teachable. He searched the world to gain wisdom. He was also a gifted builder, and it was through his great wisdom that the nation prospered. Solomon negotiated military and economic treaties not only with all his neighbours, but also nations thousands of kilometres away from which he could import goods not available in Israel. By avoiding armed conflict, he was able to use the resources of the nation to build infrastructure and develop industry. The whole nation prospered under Solomon's reign. He, like his father before him, honoured God daily. He built the most magnificent temple so that the whole nation could worship God together. Solomon firmly believed that if he followed the just ways of God, his nation would prosper. He turned out to be right. He would say later in looking back at his life ... 'Wisdom makes one wise man more powerful than ten rulers in a city' (Eccles 7:19).

Solomon's most lasting legacy was the famous book he wrote, called Proverbs. In this collection of wise sayings, he shared what he had learned from his father David and his experiences as a ruler. Some scholars believe that Proverbs was actually written to his son Rehoboam in order to prepare him to wear the mantle of leadership. Solomon wrote what he had gleaned so that future generations could also rule with wisdom and their nations could prosper. I would like to take the next few pages and look at some of Solomon's words, as I believe they hold important keys for the transformation of Zimbabwe.

> 'By me [wisdom] kings reign and rulers make decrees that are just; by
> me princes govern, and all nobles who rule on earth. I love those who
> love me, and those who seek me find me. With me are riches and hon-
> our, enduring wealth and prosperity. My fruit is better than fine gold;
> what I yield surpasses choice silver. I walk in the way of righteousness,
> along the paths of justice, bestowing wealth on those who love me and
> making their treasuries full'
>
> – PROVERBS 8:15–21 (AUTHOR'S ADDITION)

Solomon believed that a nation and its people would find success or failure based on the attitudes and the behaviour of her leaders. He was convinced that there was a direct correlation between what was in one's heart and one's actions. He believed that the quest to acquire wisdom was crucial to one's success and that wise actions produced prosperous results. He was convinced that righteousness (conformity to God's ways) brought blessing, while sin (transgression of God's ways) brought failure and ultimately death and destruction. He led his government with these truths ever before him. He didn't see God as inactive in the affairs of men and wrote soberly that, 'The LORD's curse is on the house of the wicked, but he blesses the home of the righteous' (Prov 3:33).

In other words, God is not passive when it comes to the motivations of men's hearts and their subsequent actions. He is proactive based on our choices resulting in either calamity or blessing. As we have discussed previously, God is all about personal responsibility. We each stand and fall by our own choices. Solomon wrote, 'When the righteous prosper, the city rejoices; when the wicked perish, there are shouts of joy. Through the blessing of the upright a city is exalted, but by the mouth of the wicked it is destroyed' (Prov 11:10–11). He also stated that, 'Kings detest wrongdoing, for a throne is established through righteousness' (Prov 16:12). Here Solomon warns future leaders that if you want to establish a lasting legacy, you had better rule with righteousness, i.e. integrity, justice and compassion. How many times has history witnessed the fall or death of a liberator turned tyrant after he has destroyed his country?

I remember vividly at the end of 1989 seeing the bodies of Nicolae Ceausescu, the Communist leader of Romania, and his wife after they had been executed by their own people! For 24 years he had ruled the nation with an iron fist. He had built a personality cult, erecting statues of himself and posting his picture in every building across the country. He awarded himself university degrees and military medals and listened to speeches by his comrades extolling his greatness. The problem was that underneath this propaganda machine was the truth that he and his administration were all extremely corrupt. They had raped and pillaged their own people and by using state television for misinformation, thought they had fooled everyone. Suddenly, one day their iniquities reached the tipping point and God unceremoniously removed them overnight, not only from power, but from life itself. They were executed by their own people in front of a firing squad and their bodies were buried in simple graves. The mighty Ceausescus were gone from power in a blink of an eye. The name Ceausescu lives in infamy along with the Hitlers, Stalins and Pol Pots of the 20th century.

In recent years the world watched the downfall of Saddam Hussein who, like those before him, lost everything he had built, including his life. The people celebrated for days, and every statue or image of him was either defaced or torn down. The same scenario has repeated itself across the African continent over the past 20–30 years. Initially celebrated as liberators, leader after leader fell prey to pride, greed and power and in the end they were hated by their own people and removed from power. Instead of the great legacy they had longed for, they became another sad footnote in history. 'Righteousness exalts a nation, but sin is a disgrace to any people' (Prov 14:34).

When one looks across the world stage, which countries are the most respected? It is those that attempt to take the moral high ground. It is countries that respect the rule of law where each member of the society has personal rights that are guaranteed. Exalted nations are found where justice rules and people have a record of helping others in need. Interestingly, these nations typically always have a strong Christian presence somewhere in the formative years of their history. They had leaders that reminded the nation that God cares about the motivations of the heart. What we do individually with our lives matters. How we treat our neighbours matters.

There is an obvious truth that often goes ignored: Good leadership lasts! Solomon made an interesting observation concerning political job security: 'When a country is rebellious, it has many rulers, but a ruler with discernment and knowledge maintains order' (Prov 28:2). Solomon believed that a great ruler was a Godly ruler and that a Godly ruler's government would last for many years. He would not need a military force to stay in power because the people would remain loyal to him by virtue of his strong character. People long to be led by leaders who value and rule by righteousness and justice. If a leader needs to resort to military force to stay in power, he has already lost his nation and it is only a matter of time before he will be gone as well. Solomon reminds us that:

- Love and faithfulness keep a king safe; through love his throne is made secure (Prov 20:28).

- By justice a king gives a country stability, but those who are greedy for bribes tear it down (Prov 29:4).
- If a king judges the poor with fairness, his throne will be established forever (Prov 29:14).

Solomon believed that righteousness, justice and equity were all principles that emanated from God. They were a part of God's nature and character. Those that took on these noble attributes were wise, while those that disregarded them were considered fools. He believed that leaders who truly wanted success would seek God's wisdom with all their heart. They would also encourage the people to search for understanding with the goal that these values would be fully integrated in the fabric of the nation's daily life. In order to accomplish this, the nation as a whole must seek God, asking for his grace and to be transformed by his wisdom. This was an act of humility. He proclaimed:

'For the LORD gives wisdom; from his mouth come knowledge and understanding. He holds success in store for the upright, he is a shield to those whose walk is blameless, for he guards the course of the just and protects the way of his faithful ones. Then you will understand what is right and just and fair every good path.'

– PROVERBS 2:6-9

Solomon understood that, 'Evildoers do not understand what is right, but those who seek the LORD understand it fully' (Prov 28:5), and that, 'It is the glory of God to conceal a matter; to search out a matter is the glory of kings' (Prov 25:2). It is the responsibility of a leader to search for wisdom and understanding. Passivity and arrogance are the stepping stones to disaster.

Solomon believed that a leader who wanted to see his nation prosper had to rule with equity and impartiality. Wisdom demanded it. Those at the top determined the character of a nation and its potential for prosperity. 'I [wisdom] walk in the way of righteousness, along the paths of justice, bestowing a rich inheritance on those who love me and making their treasuries full' (Author's addition, Prov 8:20–21).

If leaders chose to deal in lies, inequities and disrespect, those around them would soon take on those very same qualities. Their administrations would be polluted from top to bottom with subordinates who were only watching out for themselves, lining their pockets with bribes. For the right price they would turn their loyalties to the highest bidder, and chaos would ensue. Men, once allies, would suddenly become mortal enemies as power struggles ensued for the spoils of government. When this happens it isn't long before the nation as a whole slides into chaos, resulting in abject poverty. Under this all too common scenario, the weak and innocent always become the victims and fall prey to the wicked. Solomon warned leaders against this.

- If a ruler listens to lies, all his officials become wicked (Prov 29:12).
- The wicked accept bribes in secret to pervert the course of justice (Prov 17:23).
- It is not good to be partial to the wicked and so deprive the innocent of justice (Prov 18:5).
- It is not for kings to drink wine, not for rulers to crave beer, lest they drink and forget what has been decreed, and deprive all the oppressed of their rights (Prov 31:4–5).

Solomon stated clearly that in his mind it was the responsibility of a leader to make sure that the poor and needy were defended. From the leader's position of power it was his duty to use everything at his disposal to make sure that they were not taken advantage of by the rich and powerful. He believed it was that the courts must rule justly and not be influenced by those with power and wealth on their side.

These also are sayings of the wise: 'To show partiality in judging is not good: Whoever says to the guilty, "You are innocent," will be cursed by peoples and denounced by nations. But it will go well with those who convict the guilty, and rich blessing will come on them.'

– PROVERBS 24:23-25

For Solomon it was the role of government leaders to, 'Speak up for those who cannot speak for themselves, for the rights of all who are destitute. Speak up and judge fairly; defend the rights of the poor and needy' (Prov 31:8–9).

No man can rule a nation by himself. Governments with their huge bureaucracies have to be managed by a team of people with skills and expertise in a variety of disciplines. The most successful leaders, whether in civil government or the corporate world, are those who are a good judge of people. They know how to discern character and capacity.

Moses, another great Jewish leader whose story is recorded in the Bible, faced a crisis of leadership during his own administration. Things had reached a point where he was overwhelmed by the affairs of state and became exhausted. He took some time off to visit his father-in-law Jethro for his advice. Jethro realized that if Moses didn't start delegating, he was going to have a nervous breakdown. He advised him: 'Select capable men from all the people, men who fear God, trustworthy men who hate dishonest gain and appoint them as officials over thousands, hundreds, fifties and tens' (Exod 18:21).

A nation devoid of leaders who see themselves as servants of God is a nation doomed to certain failure.

There were two key points to Jethro's advice. First, delegate more, and second, choose wisely by picking men of character. To find men of character, one only needs to find a man who respects and honours God. US President George Washington, in addressing his countrymen, said, 'Let us with caution indulge the supposition that morality can be maintained without religion. Reason and experience both forbid us to expect that national morality can prevail in exclusion of religious principle.'

Washington believed, as did David, Solomon and Moses, that morality could come only from a heart transformed by God's grace. A nation devoid of leaders who see themselves as servants of God is a nation doomed to certain failure. While addressing the governors of the thirteen states before stepping down from the presidency in 1783, Washington prayed:

'What does God ask of man, but to do justly, to love mercy, and to walk humbly with your God? ... so as to embrace the benevolent side of human ambition. That [God] would most graciously be pleased to dispose us all, to do justice, to love mercy, and to demean ourselves with that charity, humility and pacific temper of mind, which were the characteristics of the Divine author of our blessed Religion, and without an humble imitation of whose example in these things, we [could] never hope to be a happy nation.'

Unless Zimbabwe's current leadership changes course, their days are numbered. God will not stand back and be mocked. If Zimbabwe, as a people, is ever going to change their current course, they must recognize that the land does not belong to either the blacks nor the whites; it belongs to God alone. Mankind was given a stewardship of the land and we are accountable to God for how we manage it. I think it's fair to say that if He evaluated us today, we all would fail miserably. Our only hope for a better future is humility before God and each other. As the great apostle Paul wrote: 'We all have sinned and fallen short of the glory of God' (Rom 3:23).

> *Our only hope for a better future is humility before God and each other.*

Now is not the time for blame, but for forgiveness. If we are going to turn the course of Zimbabwe around, we must come together, black and white, and invest in Zimbabwe's future – her children.

CHAPTER 15

CHILDREN ARE THE BEST INVESTMENT

The test of the morality of a society is what
it does for its children.

– DIETRICH BONHOEFFER

As a young boy, I remember my grandfather talking about the events of the Great Depression. During those gloomy years, he was an up-and-coming stockbroker on LaSalle Street in Chicago, Illinois. It was an extremely difficult time to begin a career in investments, but he persevered and became quite successful. As a young man, I listened as he described the terrible despair and heartache that families suffered in their struggle to survive during those tough times. I couldn't imagine living under those conditions, often having multiple families crammed into one dwelling and children sleeping three and four to a bed. People did whatever they could to survive.

Then one day, while discussing bad economic times, he made a comment that really took me aback. He said, 'Even in the direst of situations, there is opportunity.' This was a totally foreign concept to me and one I could not imagine being true. Then he gave me a brief history lesson on various companies that actually made money and prospered during the Depression! I was flabbergasted as all I had ever heard in school was about the high unemployment, tent cities and long soup lines. The fact that, even in the darkest of times, people found ways to create opportunities to prosper was indeed an intriguing proposition. Years later in 2008, when the financial markets melted down before the Presidential election and people were in a panic, his words rang true as companies that were financially strong were purchasing distressed companies for well below their market value. In time, their acquisitions will be worth twice or more what they originally paid for them.

> *Even in the direst of situations, there is opportunity.*

Similar to the Great Depression, the current situation on the continent of Africa can only be described as catastrophic. Without a doubt, the AIDS epidemic is the single most significant and furthest reaching health crisis of our lifetime. Its effects are not just felt in the immediate families of those infected, but through all the economic strata of African society. At the moment, a whole generation of Africans is dying at an alarming rate, leaving many young orphans. Families try to rally around the orphaned children, but often the only people left to care for them are impoverished, widowed grandmothers. In many cases, there is no family left at all and the children simply become 'street kids', living off what they can steal to survive.

Due to the nature of AIDS, it is clear to all involved that while we may stem the tide by reducing the number of new infections, this problem is not going to go away soon. The 'aftershocks' will be felt for decades to come. So where is the opportunity in this? From my perspective it is in the orphaned children. Zimbabwe's future success lies with her children and the opportunities we can create for them to change the course of their country's history. We have the chance to raise a new generation of children unpolluted by the past. With a new way of thinking, a clean heart and freedom from the bitterness of the past, this next generation could turn Zimbabwe around and put it back on track to its divine destiny. When brought up in a loving community, with a good education based on the values of the Kingdom of God and employment opportunities, these children could reshape the nation of Zimbabwe in a single generation.

How bad is the orphan crisis in Africa? To answer that question we need to first look at how bad the underlying cause is. While war and famine do play a significant role in the orphaning of children, they don't compare with the overwhelming impact of the AIDS virus. Sub-Saharan Africa is more heavily affected by HIV and AIDS than any other region of the world. An estimated 22,5 million people were living with HIV at the end of 2007 and approximately 1,7 million additional people were infected with HIV during that year. In just the past year, the AIDS epidemic in Africa has claimed the lives of an estimated 1,6 million people just in this region.

> *Without a doubt, the AIDS epidemic is the single most significant and furthest reaching health crisis of our lifetime.*

MORE THAN ELEVEN MILLION AFRICAN CHILDREN HAVE BEEN LEFT ORPHANED BY AIDS.[1]

Due to the lack of prevention and treatment options, it is expected that AIDS-related deaths are going to continue to climb dramatically over the next few decades. The result will have a devastating effect on the African family. By 2010, it is predicted that there will be around 15,7 million AIDS orphans in Sub-Saharan Africa alone.[2] The impact on African society as a whole will be significant, as its workforce and family structures become increasingly decimated. Already there are four Southern African countries with infection rates of over 20%: Botswana, Lesotho, Swaziland and Zimbabwe, where it's estimated that almost 1 in 4 are infected.

In Zimbabwe, an estimated 565 adults and children are becoming infected every day, which is roughly one person every three minutes.[3] In many cases, as one Zimbabwean doctor explained to reporters, the reality is that AIDS can now be counted amongst the country's chief concerns: 'Put simply, people are dying of AIDS before they can starve to death.'[4] The average life expectancy for women, who are particularly affected by Zimbabwe's AIDS epidemic, is 34 – the lowest anywhere in the world. Officials of the World Health Organization have admitted that since this figure is based on data collected two years ago, the real number may be as low as 30.[5] According to UN-AIDS estimates, almost 60% of the Zimbabwean adults living with HIV at the end of 2006 were female. This gender gap is even wider among young people between the ages of 15 and 24 living with HIV, of which women make up around 77%.[6] With these staggering statistics, it's no wonder that Zimbabwe, according to UNICEF,[7] has a higher number of orphans in proportion to its population than any other country in the world! AVERT, an International AIDS organization, states on their website that there are currently over 1 million orphans in Zimbabwe alone, and the number is still climbing. Zimbabwe is a nation in an unimaginably dire state.

Here is an absolute fact: We can't save everyone. Here is another absolute fact: We can save some.

While the sheer size and scope of the problem can be overwhelming and lead to paralysis, if we break things down to a more manageable level, we may see light at the end of the tunnel. Here is an absolute fact: We can't save everyone. Here is another absolute fact: We can save some. The solution to caring for the children is not a few doing a lot but a lot doing a little. Zimbabwe's children need the world community to rally to their defence, but not just through a large, Western-driven institutional solution. They need a grass roots, African community solution.

If the Zimbabwe government is able to right its ship with new leadership devoid of corruption and commits itself to managing the country with justice and integrity, I'm convinced that God will intervene on the nation's behalf. It will take the efforts of hundreds of Non-Government Organizations (NGOs) working side by side with local Zimbabweans to turn things around. If the Zimbabwean government can stabilize itself and give assurance to outside investors that what they invest will go to and stay with the people, I'm convinced that resources would flow back into the country. I also believe that the millions of Zimbabweans dispersed across the globe would return to help rebuild their homeland. These 'Diaspora', or displaced, Zimbabweans, while in the West, have been learning new skill sets and gaining understanding on how democracy and the free market system work. They have also stayed engaged with events back home and sent funds back, not only to help support their families but also their friends and neighbours. Zimbabweans think communally.

The people of The Community of Reconciliation built a working model over 20 years ago that I believe could still work today with the added dimension of the care and development of orphans. They proved that a racially integrated community could exist, prosper and impact a whole region of the country as long as it was based on the values of the Kingdom of God and hearts that were devoid of greed and selfish ambition. This is where I believe the Christian community around the world needs to join forces with the Christian community within the country to help them rebuild their nation and invest in its most valuable asset – the children.

> *Zimbabwe's future success lies with her children and the opportunities we can create for them to change the course of their country's history.*

There are a variety of workable orphanage models already operational in Africa, and I certainly do not want to 'reinvent the wheel'. At the same time, my experience in Zimbabwe and my interaction with her people has left me with what I believe are four key components that each model should incorporate if we want to ensure long-term success. Extended Family, Economy, Education and Employment are the four foundational factors that need to be looked at closely and woven into our strategies for raising Zimbabwe's next generation.

EXTENDED FAMILY

When I first visited Zimbabwe in 1984, I was struck by the strong sense of community that Africans have. The concept of the extended family is natural to them. They don't seem to work at it, as it is the essence of who they are. When facing crisis, the Africans look to their extended family first to find a solution. They find a way amongst themselves to share the load, and feel a strong sense of responsibility to be there for each other.

My wife, Elizabeth, and I recently visited an outdoor gallery of Zimbabwean sculptures that were on display at a local garden. I was particularly struck by one sculpture that graphically depicted what I've observed over the years about Zimbabweans. The name of the piece was 'He's not heavy, he's my brother', and it showed two Africans supporting their weak friend who was dying of AIDS. The imagery really moved me because it so accurately reflected the heart and soul of Zimbabweans I have met on my journeys. They care about one another and will carry each other to make it through difficult times.

I was struck once while observing Zimbabwean culture, that in some ways it more closely resembles the lifestyle of the early Christian community than our modern Western institutional-style expressions. The way they share resources, interpret family and respond to crises all reveal the sense they have of belonging to a larger, extended family. While we in the West are about the individual, they are about the community. One of the sad ironies of the early Western missionaries is that they forced the Africans to abandon their communal lifestyle because it was seen as being pagan-influenced. They were removed from their communities and 're-educated' into a Western institutional philosophy that abandoned the natural bond of relationships. This further fragmented Zimbabwean society and created a cultural rift that has yet to heal.

This institutional mindset can be seen in how we in the West have historically approached the orphan problem. We typically form an institution, raise the necessary capital, build a large structure, hire a small staff and then fill the building with as many children as it can possibly hold. People wanting to carry out their 'Christian duty' then make financial donations to the institution, helping support the poor orphans. Everyone feels good about the transaction and the fact that they have done something meaningful for the children. I want to be careful not to denigrate this model, because for the child left to die on the street, water, food and a covering over their head is the difference between life and death. In some cases, this traditional institutional model is the only option available to keep children alive.

At the same time we need to ask, 'Is this God's best?' I think many of us instinctively know that it isn't. In fact, we know from firsthand experience that there is nothing more important than the love, care and sense of security that a family brings. Every child development researcher whom I know agrees that having a father, mother and siblings to grow up with produces an emotionally healthier individual. My story comes into play here as I was adopted as a baby. I have often wondered 'what if?' What if no one had chosen me? Where would I be now and what would I be like without the love, security and guidance of loving parents. There's a high probability that I would be writing this book either from prison or not at all.

I was adopted in a time when being 'illegitimate' had a social stigma. Society has changed much from those days and today I see children like myself being celebrated and adored. It's wonderful to see them being filled with so much self-esteem and a strong sense of the love of God. I often find myself getting teary-eyed when seeing a whole family doting over a newly adopted child. For those who have adopted children, I tip my hat to you … great job! God loves orphans and those of you who have the grace to adopt bring a smile to his face. You have no idea how the destiny of each adopted child is changed by that one act of kindness.

It is my feeling that Zimbabweans are more inclined to adopt their orphaned and abandoned children into their own communities than send them off and institutionalize them. In light of that, I would like to propose a model that is more in harmony with the African communal expression of looking after each other. I believe that there are many families and communities in Zimbabwe that would gladly adopt and care for orphaned or abandoned children. From what I've seen so far, Zimbabweans all over the world feel a strong sense of responsibility to their next generation. They are committed to being a part of the solution and are willing to take on the responsibility of caring for their own; they simply need help doing it. They cannot carry the load alone; they need us to come alongside and pick them up because they aren't heavy, they are our brothers.

ECONOMY

In discussing this vast topic in depth with my African friends, they have pointed out to me that economics play a huge role as the glue that holds their communities together. As my Zimbabwean friend Muchengetwa Bgoni has succinctly stated, 'We are a community, because we have to be a community; we cannot survive on our own.' We in the West are by and large independently wealthy, which gives us a strong sense of autonomy. The number one factor that causes American families to split up and spread across the country is the pursuit of wealth. We go where there are jobs and opportunity. It's rare these days to see a community manufacturing facility in the US where three generations of the same family have worked. What has been lost in our pursuit of wealth is that sense of being connected to an extended family and a community. We don't feel responsible for each other because we feel each person has the ability to take care of themselves. Our sense of community is 'every man for himself'. We come home for the holidays to briefly reconnect with family and then head back to our own niche that we have carved out.

We are a community, because we have to be a community; we cannot survive on our own.

I submit to you that the key to solving the orphan problem is actually by solving the community economic problem. Zimbabweans will adopt their lost children if they can afford to take care of them. The issue is not if they are willing but if they are able. The solution to caring for and developing the next generation is to raise strong Christian communities that will look after them and give them a sense of belonging to a larger unit. These communities need three basic elements to sustain themselves and the children: land, water and agriculture.

LAND

As we've already documented, the land redistribution policies of the last 20 years in Zimbabwe have been disastrous. The land was first taken out of greed and then taken again out of anger and resentment. In the midst of this ownership tug-of-war, it has ultimately been torn apart and destroyed. It now lies dying and can't feed the people. In this dance of insanity, everyone has lost. Those who knew how to work the land were driven off; those who didn't are letting it die a slow death. The result has been the utter collapse of the agricultural sector across the whole country. While I do understand where the anger comes from, and in many cases it's justified, solving a problem by more angry, unjust acts is simply a recipe for more disaster. No one wins, everyone loses!

While the Mugabe government continues to insist that the country doesn't need help from the West, I suspect that is more about the fear of losing power than what is best for the people. Zimbabwe desperately needs an influx of new people with macro and micro agricultural skills.

The issue is not if they are willing but if they are able.

Their skin colour should be irrelevant. What is in their heart is critical. It is important that each of us understands that God has entrusted the land to the people of Zimbabwe, whoever they may be, and it is their responsibility to cause it to flourish. Mankind's accountability has not changed since the Garden of Eden. If the Zimbabwean government would establish a rule of law whereby men could be assured that justice, fairness and equity would always prevail, many would come to help rebuild the country. Zimbabwe was at one time the 'breadbasket of Africa' and she can be that again.

The primary focus of the next chapter in the history of Zimbabwe should be on restoring the commercially viable farms to productivity so the nation can feed itself. While this is taking place, Zimbabweans need to be trained in farm management, so that one day they can manage their own farms. As skilled African farmers emerge, they need to be allowed and enabled to purchase farmland of their own to manage, adjacent or near these larger farms. The produce from these smaller farms could then be sold to a community co-op which in turn would sell to larger concerns. Zimbabwe needs to return to its community roots, roll up its sleeves and work as a community.

If every family were able to own land, or at a minimum, have a decent place to live and be able to put food on the table, they would gladly extend their families and care for more children. If the Zimbabwean government were to work with NGOs to establish strong, viable communities around its agricultural lands, it would ensure that there was always a skilled workforce within walking distance.

In this dance of insanity, everyone has lost.

In the case of the Community of Reconciliation, the wages weren't always in the form of money, but sometimes produce. Everyone who worked in the community gardens took home fresh fruit and vegetables daily to feed their families. Others tended cattle and were given fresh meat. They even developed a highly successful poultry business. The productivity was so high that the excess was sold on the city markets, generating the cash they needed to purchase more seed, animals, tools and farm implements. With the help of donations from overseas, we were able to build dwellings on the farmlands so that everyone could live near where they worked. This community setting was a natural way of life for the Zimbabweans, and they prospered.

Contrary to the propaganda that has come out of the Mugabe government, there were and are many Americans and Europeans who have been very fair in their dealings with Africans. Certainly not all of them, but there were men like John Russell who treated all his employees the same, no matter their skin colour. There were white farmers in the country who cared about the plight of the African farmer and wanted to help them but were driven out by the government in anger. For the sake of the children we need to get past the past and move forward under a renewed sense of the fact that 'we are a community made of a variety of people' or as we say in the racially diverse United States, 'We are one nation under God.'

WATER

In every corner of the world it could be said that 'water is life'. Civilizations cannot exist without it, people can't live without it. Water has been at the root of conflict after conflict throughout the whole of human history. World wars have been fought over it. It is the most valuable commodity in the world. Even in a nation like the United States with its abundant water resources, states are continually fighting over how those resources are appropriated.

In Africa, water is the difference between life and death every day for each individual. Obtaining water, for many, occupies a good portion of their day. In Africa, access to water is limited and therefore severely restricts development. How a nation manages its water resources directly affects its ability to prosper. Below are some interesting facts concerning water that I have collected over the years. Hopefully they will give you some perspective as to how important clean water is to a society.

- More than 50% of Africa's people lack access to safe drinking water.
- Of all the renewable water available in Africa each year, only 4% is used because most Africans lack the wells, canals, pumps, reservoirs and other irrigation systems to access it.
- In developing countries, one person uses an average of ten litres of water per day. In the United States, one person uses an average of 260–300 litres during the same time period.
- Each flush of a toilet in the West uses the same amount of water that one person in the Third World uses all day for washing, cleaning, cooking and drinking.
- In the past ten years, diarrhoea caused by bad water has killed more children worldwide than all the people lost to armed conflict since World War II.

- Twelve million people die each year from the lack of safe drinking water, including more than three million who die from water-borne diseases.
- Over 80% of the diseases in developing countries are related to poor drinking water and sanitation.
- 1,5 billion people in the world are suffering from parasite infections due to the presence of solid human waste in the environment. These infections can cause malnutrition, anaemia and delayed growth. Many of them could be controlled with improved hygiene, clean water and sanitation.
- The average distance a woman in Africa and Asia walks to collect water is 6 km.
- The weight of water that women in Asia and Africa carry on their heads is equivalent to the maximum baggage weight allowed by most airlines: 20 kg.
- Women are the primary caretakers for those who fall ill from water-related diseases, reducing their time available for education and productive economic efforts.
- One-third of women in Egypt walk more than an hour a day for water; in other parts of Africa, the task can consume as much as eight hours.
- Medical research has documented cases of permanent damage to women's health as a result of carrying water, such as chronic fatigue, spinal and pelvic deformities, and effects on reproductive health including spontaneous abortion.
- In some parts of Africa, women expend as much as 85% of their daily energy getting water. This exhausting work has increased incidences of anaemia and other health problems.

Needless to say, clean, accessible water is crucial. If we are going to attempt to establish agrarian-based communities that can sustain families capable of raising orphaned children, clean water is a key component. The United Nations and governments like that of Norway have tried to help institute water development projects all through Africa over the years.

The same problem plagues these projects as other government-sponsored projects, and that is government corruption. The funds never get to the people they are intended to help. There is a huge opportunity here for the Christian community that walks in integrity. Not only is the authentic Christian governed by accountability to God, and therefore must act with integrity, but also has the heart and soul of their leader Jesus, and is therefore motivated by compassion. The UN and other international aid agencies are frustrated by the corruption issue; they are looking for people to work with who have integrity and can be trusted. There are millions of dollars of resources available for those who can be proven trustworthy and capable.

With Zimbabwe's erratic rainfall, wells, weirs and dams are a key to increased agricultural productivity and a healthier population. The Zambezi River is a huge yet virtually untapped resource. At the centre of every community should be fresh, clean water wells. Land surrounding these communities needs to be surveyed for potential opportunities to build weirs or dams to catch the runoff during the rainy season. The Israelis proved that the desert can blossom when water resources are properly managed. They developed drip irrigation to preserve their limited water supplies and used it strategically so that there would be no waste. I watched firsthand as my friends at the community turned land ravaged by overuse and drought into a Garden of Eden, simply by properly managing water. It can be done; it must be done. Zimbabwe's leaders need to stop being self-centred and stop thinking short-sightedly. They need to look at the future and act for their children and their children's children.

AGRICULTURE

I know that there are many in Zimbabwe who want to see the nation become more industrialized, and I think that some day that can happen. The problem is that you have to start with what you have to work with. At the moment the nation cannot even feed itself, and complicating the problem is the fact that AIDS is devastating the workforce. Zimbabwe needs to think and strategize in light of the realities on the ground and not what everyone else is doing. In the developing days of the US, 80% of the population was involved in agriculture of some form. It's where every developing nation must focus its resources in order to build a strong foundation. Development needs to focus on getting every community self-supported agriculturally and educating its next generation on the best land and water management skills available. We in the West could contribute significantly by helping establish schools of agriculture and sharing our expertise. In recent years the knowledge of farming in arid climates has increased exponentially. Organic farming opens the door for many in areas where manufactured fertilizers and pesticides aren't available.

One of the issues that has plagued Africa over the years has been the refusal of its leadership to think long-term. When one is driven by greed and selfish ambition, all that one thinks about is, 'What do I get out of this?' The focus is instant gratification. This ravenous beast has destroyed Zimbabwe and we are going to have to come together out of the ruins and rebuild from the ground up. Agriculture is the foundation stone that all else will lie upon. Zimbabwe's next generation of leaders must change their nomadic tribal mindset from living for today and carving out a personal kingdom, to building a future for their children tomorrow in the form of a prosperous nation. This will take hard work and personal sacrifice, but like those who have gone before, the children will not let your name be forgotten. You will become the true fathers of Zimbabwe.

EDUCATION

The next key component in preparing Zimbabwe's children for the future is education. We must invest in schools and teachers. Every community needs to have a strong school that is focused on raising a new generation of children that looks forward to what lies ahead and is not enslaved to the angry attitudes of the past. If children are taught to look for opportunity, they will find it. If Zimbabwe is to prosper, and get free from the chains of corruption, its children need to be trained in the ways of the Kingdom of God. Jesus needs to be their model, not Mugabe.

The values, morals and ethics they need to learn will be the foundation stones on which their communities will be built and prosper. Without these values instilled, Zimbabwe's next leaders will carry on the corrupt practices of their predecessors, and all Zimbabweans will continue to suffer under the slavery of poverty for generations to come. As I have documented earlier, there is a historical record and personal testimony on file of three great world leaders, being David, Solomon and Moses, who each built governments on the principles of justice. When righteousness reigns, nations prosper.

Besides establishing a right heart and learning how to respect and honour each other, career skills are an equally important component in a child's education. There is a sad problem in Africa that needs to be rectified. I have met countless Western educated Africans with multiple degrees walking around in suits and carrying briefcases and yet unemployed. Africans go overseas to train in areas where there are no jobs! What is the sense of a degree in computer engineering when your village has no electricity?

If children are taught to look for opportunity, they will find it.

Coming home with a college degree creates another problem I've observed; one rooted in pride. For some Africans, a degree makes them unwilling to roll up their sleeves and work side by side with their brothers in manual labour. They see it as beneath them. They would rather go hungry than be seen doing physical work. This attitude has to change. Not only is it condescending, it's counterproductive. Remember the example that Jesus set: those who want to lead must take on the heart and work-ethic of a servant.

Children must be trained in skills they can use to make a living in the current economic development stage of the country. I would suggest that what we started to do in the 1980s at The Community of Reconciliation needs to be revisited. By apprenticing in the areas of agriculture, wood working, metal working, basket weaving, knitting, etc., everyone found a practical skills that could be used to at least sustain a family. In an agrarian-based economy, there are many support industries that can be developed to help sustain it. Zimbabwe needs engineers who can develop and manage its water resources. It needs teachers who understand by sowing the right values into the children now, the whole country will reap a bountiful harvest later. With the devastation of the AIDS crisis, all medical disciplines will be in huge demand.

EMPLOYMENT

I think hope is important. If children grow up in a world of 80% unemployment, what is their incentive to want to learn? What is the point if it gets them nowhere? If properly educated in trade skills, even if there is not a position open in an existing company, one can still make products that can be sold on the open market, directly to the consumer.

Zimbabwe must focus its development on water resources that in turn will bring renewed life to a dry and weary land. When that land has been replenished it will become productive and create job opportunities for even more Zimbabweans as they sow and reap. As the children who are being educated graduate, there will plenty of opportunities to find work as more and more land is reclaimed and the agricultural sector grows.

In countries like China and India as their populations continue to grow, they are finding it increasingly difficult to feed their people. There are business opportunities in the agricultural sector for Zimbabweans to supply these burgeoning populations with food. There are huge opportunities ahead for Zimbabwe if she can think and plan appropriately. Zimbabwe's leadership needs to change the mindset of its people from being victims to entrepreneurs. This starts with leaders who have left behind the 'chief' mentality and understand that leadership is really about serving the people, not the other way around.

THE SIGNIFICANCE OF WOMEN

If Zimbabwe is to change course and realize its destiny, all of its people must come together and humble themselves before God and each other. Hand in hand, together, they must build a better future for their children. African politics has historically been dominated by men. The results haven't exactly been stellar as the male hormone testosterone seems to have been the driving force behind so much of the conflict that has ravaged the continent. Maybe Africa needs to look to its mothers for help in leadership.

One universal truth that I have observed in every culture in the world is that mothers care more about their children than about themselves. Within a mother's heart is an innate understanding of the heart of Jesus who, for the sake and welfare of others, laid his life down. I have watched mothers for years do the extraordinary for the welfare of their children. I think Africa's mothers must speak up, for they carry within their souls so much of what Africa needs to heal itself.

For those of you who may still doubt that there is something spiritually diabolical at work, please take a look at the facts. Women make up around 77% of people between the ages of 15 and 24 living with HIV.[8] Women and children are under an all-out assault! This attack is not about hamstringing a nation or a continent so that it walks with a limp. It is about destroying it so that it ceases to exist. Kill the mothers so that they can't reproduce and orphan the children so that they die from abandonment and starvation. I can't say it any clearer …

> *I think Africa's mothers must speak up, for they carry within their souls so much of what Africa needs to heal itself.*

THIS IS SPIRITUAL GENOCIDE!

It is my contention that we in the Christian community cannot sit back and feel sorry for the Zimbabweans. Whether we like it or not, by virtue of our spiritual bond at the foot of the cross, we cannot remain passive. We who are strong are required by the love of God to use whatever means possible to fight on behalf of our brothers and sisters in Zimbabwe who are under assault. 'This is what the LORD Almighty said: "Administer true justice; show mercy and compassion to one another"'(Zech 7:9).

> *Whether we like it or not, by virtue of our spiritual bond at the foot of the cross, we cannot remain passive.*

CHAPTER 15 ENDNOTES

1. UNAIDS, '2007 AIDS Epidemic Update'.

2. UNAIDS/ UNICEF/ USAID, 'Children on the Brink 2004: A joint report of new orphan estimates and a framework for action'.

3. World Health Organization (December 2005), 'Zimbabwe country profile for HIV/AIDS treatment scale up'.

4. The Sunday Times (April 2nd 2006) 'Desperate mothers throw away 20 babies a week as Zimbabwe starves'.

5. The Independent (17th November 2006), 'How AIDS and Starvation Condemn Zimbabwe's Women to Early Grave'.

6. UNAIDS (2006) 'Report on the global AIDS epidemic'. Accessed 13th March 2008.

7. Association of Zimbabwe Journalists (19th November 2006), 'Zim has Highest Orphan Rate: UN Official'.

8. UNAIDS (2006) 'Report on the global AIDS epidemic'. Accessed 13th March 2008.

CHAPTER 16

THE BAND OF BROTHERS

From this day to the ending of the world,
But we in it shall be remembered –
We few, we happy few, we band of brothers.

– WILLIAM SHAKESPEARE

A mazingly, this rather eventful journey surrounding the people of
Zimbabwe actually fits within the context of an even broader story
that I'd like to share with you as I believe it is relevant. In 1983, a year before
I first went to Zimbabwe, I had a rather unusual encounter with God that
significantly changed my religious paradigm. As a 25-year-old with a year of
Bible School under my belt, I found myself planting a church with a friend.
The learning curve was steep but the lessons invaluable. As with most young
men with aspirations for ministry, I studied the scriptures long and hard to
become well versed in them. I read the leading Christian authors of the ages
and soon developed a 'clear view' of how God interacted with mankind. Little did I understand how religious and overly spiritualized my perspective
was at the time.

It was a strange encounter during a Sunday morning church service
that would begin a significant paradigm shift for me. I had fallen into the
subtle and dangerous religious trap of 'overestimation of self', otherwise
called arrogance. Since I was in full-time ministry, I saw myself as on a
different plane from the congregation. It was clear to me that if one was
truly committed to the establishment of the Kingdom of God, one would

need to be in full-time ministry to do so. As I closed my eyes for a moment while on the stage during worship, I had no idea that when I opened them everything would look different.

The people you see standing on the outside are vital to my divine purposes and none of them will ever be on staff at a church. Now go and find them and teach them my ways.

As I stood there entering into the sweet melodies of worship, I was interrupted by an inner voice that told me to open my eyes and look at the congregation and 'tell me what you see.' After doing a quick inventory of my mental faculties to see if I was in fact lucid, I slowly opened one eye to make sure I was still at church, awake and not dreaming. Then, with both eyes opened, I observed something that I had never noticed before; two very distinct groups. They were spread out in front of me in a half-circle and I became keenly aware that there was a distinct inner circle of about one-third of the congregation. These were what I called the die-hards; the most committed people, aspiring to the noble pursuit of ministry and already involved in some capacity of leadership. Standing on the outside, making up the remaining two-thirds, were those who simply attended church and for the most part were pursing less noble ambitions such as business careers. Of course, I knew very few of these people as they were not a priority. It was then I heard a charge from this same inner voice. 'The people you see standing on the outside are vital to my divine purposes and none of them will ever be on staff at a church. Now go and find them and teach them my ways.'

I was speechless for two reasons. First, I had just had a very strong voice speak to me and that was in itself unnerving. Second, it was very clear that I had no idea what God's way was, as He had just blown my religious paradigm away. How could people not in full-time ministry be as important as those of us that were? After all, were we not the committed ones, the die-hards?

I was certainly dazed and confused but also insatiably curious as to what this all meant. Mystified but hooked by this encounter, I decided to head back to the instruction manual to reread it, as I obviously had missed something. I started in Genesis and as I continued reading I realized for the first time that the Old Testament 'Heroes of the Faith' were in fact not priests or even in the ministry!

These were men God used in the secu-lar arena and they would have never been on staff at a church. In fact, most of them would not have even been home group leaders, and yet God used them in signifi-cant ways. At first I was surprised and then inspired to the point that I had to share this with others. I went in pursuit of these fringe-dwellers at the church to share what I had discovered with them. Many of these relationships have remained to this day and I am grateful for each and every one as it has been quite a journey we have all been on.

> *The Old Testament*
> *'Heroes of the Faith' were*
> *in fact not priests or even*
> *in the ministry!*

THE JOSEPH COMPANY

As time went on, it became clear to me that something more was hap-pening. While we were discovering a new perspective on God's way, it was how we were doing it that touched my heart – together as a group of men. I decided to give it a conceptual name and called it the 'Joseph Com-pany'. My reasoning was that I identified with the biblical character of Joseph more than any other. Many of the experiences he went through seemed to parallel my own life and the lives of the men I was meeting with. Over the years those parallels have continued in ways that have deep-ly and profoundly affected me, and one day in eternity when we meet, I have a feeling we will be able to finish each other's sentences.

For me, the Joseph Company was not a business entity or even a min-istry organization, but a type of calling outside the walls of the ecclesias-tical world in the business and political sectors. The focus was about men who would band together to fulfil God's purpose for their lives and

influence the realms of secular society with Kingdom values and principles. It was not the 'how' that was the only focus; the 'who and what' were
equally important. Who had God brought together in friendship and what
purpose did they have together? Even as a young man I had begun to see
the subtle corruption that wealth and power could bring. I was deeply
concerned that the men of the Joseph Company would lose their focus
on others while building personal wealth. I did not want them to lose
their heart in the process. Without God's heart of compassion focused
outward on others in need, the focus turns inward and it all becomes
about me. Men become consumed with God's blessing and prosperity as
a means of increasing their own empire, and what looks so good on the
outside is insidiously self-centred on the inside.

It's now been twenty-five years and a lot of miles since we 'Josephs'
started out on this journey. As we continue to meet over breakfast or lunch,
each of my friends has asked with genuine heartfelt concern about other
long-time friends we have in common. I have recently been asking myself,
why now, after all these years do we still sense this depth of love and concern for one another? We are scattered across the city, the nation and the
world, yet there seems to be some invisible
tie that continues to hold us together. I have
a few theories and all of them have to do
with age.

*The focus was about men
who would band together
to fulfil God's purpose for
their lives and influence
the realms of secular
society with Kingdom
values and principles.*

It seems to me that as young men we
tend to focus on the 'what and how' because we are so driven to achieve and gain
status. We struggle so hard to figure out
who we are. We need to accomplish significant feats so that we feel that we are significant. We need to impress others.

Relationships are important only in that
they help us gain the significance that we so desperately seek. It is hard to
admit, but we Christians use people to get what we want as much as anyone else. We live in a consumer-driven culture and we are trained from

childhood to consume relationships as well. So what has changed now?

As we get older we begin to suffer the pain of loss. We have lost parents, siblings, wives, children and friends. We have learned the pain of losing those we love and faced our own frail humanity as some of us have faced death ourselves. Our priorities have significantly changed, our values have been restructured, and how we see life has taken a huge paradigm shift. We are less interested in show and more interested in substance. We are more thoughtful and introspective; looking for answers on how to spend the rest of our days. We find ourselves asking these types of questions ...

- What do I want to leave behind; what is my legacy?
- Have I made a real difference in someone else's life?
- Does my life matter; what have I done with it?

Even though we are bruised and battered and may feel our age, there are some of us who are actually in a better place. We have certainly added perspective to the mix. We are entering into a potentially wonderful time of our lives. Our children are grown and most have left the nest. While we may have less energy, we do have more time and resources. So what are we doing? Are we building castles for ourselves with a custom moat included to protect ourselves from the big bad world?

Are we building castles for ourselves with a custom moat included to protect ourselves from the big bad world?

I also think that failure has had a huge impact on shaping us as men. We have come face to face with our weaknesses. Being a father and raising children is at times a terribly humiliating experience in failure. Business failures, church failures and relational failures are all seen in the rear view mirrors of our lives. These failures, of course, were virtually non-existent when we were in our twenties. Later, when we started to experience failure, we were convinced it could not possibly be our fault, so we blamed it on everyone else.

We have now all come to the painful realization that we are in fact fallible and very human. We are men with clay feet. We have discovered that we are downright terrible at some things but then that is OK. We have hurt people (even the ones we love) and done some really stupid things. A lot of us have gone from thinking how lucky God was to have us on his side to just hoping that we have not screwed it all up! This is called humility, and it takes a good thirty years to even begin to understand it.

> *I also think that failure has had a huge impact on shaping us as men. We have come face to face with our weaknesses.*

If you have been misunderstood, thrown into a pit in life, falsely accused, punished for having integrity and been forgotten after doing a favour, you are a Joseph. If this is your journey, then like Joseph you understand humility, and when your brothers are starving and come asking for food, your heart cannot help but be moved to compassion.

An Historical Legacy

There was a point on my journey to understanding how God uses people when I wondered if God's interaction with what I will call the 'biblical career executives' was limited to the dispensation of the Old Testament. Would He ever use another Abraham, Joseph, Moses or David to make an impact on the world? I wondered if, with the formation of the Church concept, things had changed.

Did the new emerging 1st century model called the Church do away with God using men and women in the marketplace? Was it now up to full-time pastors and ministers to fulfil this role? Many of my ministry colleagues reassured me that it was, but I wasn't so sure. Soon I realized that I had the answer to my own question. Why would God have asked me to find them if He didn't intend to use them? This was all the motivation I needed to research these types of men through modern history.

I was convinced that God was still using them, but where were they and who were they?

You would have thought I was mining for gold as I pored over hundreds of books in search of people with this type of Joseph calling. Each book had the same story; it was the preachers and their messages that made the difference. However, one day while reading a book on revival, the author referenced a group of businessmen by name who worked hand-in-hand with the revivalist Charles Finney. That was the key I needed. From there I discovered that the past 200 years of history have left us today with an enormous legacy. Something has been handed down to us. A torch has been passed. I would like to highlight two groups here that exemplify what I am talking about.

THE CLAPHAM SECT

This was a group (a 'company') of English friends and colleagues ('brothers'), who worked together from around 1790–1830 to take up various causes they felt central to establish-

A lot of us have gone from thinking how lucky God was to have us on his side to just hoping that we have not screwed it all up!

ing the Government of God on earth. They were men who believed in the cause of the Justice of God and looked for ways to see it established in England. They were bankers, lawyers, businessmen, politicians, playwrights and authors, many who initially did not see themselves as the type of material God could use to make a difference. In their case they felt the call from God to take on the issue of the injustice of slavery.

Clapham was a small town just south of London where the two most prominent members resided. Henry Thornton was a highly successful merchant banker. William Wilberforce was the parliamentarian who championed their cause in the British Government. Through their efforts and those of their 'company of brothers', the Slave Trade Act was passed in England in 1807, abolishing slavery. They continued with the battle and after many more years of campaigning, they were victorious with the total emancipation of British slaves with the passing of the Slavery Abolition Act in 1833. They also campaigned vigorously for Britain to use its influence to eradicate slavery throughout the world. As a company of men they also took up such causes as Penal Reform and evangelizing India.

The movie *Amazing Grace*, released in 2006, recalls the story of the life of William Wilberforce. As he struggles with his own frail humanity, he has to overcome his inner demons and in the end decides to take a stand on God's side. John Newton, the ex-slave trader and author of the now famous hymn 'Amazing Grace', was a rector in London and exerted a huge influence on Wilberforce. While Wilberforce's name is associated with the victory, it was a team effort, as each of the 'company of brothers' played a key role in building the case that eventually set the captives free.

THE ASSOCIATION OF GENTLEMEN

In the United States, brothers Arthur and Louis Tappan, who were dry goods and silk merchants during the 1820–30s in New York City, rallied their 'company of brothers' in business together. They took on a variety of causes including the abolition of slavery, the sex trade and chemical dependency. They were men of such integrity that they refused to do business in the generally accepted custom of the day, which was to have different prices for customers depending on their status. The Tappans, on the principle of integrity, advertised 'One Price for All'. Due to their unwavering commitment to integrity, they became the most trusted merchants on the east coast. Even those who hated their religious philosophy on various social issues still did business with them as they knew they could be trusted.

They built churches for the poor and turned the established religious thinking of the day upside down. They abolished the 'pew tax', enabling the poor to come to church for free. Can you imagine it? What a radical idea! They formed not-for-profit organizations, founded newspapers and built universities, all in an effort to establish the Government of God on Earth. This company of men grew increasingly frustrated with the church politics of the day. They felt that they needed a spokesman as radical and open-minded as they were, and recruited Charles Finney. They built his churches and financed his revivals. When they felt he was out of line by segregating his congregation, as was the custom of the day, they confronted him and made him change.

Stephen Spielberg produced a movie in 1997 called *Amistad*. It is the story of a group of slaves who revolted on their slave ship and were later captured. Stellen Skarsgard plays Louis Tappan, who not only financed the slave's defence but was instrumental in recruiting ex-President John Quincy Adams to argue the case before the US Supreme Court.

THE BAND OF BROTHERS

It was in 2001, after watching the HBO mini-series *Band of Brothers*, that many of the principles, concepts and feelings that I had had over the years started to come together. I slowly formed a more comprehensive picture of what I wanted my life to be about. A vision slowly emerged about what legacy I wanted to leave behind for future generations, and who I wanted to do it with. The story from the Band of Brothers series is about a group of men called 'Easy Company' and everything they went through together during the Second World War.

It made me think again about so many of the things stored away in my own heart. If my suspicions are right, I think many of you reading this are also feeling a tugging or burning in your own heart. I believe many of us who have reached middle age are at another crossroads in our lives. We all have important choices to make and I am about to suggest one.

There are a number of key correlations between everything that the men of Easy Company went through in the battle for the liberation of Europe, and the battle that the Christian Community currently wages on earth for the establishment of the Kingdom of God. The word 'Kingdom' seems like such an archaic word so every once in awhile I like inserting the word 'Government'. I think it is more culturally relevant today.

So what is it that makes the concept of the Band of Brothers so appealing to me? At the core is a group of ordinary men, called on to do extraordinary things together, in order to reach a common goal. I see this same theme in the group or 'company' of men that Jesus chose to have at his side. They too were ordinary guys brought together from different backgrounds to fulfil a common purpose. This is such an interesting group – family members, business associates and men looking for a cause worth fighting for. The fervent ones we know as 'zealots'. It is clear by their nicknames and their actions that they were all passionate men. They were all looking for a cause and Jesus knew it and gave them one much bigger than they had ever imagined. They spent three years with Jesus on an incredible high, watching Him gather crowds, perform miracles and share profound words of insight, only to be left feeling abandoned and confused by his death. Then, encouraged by his resurrection, but still not sure what to do, they hid out together in Jerusalem until the Holy Spirit united their hearts and opened their eyes to a cause worth laying their lives down for. These were ordinary men called to do extraordinary things, and because of their faith they did!

I believe many of us who have reached middle age are at another crossroads in our lives.

At the core is a group of ordinary men, called on to do extraordinary things together.

Jesus must have seen something deep within them at the very core of their heart. It is interesting to note that it's possible that half of the group was related to someone else in the group. In other words, they had an existing bond before Jesus brought them together to fulfil a common purpose. It certainly wasn't their personal wealth or skills that Jesus was after, as there were certainly others wealthier and more talented. I suspect He saw something in their hearts that caused Him to trust them with the keys of his Kingdom.

What were those keys? I believe them to be the values and principles that God's Government is built on. To know and understand these values and principles is to know God's heart, as this is where they are kept. Have you ever thought about what the Government of God would look like on earth? I imagine that while we may not know exactly the form it would take, we do know that it would be built on a number of key principles, none less important than that of Justice. Wasn't this also what the 'Band of Brothers' in Easy Company was fighting for; to fight back the armies of tyranny and destroy the oppressor so that Justice was established and the downtrodden and captive could be set free?

This whole concept of the Band of Brothers really touches something at the core of my soul as I see myself as very ordinary while my heart wants to do something extraordinary alongside other ordinary guys.

I am bored with normal and ordinary. Mundane is getting old. I am tired of solely pursuing a business career and accumulating material goods. I ask myself, 'To what end?' What is the point or purpose of it all? I cannot take anything with me, and in the end what will I have to show for it all? Solomon summed it all up rather succinctly as meaninglessness. He asked, 'What does man gain from all his labour at which he toils under the sun?' (Eccles 1:3). Meaninglessness is not how I want my life to be summed up.

I suspect He saw something in their hearts that caused Him to trust them with the keys of his Kingdom.

Is God giving me pats on the back for all the great business deals I am doing or how much wealth I'm accumulating? Does He really care about my portfolio or my retirement plan? Or is He observing what I have done with what He entrusted to me? How does what I do everyday build his Government here on earth? Am I building 'Heaven on Earth' like I pray for daily in the 'Lord's Prayer'? These are the questions that fill my thoughts and make me re-evaluate where my heart is. Jesus said, 'Where your treasure is, there your heart will follow' (Luke 12:34). I ask myself, what then is really important to me; where is my heart?

As I have pondered these questions I have come to a number of important conclusions about myself:

1. I care about the plight of the *Oppressed Poor* and would like to see what I can do to help alleviate their suffering. It seems to me that God is doing a work in my heart that must be expressed in a tangible way.
2. I think it is in the nature of all men to build in some form or fashion. I want to build something for the oppressed poor that will make a significant difference in their lives. With the understanding I now have, it must be built on the principle or foundation of *Justice*.
3. I also want to do it with my long-time friends who are my *Band of Brothers*. I want to see others find both their Band of Brothers and a purpose together. I believe that God is not done with us, and we may in fact just be getting started.
4. I want to do it from a right heart; the heart of *Compassion*, as this is genuine and brings Life for all involved.

It is essential if we are to go on this journey together, that we all understand the heart of God when it comes to the oppressed poor and those who fight on their behalf.

THE SIGNIFICANCE OF RELATIONSHIPS AND A PURPOSE

In this current season of my life, I have been on a very significant personal journey. As I have shared, it is one that has me thinking a lot about who I am, what I want to do with the remaining years of my life and how I want to be remembered.

I have been making a point of reconnecting with many dear friends who go back through the years. As a man, I have come to see how we men tend to let our relationships drift away from us if they aren't functionally relevant. In the process I've discovered something profound and meaningful. After not seeing each other, in some cases for years, I still have a deep sense of love, respect and connection with each and every man. As I sit in their presence this deep sense of 'brotherhood' sweeps over my soul. Some of these relationships go back as far as 1977. The interesting thing I've discovered recently is that there is still a deep heartfelt bond that connects many of us. Why? Each of these friends asks about the other, which tells me that they still feel the unspoken bond as well. Each laments that they do not see enough of their old friends. As I listen I heard something calling out from deep inside of each man.

As we catch up and share the journeys of our lives, we all have in common 'glorious victories and humiliating defeats'. We have all raised families, had careers and struggled to find our place in God's divine plan. While we were together in our younger years, we tried to do something significant for God by fulfilling the visions and purposes of others. While most of it was good, it wasn't always fulfilling, as it was often not based on the values and principles that resonated within our own hearts. In some cases it led to disillusionment and discouragement. Then, over the years, we have scattered to various places trying to find our own destiny and, in many cases, have lost touch with each other or have had very little interaction.

Not only is there the longing for camaraderie, there is also a wondering of what still lies ahead for us all. Was our history together a thing of the past or is there still some destiny to fulfil as a group? Are we past our 'use by date' or is there something still left for us to do together? I think each and every man has asked these questions and wondered what any of it means.

We are all in that stage of life that naturally tends to shift our inner focus from offence to defence. We realize that most of our life is behind us and that we may have twenty years at best left in the marketplace. Retirement becomes our priority and investments become increasingly important. We start erecting our castle, complete with moat, and prepare to defend ourselves against the forces of nature that want to take it all away from us. Fear can often be the driving force behind our decisions. We tend to want to isolate and insulate ourselves from much that is going on out there in the world, as most of it is out of our control. The more I thought about it, the more it dawned on me how self-centred and self-serving this all feels. Not that those things are not important, but they could very well dominate a man's soul to the point where he turns himself into a self-centred Scrooge and not even realize it. It would be very easy for us all to find ourselves increasingly relationally isolated as we focus our energies on building the nest egg.

Are we past our 'use by date' or is there something still left for us to do together?

It is my contention that there is a healthy balance to keep oneself from falling too far down the well of self-centredness, and that is to find ways to serve and help others. I think it is also helpful to keep ourselves exposed to the global picture. Ninety-five percent of the world has no concept of retirement. Retirement is the result of the prosperity of our Western culture and, like so many things, a product that our self-centred, consumer-driven world has sold us. This does not make it wrong, but it does raise some interesting questions about how one wants to spend the later years of one's life and with whom.

There is a healthy balance to keep oneself from falling too far down the well of self-centredness, and that is to find ways to serve and help others.

In 2001, around the same time as the *Band of Brothers* mini-series came out, a Christian counsellor, John Eldredge, published his book, *Wild at Heart*. While the book has had its share of critics over John's use of scripture to make his points, I think there is little doubt that the book's wild popularity is due to the fact that it struck chords of truth in men's hearts. Across the world it touched them at the core of their soul as they each identified and got back in touch with their God-created nature. Instead of feeling guilty or ashamed about it, they celebrated it!

In summarizing, John's book states that men need to find three things in order to find fulfilment:

1. *A battle to fight:* A cause outside of themselves to fight for – something noble and on behalf of others who have need of them.
2. *An adventure to live for:* This cause must have a sense of adventure and danger – it cannot be easy to accomplish or too safe.
3. *A beauty to fight for:* There must be someone worth fighting for – someone who can appreciate the sacrifice made.

To quote from the book, 'If a man is ever to find out who he is and what he is here for, he has got to take that journey for himself. He has got to get his heart back.'

I think there are a lot of middle-aged men out there who still need to take that journey. There is a world of battles to fight, adventures to go on and beauties to rescue, but often in the most unexpected places. I can think of nothing more exciting or noble than putting men in need of battles together with people who need rescuing. The personal reward would be life-changing, and I believe that in the end they would get their hearts back.

CHAPTER 17

COMPASSIONATE JUSTICE

Administer true justice, show mercy and
compassion to one another.

– ZECHARIAH 7:9

W hen we began the process of setting up our organization to fight on behalf of the oppressed poor, we thought long and hard as to what to name it. After trying on a whole host of names, nothing quite seemed to fit. It was important that the name accurately reflected what was in our hearts. After pondering for a few days, the two words that seemed to encapsulate our burden were 'compassion' and 'justice'. I was convinced that while these words certainly summarized the motivation and goal, there was no possible way the name would be available for incorporation. Much to my surprise, not only were they available, but I could barely find the two words being used together anywhere. I also discovered the same situation when we set up our website at **www.compassionatejustice.com**.

Once we were up and running, I started receiving e-mails and phone calls from friends and associates commenting on the unusualness of the name. This perplexed me at first until one of my close friends explained that for most people the word justice means vindication. To them the thought of justice evokes feelings of something cold, sterile, legal, insensitive or even harsh. In some cases we think it's violent and want or demand justice when we are wronged. Place this next to 'compassionate' and it can certainly cause confusion, so let me try to give some clarification and understanding.

THE SIGNIFICANCE OF JUSTICE IN HIS OWN WORDS

A few years ago, in an effort to get a grasp on the significance to God of the principle of justice, I set out to do a Bible study. I was hoping to find a few choice nuggets from which to glean some understanding of the issue. I soon discovered was that those nuggets were not hard to find and in fact, there was a rich gold vein of material. There were hundreds of verses that clearly stated God's thoughts on the matter.

What became resoundingly clear when I completed the study was that this issue of justice was no secondary matter to God. In fact it was of utmost priority to Him. Surprisingly, He not only had a lot to say on the matter, He was committed to action on behalf of those who were victims of injustice and those who chose to fight on behalf of the victims.

After some thought, I decided to put a little booklet together that compiled all of the scripture nuggets I had found. I called it 'The Ministry of Compassion' which I felt embodied itself in the only human example we have of God the Father, which was Jesus. There is no narrative in the booklet as I thought it important for these scriptures to speak for themselves. I simply compiled them in one place and sorted them into groups that address the various facets of God's heart. (The booklet can be downloaded free of charge from our Compassionate Justice website.)

What became resoundingly clear when I completed the study was that this issue of justice was no secondary matter to God.

For the sake of space here in the book, I have chosen to include just a few of these scriptures, but have listed the references for the others at the end of the chapter. I think you will find, as I did, that God has a lot of emotional energy in his heart concerning the poor. They need justice. They need it dispensed through our efforts. If we choose to take up the cause we will have someone in our corner who has more invested in this mission than we do.

GOD IDENTIFIES WITH THE SUFFERING OF THE OPPRESSED

He feels their pain, their aloneness and their feeling of hopelessness. God understands suffering; so should we!

Though I cry, 'I've been wronged!' I get no response; though I call for help, there is no justice.

— JOB 19:7 (AUTHOR'S EMPHASIS)

Men cry out under a load of oppression; they plead for relief *from the arm of the powerful.*

— JOB 35:9 (AUTHOR'S EMPHASIS)

Look to my right and see; no one is concerned for me. *I have no refuge; no one cares for my life.*

— PSALM 142:4 (AUTHOR'S EMPHASIS)

A poor man's field may produce abundant food, but injustice sweeps it away.

— PROVERBS 13:23 (AUTHOR'S EMPHASIS)

Woe to those who make unjust laws, to those who issue oppressive decrees, *to* deprive the poor of their rights *and* withhold justice *from the oppressed of my people,* making widows their prey and robbing the fatherless.

— ISAIAH 10:1-2 (AUTHOR'S EMPHASIS)

Now this was the sin of your sister Sodom: She and her daughters were arrogant, overfed and unconcerned; they did not help the poor and needy.

– EZEKIEL 16:49 (AUTHOR'S EMPHASIS)

This is what the Lord says: 'For three sins of Israel, even for four, I will not turn back my wrath. They sell the righteous for silver, and the needy for a pair of sandals. They trample on the heads of the poor *as upon the dust of the ground and* deny justice to the oppressed.'

– AMOS 2:6–7 (AUTHOR'S EMPHASIS)

When he saw the crowds, he had compassion on them, *because they were harassed and helpless, like sheep without a shepherd.*

– MATTHEW 9:36 (AUTHOR'S EMPHASIS)

GOD HAS ISSUED A RALLYING CALL TO ACTION

… for a cause worth fighting for on behalf of a people who cannot fight for themselves.

'Because of the devastation of the afflicted, because of the groaning of the needy, now I will arise,' says the Lord; 'I will set him in the safety for which he longs.'

– PSALM 12:5 (AUTHOR'S EMPHASIS)

A father of the fatherless and a judge for the widows is God in his holy habitation. God makes a home for the lonely.

– PSALMS 68:5–6 (AUTHOR'S EMPHASIS)

The Lord protects *the strangers; He* supports *the fatherless and the widow; but He* thwarts *the way of the wicked.*

– PSALM 146:9 (AUTHOR'S EMPHASIS)

312

He who oppresses the poor reproaches his Maker, but he who is gracious to the needy *honours Him.*

– PROVERBS 14:31 (AUTHOR'S EMPHASIS)

Do not exploit the poor because they are poor and do not crush the needy in court, *for the Lord will take up their case* and will plunder those who plunder them.

– PROVERBS 22:22–23 (AUTHOR'S EMPHASIS)

Learn to do right! Seek justice, *encourage the oppressed.* Defend the cause *of the fatherless, plead the case of the widow.*

– ISAIAH 1:17 (AUTHOR'S EMPHASIS)

The poor and needy search for water, but there is none; their tongues are parched with thirst. But I the Lord will answer them; *I, the God of Israel, will not forsake them.*

– ISAIAH 41:17 (AUTHOR'S EMPHASIS)

This is what the Lord says: 'Maintain justice and do what is right, *for my salvation is close at hand and my righteousness will soon be revealed.'*

– ISAIAH 56:1 (AUTHOR'S EMPHASIS)

'Is this not the fast which I chose, to loosen the bonds of wickedness, to undo the bands of the yoke, and to let the oppressed go free, and break every yoke? Is it not to divide your bread with the hungry, and bring the homeless poor into the house; when you see the naked, to cover him; and not to hide yourself from your own flesh?'

– ISAIAH 58:6–7 (AUTHOR'S EMPHASIS)

I myself will tend *my sheep and have them lie down, declares the Sovereign Lord. I will* search *for the lost and bring back the strays.*

I will bind *up the injured and* strengthen *the weak, but the sleek and the strong I will destroy. I will shepherd the flock with justice.*
— EZEKIEL 34:15–16 (AUTHOR'S EMPHASIS)

Then the Lord said to him, 'Now then, you Pharisees clean the outside of the cup and dish, but inside you are full of greed and wickedness. You foolish people! Did not the one who made the outside make the inside also? But give what is inside the dish to the poor, and everything will be clean for you.'
— LUKE 11:39–41 (AUTHOR'S EMPHASIS)

Finally, all of you, live in harmony with one another; be sympathetic, love as brothers, be compassionate *and humble.*
— 1 PETER 3:8 (AUTHOR'S EMPHASIS)

Religion that God our Father accepts as pure and faultless is this: to look after *orphans and widows in their distress and to keep oneself from being polluted by the world.*
— JAMES 1:27 (AUTHOR'S EMPHASIS)

GOD IS COMMITTED TO THOSE THAT TAKE UP THE CAUSE OF JUSTICE

… and defend the oppressed. He will fight for them as well.

Commit your way to the Lord; trust in him and he will do this: He will make your righteousness shine like the dawn, the justice of your cause *like the noonday sun.*
— PSALM 37:5–6 (AUTHOR'S EMPHASIS)

… *blessed is he who is kind to the needy.*
— PROVERBS 14:21

*He who is kind to the poor lends to the Lord, and he will reward him
for what he has done.*

– Proverbs 19:17

*A generous man will himself be blessed, for he shares his food with
the poor.*

– Proverbs 22:9

*He who gives to the poor will lack nothing, but he who closes his eyes
to them receives many curses.*

– Proverbs 28:27

*Blessed is he who has regard for the weak; the Lord delivers him in times
of trouble. The Lord will protect him and preserve his life; he will bless
him in the land and not surrender him to the desire of his foes. The Lord
will sustain him on his sickbed and restore him from his bed of illness.*

– Psalm 41:1–3

*Therefore, O King, be pleased to accept my advice; Renounce your sins
by doing what is right, and your wickedness by being kind to the oppressed. It might be that your prosperity will continue.*

– Daniel 4:27

*Cornelius stared at him in fear. 'What is it, Lord?' he asked. The an-
gel answered, 'Your prayers and* gifts to the poor have come up as
a memorial offering before God.'

– Acts 10:4 (Author's emphasis)

God is not unjust; he will not forget your work and the love you have
shown Him as you have helped his people *and continue to help them.*

– Hebrew 6:10 (Author's emphasis)

THE SIGNIFICANCE OF JUSTICE AS A CALLING

After reading the volume of references, there can be no denying that justice is supremely important to God. It is equally imperative that we understand there is a very big difference between Civil Law and Biblical Justice. Howard Zehr, a Mennonite author, wrote in his book, *Changing Lenses*, 'The test of justice in the biblical view is not whether the right rules are applied in the right way,' instead, 'Justice is tested by the outcome. The tree is tested by its fruit ... Does the outcome work to make things right? Are things being made right for the poor and the least powerful, the least "deserving"? Biblical justice focuses on right relationships, not right rules.'

In other words, when it comes to dispensing justice, God is proactive.

I was struck by his use of the word 'relationships' as this speaks directly to one of the core values of the Band of Brothers. Here we clearly see again that God's emphasis is on having a 'right heart' and not just having 'right form'.

We have all experienced the frustration of seeing someone who was, by their behaviour obviously guilty, but due to a legal technicality the court was forced to find them not guilty. This gets under our skin and makes us very angry. Everything inside us screams that this is not justice. We are sure that Lady Justice is blind. This is Legal Justice, not Biblical Justice.

In order to understand God's heart for the oppressed poor, one has to understand that it is based on the principle of justice which is a part of his 'genetic code' and expressed through the writings of the Scriptures. In the dispensation of the Old Testament, the writer of the Psalms declared, '[The Lord] executes justice for the oppressed; [He] gives food to the hungry. The Lord sets the prisoners free; the Lord opens the eyes of the blind' (Author's additions, Ps 146:7–8).

In other words, when it comes to dispensing justice, God is proactive. This is an issue that is pre-eminent in his heart, foremost in his mind and must be expressed continually in his followers. It is who He is. When

316

He introduced himself to Moses in the burning bush as 'I Am', He could have added the word justice among many others. 'I Am Justice.'

As we discussed earlier in the book and by way of reminder, hundreds of years later, Jesus characterized his earthly ministry by service to the poor, the outcasts and the downtrodden, thereby establishing justice.

> *The Spirit of the Lord is upon me, because he has anointed me to bring good news to the poor. He has sent me to proclaim release to the captives and recovery of sight to the blind, to let the oppressed go free, to proclaim the year of the Lord's favour.*
>
> – LUKE 4:18-19

I have seen this quote spiritualized to the point that it is unrecognizable. It has been used to justify so many self-serving fund-raising programmes within the church. I don't think it needs interpretation, I think it means exactly what it says. Jesus came for the poor and those in need. He came to let the oppressed go free.

THE 'OPPRESSED POOR' DEFINED

It's my heart's desire to be on God's side of this battle for justice. I have a particular burden that occupies my heart; it is my desire to fight on behalf of the oppressed poor.

It is not that I do not have compassion on all the poor because I most certainly do. For me, however, something rises in my heart when I see powerful forces taking advantage of the weak and desperate situations of the poor in order to fulfil their

Biblical justice focuses on right relationships, not right rules.

own agenda. Honestly, it makes me angry as I see it as a great injustice. I find myself wanting to be an active participant in seeing that justice is established on behalf of those people too weak to fight for themselves.

So that there is no misunderstanding, I define the oppressed poor or, as the Bible sometimes refers to them, 'the downtrodden', as those whose plight is not a choice of their own making. Nor is it a consequence of their actions or attitudes, but the result of being up against forces much too powerful for them to overcome on their own.

In my mind the strong forces that oppress the poor could be summarized into the following five groups:

1. *Political Oppression:* In these situations, governments, dissidents, rebels or warlords are in conflict with each other for control of a region. This results in innocent people, uninterested in the politics of it all, who are just trying to survive, getting caught in the crossfire. The outcome is that they lose their homes, livelihood and life itself. I personally witnessed this in Guatemala in the 1980s, where hundreds of women were left widowed after their husbands were killed by political dissidents coming over the border from southern Mexico. Africa too has seen its share of political struggles in Zimbabwe, Rwanda, Liberia and today in Darfur. My friends were tragically murdered by misguided political activists.

2. *Economic Oppression:* These are scenarios where people are living under economies where the country's infrastructure has been destroyed by incompetent or greedy leaders so that they cannot make a living or put food on the table. Zimbabwe would certainly be a dramatic case in point. The leadership of the country has destroyed one of Africa's most prosperous countries within a decade. Economic turmoil often results in women being forced into prostitution to survive. Currently the sex slave trade of Eastern Europe and Asia is imprisoning and shipping young women and children overseas who rarely reach the age of 30 before dying of disease, drug overdose or are murdered. Women are often the worst victims of economic oppression.

3. *Religious Oppression:* Historically, this has been the most common source of war and oppression and it continues today in many countries. More people have died in the 'name of God' than any of

318

us can imagine. Sadly, the Church has more often been a 'prophet of oppression' than a liberator of the poor. It has sided with political leaders and ideologies that have enslaved people. One needs to go no further than the Apartheid politics of South Africa. We continue to see the age-old battles in the Middle East. We've witnessed the brutality of the Taliban in Afghanistan as they attempt to enslave whole people groups to their religion. It was just a few years ago that we saw the mass graves from the Genocide going on in Eastern Europe that was called 'Ethnic Cleansing' which was really a cover up for 'Religious Cleansing'. Religious wars have had devastating consequences and never resulted in changing much for very long. A lot of lives have been lost in vain.

4. *Cultural Oppression:* The historical cultural prejudices of the caste system I witnessed in India, or the rejection of working widows or single mothers in the marketplace because of their gender, has lead to widespread global poverty. Children are often casualties in these situations. In Guatemala, many of us worked to balance the Scales of Justice by building homes for widowed families living in caves and sewer pipes because the women were not allowed to work.

5. *Natural Oppression:* The force of natural disasters such as earthquakes, floods, hurricanes, tornadoes and droughts that have destroyed everything in their path, leaving people homeless and starving, are a huge problem. In the United States we have recently witnessed the devastation of Hurricane Katrina. In the case of Indonesia one earthquake in the ocean released a tsunami that killed nearly 300 000 people within a few hours. In Africa, drought and the lack of water lead to widespread starvation and disease. Often the water is just under their feet but they cannot reach it or they can't afford to build the dams to catch it and store it in the rainy season.

I believe that God has invited all of us to the battle; it is now simply a matter of us responding.

THE ORPHAN AND WIDOW

It seems clear that, in God's heart under the general heading of the 'Oppressed Poor', there are two groups that are a priority to Him. They are addressed countless times in the scriptures and nothing gets his ire up more than people who take advantage of them. On the other side of the equation, I also think that nothing touches his heart more deeply than those who seek justice on their behalf.

I am referring to the orphan and the widow. These two groups of society are the weakest and most vulnerable under oppression. Orphans were brought into the world without a say in the matter. Whether their parents were the victims of war, starvation, AIDS or just abandoned them, they are powerless to fight for themselves. Unless someone comes to their aid, they have a death sentence hanging over their heads.

> *I also think that nothing touches his heart more deeply than those who seek justice on their behalf.*

The same could be said of widows. They too are in a sad situation, but not by any choice of their own. Often in the later years of their lives, without the physical strength to work, or being unable to work due to cultural prejudices, they are abandoned and alone. They are seen as a liability and not a productive member of the community.

The scriptures are very straightforward about how God sees them and their situation and leaves little to question. In fact our actions toward these two groups significantly define how God views the reality of our faith. The elder James laid it out rather plainly when he wrote, 'This is pure and undefiled religion in the sight of our God and Father, *to visit orphans and widows in their distress*, and to keep oneself unstained by the world' (*Author's emphasis*, Jas 1:27).

The prophet Isaiah proclaimed, 'Learn to do right! Seek justice, encourage the oppressed. Defend the cause of the fatherless, plead the case of the widow' (Isa 1:17). In looking at this quote further, I noticed that he actually laid out a great strategy for taking up their cause:

- *Learn to:* In other words, get proactive and learn about the plight of the orphan and the widow in our world. Do your research; ignorance is no excuse.
- *Do right:* This is quite clear-cut. Doing is an action word. What do we do? The right thing on their behalf! There's no room for passivity here.
- *Seek justice:* This is another proactive action word. This is not waiting for it to come to you. This is about you taking the initiative to look for ways to establish justice on others' behalf.
- *Encourage the oppressed:* Again, we are exhorted to be proactive and not to keep our mouths shut. Silence, in this case, is deadly!
- *Defend the orphan:* Another action word. In fact, it's a command to be proactive and fight on behalf of the orphan.
- *Plead the case for the widow:* I think it is quite clear by now that God is expecting us to be proactive and aggressively pursue pleading the case for the widow and the orphan.

Martin Luther King said, 'The ultimate tragedy is not the oppression and cruelty by the bad people, but the silence over that by the good people.'

The Dream in My Heart

As Martin Luther King did, I have a dream in my heart and it is that ...

... God would once again unite the hearts of the Band of Brothers, their wives and their children to bring them together for a *noble* cause.

... God would re-ignite the hearts of the Band of Brothers and give them back the *passion* and *vision* that has grown dim or been lost.

... Bands of Brothers all over the world would come together and form a group or 'company' to do, at God's bidding, something *significant* for someone else in need.

... The Band of Brothers would take up a *cause*, saddle themselves up for an adventure and rescue someone in real distress.

When I dream of making a significant impact, I do not mean that it is necessarily a large scale cause. What I mean is that it has an impact on someone's life that makes a significant difference to them. It needs to be something meaningful; something of substance that changes a person's life forever; something they will never forget.

I believe that all over the world there are Bands of Brothers that God has tied together at the heart. They are natural, God-ordained relationships that have come together for a purpose that may not yet be discovered. I think most of us have thought of them selfishly as though they were created for our benefit or gain, but what if that's not the case?

Could there be an untapped potential to fulfil a bigger purpose? Maybe God has been orchestrating these relationships so that one day these ordinary men, in these ordinary relationships, could band together to do something extraordinary in someone else's life. God knows the real need that's out there for men like us to band together and to fight on the side of justice on behalf of the oppressed.

I ask you, 'We few, we happy few, we band of brothers;' will you help us take up the cause of the orphan and widow in Zimbabwe?

So we can ...

Administer true justice, show mercy and compassion to one another.

– ZECHARIAH 7:9

SCRIPTURE REFERENCES FOR:

'THE MINISTRY OF COMPASSION'

THE BURDEN

Job	12:5
	19:7
	22:5–9
	24:2–12
	30:3–4
	30:16–17
	30:27
	31:16–23
	35:9
Psalms	14:6
	31:10
	38:8–10
	142:4
Proverbs	13:23
	14:20
	18:23
	21:13
Ecclesiastes	4:1
	9:13–16
Isaiah	1:23–27
	3:14–15
	10:1–2
	32:7
Jeremiah	5:26–31

Lamentations	2:11–12
	2:19
	4:4
	4:9–10
Ezekiel	16:49
	22:6–7
	22:24–30
	34:1–6
Amos	2:6–7
	4:1
	5:11–12
Zechariah	7:9–14
Malachi	3:5
Matthew	9:36
	15:32
Luke	11:42
1 Corinthians	4:11
Hebrews	13:3

THE PRAYERS

Psalms	5:2
	10:12–18

325

	17:6–7		102:17
	28:2		102:19–20
	35:10		103:6
	36:5–9		103:13
	40:17		107:8–9
	44:23–26		109:30–31
	60:5		111:4–5
	60:11		113:7
	72:1–4		119:49–50
	72:12		140:12
	74:18–21		145:8–9
	79:11		146:5–9
	82:2–5		
	94:3–7	Proverbs	28:8
	119:147		29:26
Isaiah	16:3	Isaiah	11:2–4
	63:15		14:3–4
			28:5–6
Hosea	14:3		30:18
			32:1–8

THE PROMISES

			41:10
Deuteronomy	10:17–18		41:17
	26:7		49:8–10
			51:4–5
Job	36:15		61:1
2 Samuel	22:31	Ezekiel	34:15–16
Psalms	9:9	Zechariah	9:11–12
	9:12		
	12:5	Luke	18:7–8
	22:24		
	34:6	John	14:12–13
	34:18		
	37:5–6	Acts	10:4
	37:14–15		
	68:5–6		

THE COMMAND

	69:33	Exodus	23:1–9

Leviticus	19:15		1 John	3:16–18
	19:34			
	25:35–37		## THE REWARD	
Deuteronomy	15:4–11		Job	29:11–14
	24:10–22			
	26:12–13		Psalms	41:1–3
				112:1–9
Proverbs	14:31			
	22:22–23		Proverbs	14:21
	29:7			19:17
	31:8–9			22:9
				28:27
Isaiah	1:17			29:14
	56:1			
	58:5–12		Daniel	4:27
Jeremiah	7:3–7		Matthew	25:31–46
	21:11–12			
	22:3–5		Hebrews	6:10
	22:15–16			
Matthew	6:1–5			
	19:21			
Luke	6:27–38			
	10:25–37			
	11:39–41			
	12:3			
	14:12–23			
Romans	12:13			
2 Corinthians	8:3–8			
Galatians	6:2			
Colossians	3:12			
James	1:27			
	2:1–7			

MAP OF AFRICA HIGHLIGHTING ZIMBABWE

MAP OF ZIMBABWE

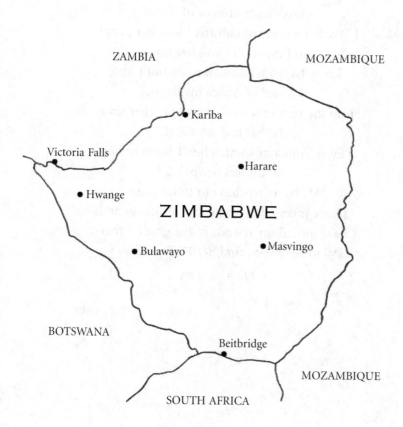

ZAMBIA

MOZAMBIQUE

● Kariba

Victoria Falls

●Harare

● Hwange

ZIMBABWE

● Bulawayo

●Masvingo

BOTSWANA

Beitbridge
●

MOZAMBIQUE

SOUTH AFRICA

I love the continent of Africa.
I love her variety of culture, I love her people
and I especially love her music.
I may have a white skin color but I have
the soul of Africa inside me.
From the very first day I set foot on her shores
she has had my heart.
Even from afar I watch her, I listen to her
and I feel her pain.
My heart reaches out toward her.
I have invested my time, my resources and
I have buried my friends in the ground there,
All to see Africa find her Divine destiny.

– BOB SCOTT

For more information on the author Bob Scott and
Compassionate Justice International, please visit:

www.savingzimbabwe.com
www.compassionatejustice.com

COMPASSIONATE
JUSTICE
INTERNATIONAL

We would like to hear from you.
Please send your comments about this book to us at:
reviews@struikchristianmedia.co.za

Christian Republic is a vibrant online resource website for Christians. It's a friendly platform for Christians of all ages, races all walks of life and all denominations to interact and access cutting edge resources online.

Main Features on the website include:

- Christian Events
- Church Finder
- Daily Devotionals
- Prayer Requests
- Online Shop

Visit the online shop today at
www. christianrepublic.co.za and buy
this book and many other exciting
Struik Christian Media releases on line.

CHRISTIAN REPUBLIC
www.christianrepublic.co.za